William Shakespeare

Doubtful Plays of William Shakespeare

William Shakespeare

Doubtful Plays of William Shakespeare

ISBN/EAN: 9783742808288

Manufactured in Europe, USA, Canada, Australia, Japa

Cover: Foto ©Andreas Hilbeck / pixelio.de

Manufactured and distributed by brebook publishing software (www.brebook.com)

William Shakespeare

Doubtful Plays of William Shakespeare

COLLECTION
OF
BRITISH AUTHORS

TAUCHNITZ EDITION.

VOL. 1041.

DOUBTFUL PLAYS OF WILLIAM SHAKESPEARE.

IN ONE VOLUME.

DOUBTFUL PLAYS

OF

WILLIAM SHAKESPEARE

LEIPZIG
BERNHARD TAUCHNITZ
1869.

INTRODUCTORY REMARKS.

BESIDES the 37 Dramas, genuine or assumed to be so, which are contained in most editions of Shakespeare's works, (including the volumes edited by the late Rev. A. Dyce in the Tauchnitz Collection), there are a number of other plays dating from Shakespeare's time, which are, with more or less justice, partially or wholly ascribed to him. In a chronological order, i. e. according to the dates when they are known to have been first performed, printed, mentioned, or entered in the Stationers' Registers, they are the following 15 plays:

1. *The Arraignment of Paris.*
2. *Arden of Feversham.*
3. *George-A-Greene.*
4. *Locrine.*
5. *King Edward III.*
6. *Mucedorus.*
7. *Sir John Oldcastle.*
8. *Thomas Lord Cromwell.*
9. *The Merry Devil of Edmonton.*
10. *The London Prodigal.*
11. *The Puritan; or, the Widow of Watling Street.*
12. *A Yorkshire Tragedy.*
13. *Fair Em.*
14. *The Two Noble Kinsmen.* (Supposed to be written by Fletcher and Shakespeare.)
15. *The Birth of Merlin.* (Supposed to be written by Shakespeare and William Rowley.)

INTRODUCTORY REMARKS.

These 15 plays, according to the more or less doubtful authorship of Shakespeare or his participation in them, are designated in the literary world as "Spurious" or "Doubtful Plays." In the present volume, which is intended to serve as a supplement to Shakespeare's works, I have, at the desire of the publisher, selected those six pieces, which, according to my firm conviction, bear the most unmistakable traces of Shakespeare's authorship. To specify the reasons which have guided me in my selection and determined me to admit these and reject others, would carry me too far here; it may suffice for my purpose to let each of the plays admitted in this collection bear as a motto what Capell says with reference to King Edward III., the drama which I have placed at the head of this series:

"But, after all, it must be confessed that its being his work must be conjecture only, and matter of opinion; and the reader must form one of his own, guided by what is now before him, and by what he shall meet with in perusal of the play itself."

Let me only add that a reprint of the so-called Doubtful Plays finds ample justification in the fact that, quite irrespective of the question of Shakespeare's authorship or participation in them, there are among the plays included in this volume, as well as among those excluded, some which, though they should eventually turn out to be not genuinely Shakespearian, yet, from their own intrinsic merit, may assert their claims to this day to be received as genuine dramatic productions.

MAX MOLTKE.

Leipzig, August 27, 1869.

CONTENTS

	PAGE
KING EDWARD III	1
THOMAS LORD CROMWELL	77
LOCRINE	131
A YORKSHIRE TRAGEDY	195
THE LONDON PRODIGAL	219
THE BIRTH OF MERLIN	279

KING EDWARD III.

DRAMATIS PERSONÆ.

EDWARD III., king of England.
EDWARD, prince of Wales, his son.
Earl of WARWICK.
Earl of DERBY.
Earl of SALISBURY.
Lord AUDLEY.
Lord PERCY.
LODOWICK, Edward's Confident.
Sir WILLIAM MOUNTAGUE.
Sir JOHN COPLAND.
Two Esquires, and four Heralds, English.
ROBERT, stiling himself Earl, of ARTOIS.
Earl of MONTFORT.
GOBIN DE GREY.
JOHN, king of France.
CHARLES, and PHILIP, his sons.
Duke of LORRAIN.
VILLIERS, a French lord.
King of Bohemia, and A Polish Captain, } Aids to King JOHN.
Six Citizens of Calais.
A French Captain, and some poor Inhabitants, of the same.
Another Captain; a Mariner.
Three Heralds, French.
DAVID, king of Scotland.
Earl DOUGLAS; and two Messengers, Scotch.

PHILIPPA, Queen to King EDWARD.
Countess of SALISBURY.
A French Woman and two Children.

Lords, and divers other Attendants; Heralds, Officers, Soldiers, &c.

SCENE—*dispers'd; in England, Flanders, and France.*

ACT I.

SCENE I. *London. A room of state in the palace.*

Flourish. Enter King EDWARD, *attended;* Prince of WALES, WARWICK, DERBY, AUDLEY, ARTOIS, *and others.*

Edw. Robert of Artois, banish'd though thou be
From France, thy native country, yet with us

Thou shalt retain as great a signiory;
For we create thee Earl of Richmond here.
And now go forwards with our pedigree:
Who next succeeded Philip le beau?
   Art. Three sons of his; which all, successively,
Did sit upon their father's regal throne;
Yet dy'd, and left no issue of their loins.
   Edw. But was my mother sister unto those?
   Art. She was, my lord; and only Isabelle
Was all the daughters that this Philip had:
Whom afterward your father took to wife;
And, from the fragrant garden of her womb,
Your gracious self, the flower of Europe's hope,
Derivèd is inheritor to France.
But note the rancour of rebellious minds.
When thus the linage of le beau was out,
The French obscur'd your mother's priviledge;
And, though she were the next of blood, proclaim'd
John, of the house of Valois, now their king:
The reason was, They say, the realm of France,
Replete with princes of great parentage,
Ought not admit a governor to rule,
Except he be descended of the male;
And that's the special ground of their contempt,
Wherewith they study to exclude your grace:
But they shall find that forgèd ground of theirs
To be but dusty heaps of brittle sand.
Perhaps, it will be thought a heinous thing,
That I, a Frenchman, should discover this:
But heaven I call to record of my vows;
It is not hate, nor any private wrong,
But love unto my country, and the right,
Provokes my tongue thus lavish in report:
You are the lineal watchman of our peace,
And John of Valois indirectly climbs:
What then should subjects, but embrace their king?
And wherein may our duty more be seen,

Than, striving to rebate a tyrant's pride,
Place the true shepherd of our common-wealth?
   Edw. This counsel, Artois, like to fruitful showers,
Hath added growth unto my dignity:
And, by the fiery vigour of thy words,
Hot courage is engender'd in my breast,
Which heretofore was rak'd in ignorance;
But now doth mount with golden wings of fame,
And will approve fair Isabelle's descent
Able to yoke their stubborn necks with steel
That spurn against my sov'reignty in France.—
                                          [*Cornet within.*
A messenger?—Lord Audley, know from whence.
                                  [*Exit Audley, and returns.*
   Aud. The duke of Lorrain, having cross'd the seas,
Intreats he may have conference with your highness.
   Edw. Admit him, lords, that we may hear the news.—
                      [*Exeunt Lords. King takes his state.*

Re-enter Lords; *with* LORRAIN, *attended.*

Say, duke of Lorrain, wherefore art thou come?
   Lor. The most renownèd prince, King John of France,
Doth greet thee, Edward: and by me commands,
That, for so much as by his liberal gift
The Guyenne dukedom is entail'd to thee,
Thou do him lowly homage for the same:
And, for that purpose, here I summon thee
Repair to France within these forty days,
That there, according as the custom is,
Thou mayst be sworn true liege-man to the king;
Or, else, thy title in that province dies,
And he himself will repossess the place.
   Edw. See, how occasion laughs me in the face!
No sooner minded to prepare for France,
But, straight, I am invited; nay, with threats,
Upon a penalty, enjoin'd to come:
'Twere but a foolish part, to say him nay.—

Lorrain, return this answer to thy lord:
I mean to visit him, as he requests;
But how? not servilely dispos'd to bend;
But like a conqueror, to make him bow:
His lame unpolish'd shifts are come to light;
And truth hath pull'd the vizard from his face,
That set a gloss upon his arrogance.
Dare he command a fealty in me?
Tell him, the crown, that he usurps, is mine;
And where he sets his foot, he ought to kneel:
'Tis not a petty dukedom that I claim,
But all the whole dominions of the realm;
Which if with grudging he refuse to yield,
I'll take away those borrow'd plumes of his,
And send him naked to the wilderness.

Lor. Then, Edward, here, in sight of all thy lords,
I do pronounce defiance to thy face.

Pri. Defiance, Frenchman? we rebound it back,
Even to the bottom of thy master's throat:
And,—be it spoke with reverence of the king
My gracious father, and these other lords,—
I hold thy message but as scurrilous;
And him, that sent thee, like the lazy drone,
Crept up by stealth unto the eagle's nest;
From whence we'll shake him with so rough a storm,
As others shall be warned by his harm.

War. Bid him leave off the lion's case he wears;
Lest, meeting with the lion in the field,
He chance to tear him piece-meal for his pride.

Art. The soundest counsel I can give his grace,
Is, to surrender ere he be constrain'd:
A voluntary mischief hath less scorn,
Than when reproach with violence is born.

Lor. Degenerate traitor, viper to the place
Where thou wast foster'd in thine infancy,
[*Drawing his sword.*
Bear'st thou a part in this conspiracy?

Edw. Lorrain, behold the sharpness of this steel:
[*Drawing his.*
Fervent desire, that sits against my heart,
Is far more thorny-pricking than this blade;
That, with the nightingale, I shall be scar'd,
As oft as I dispose myself to rest,
Until my colours be display'd in France:
This is thy final answer; so be gone.
　Lor. It is not that, nor any English brave,
Afflicts me so, as doth his poison'd view;
That is most false, should most of all be true.
[*Exeunt Lorrain, and Train.*
　Edw. Now, lords, our fleeting bark is under sail:
Our gage is thrown; and war is soon begun,
But not so quickly brought unto an end.—

Enter Sir WILLIAM MOUNTAGUE.

But wherefore comes sir William Mountague?
How stands the league between the Scot and us?
　Mou. Crack'd and dissever'd, my renownèd lord.
The treacherous king no sooner was inform'd
Of your withdrawing of our army back,
But straight, forgetting of his former oath,
He made invasion on the bordering towns:
Berwick is won; Newcastle spoil'd and lost;
And now the tyrant hath begirt with siege
The castle of Roxborough, where enclos'd
The countess Salisbury is like to perish.
　Edw. That is thy daughter, Warwick, is it not;
Whose husband hath in Bretagne serv'd so long,
About the planting of lord Montfort there?
　War. It is, my lord.
　Edw. Ignoble David! hast thou none to grieve,
But silly ladies, with thy threat'ning arms?
But I will make you shrink your snaily horns.—
First, therefore, Audley, this shall be thy charge;
Go levy footmen for our wars in France:—

And, Ned, take muster of our men at arms:
In every shire elect a several band;
Let them be soldiers of a lusty spirit,
Such as dread nothing but dishonour's blot:
Be wary therefore; since we do commence
A famous war, and with so mighty a nation.—
Derby, be thou embassador for us
Unto our father-in-law, the earl of Hainault:
Make him acquainted with our enterprize;
And likewise will him, with our own allies,
That are in Flanders, to solicit too
The emperor of Almaigne in our name.—
Myself, whilst you are jointly thus employ'd,
Will, with these forces that I have at hand,
March, and once more repulse the trait'rous Scots.
But, sirs, be resolute; we shall have wars
On every side:—and, Ned, thou must begin
Now to forget thy study and thy books,
And ure thy shoulders to an armour's weight.

   Pri. As cheerful sounding to my youthful spleen
This tumult is of war's encreasing broils,
As, at the coronation of a king,
The joyful clamours of the people are,
When, ave, Cæsar! they pronounce aloud;
Within this school of honour I shall learn,
Either to sacrifice my foes to death,
Or in a rightful quarrel spend my breath.
Then cheerfully forward, each a several way;
In great affairs 'tis naught to use delay.

                                              [*Exeunt.*

        SCENE II. *Roxborough. Before the castle.*

Enter Countess *of* SALISBURY, *and certain of her People, upon the walls.*

   Cou. Alas, how much in vain my poor eyes gaze
For succour that my sovereign should send!

Ah, cousin Mountague, I fear, thou want'st
The lively spirit, sharply to solicit
With vehement suit the king in my behalf
Thou dost not tell him, what a grief it is
To be the scornful captive to a Scot;
Either to be woo'd with broad untunèd oaths,
Or forc'd by rough insulting barbarism:
Thou dost not tell him, if he here prevail,
How much they will deride us in the north;
And, in their vile, uncivil, skipping jigs,
Bray forth their conquest, and our overthrow,
Even in the barren, bleak, and fruitless air.

Enter King DAVID, and Forces; with DOUGLAS, LORRAIN, and others.

I must withdraw; the everlasting foe
Comes to the wall: I'll closely step aside,
And list their babble, blunt, and full of pride.
                        [*Retiring behind the works.*

Dav. My lord of Lorrain, to our brother of France
Commend us, as the man in Christendom
Whom we most reverence, and entirely love.
Touching your embassage, return, and say,
That we with England will not enter parley,
Nor never make fair weather, or take truce;
But burn their neighbour towns, and so persist
With eager roads beyond their city York.
And never shall our bonny riders rest;
Nor rusting canker have the time to eat
Their light-borne snaffles, nor their nimble spurs;
Nor lay aside their jacks of gymold mail;
Nor hang their staves of grainèd Scottish ash
In peaceful wise upon their city walls;
Nor from their button'd tawny leathern belts
Dismiss their biting whinyards,—till your king
Cry out "Enough; spare England now for pity."
Farewell: and tell him, that you leave us here

Before this castle; say, you came from us
Even when we had that yielded to our hands.
 Lor. I take my leave; and fairly will return
Your acceptable greeting to my king. [*Exit Lorrain.*
 Dav. Now, Douglas, to our former task again,
For the division of this certain spoil.
 Dou. My liege, I crave the lady, and no more.
 Dav. Nay, soft ye, sir, first I must make my choice;
And first I do bespeak her for myself.
 Dou. Why then, my liege, let me enjoy her jewels.
 Dav. Those are her own, still liable to her,
And, who inherits her, hath those withal.

   Enter a Messenger, *hastily.*

 Mes. My liege, as we were pricking on the hills,
To fetch in booty, marching hitherward
We might descry a mighty host of men:
The sun, reflecting on the armour, shew'd
A field of plate, a wood of pikes advanc'd;
Bethink your highness speedily herein:
An easy march within four hours will bring
The hindmost rank unto this place, my liege.
 Dav. Dislodge, dislodge, it is the king of England.
 Dou. Jemmy my man, saddle my bonny black.
 Dav. Mean'st thou to fight, Douglas? we are too weak.
 Dou. I know it well, my liege, and therefore flee.
 Cou. My lords of Scotland, will ye stay and drink?
      [*Rising from her concealment.*
 Dav. She mocks at us; Douglas, I can't endure it.
 Cou. Say, good my lord, which is he, must have the
    lady;
And which, her jewels? I am sure, my lords,
Ye will not hence, till you have shar'd the spoils.
 Dav. She heard the messenger, and heard our talk;
And now that comfort makes her scorn at us.

   Enter another Messenger.

 Mes. Arm, my good lord; O, we are all surpriz'd!

Cou. After the French ambassador, my liege,
And tell him, that you dare not ride to York;
Excuse it, that your bonny horse is lame.
　　Dav. She heard that too; Intolerable grief!—
Woman, farewell: Although I do not stay,—
　　　　　　　　　　　[*Alarums.   Exeunt Scots.*
　　Cou. 'Tis not for fear,—and yet you run away.—
O happy comfort, welcome to our house!
The confident and boist'rous boasting Scot,—
That swore before my walls, he would not back
For all the armèd power of this land,—
With faceless fear, that ever turns his back,
Turn'd hence against the blasting north-east wind,
Upon the bare report and name of arms.

　　　　　　Enter MOUNTAGUE, *and others.*

O summer's day! see where my cousin comes.
　　Mou. How fares my aunt? Why, aunt, we are not Scots;
Why do you shut your gates against your friends?
　　Cou. Well may I give a welcome, cousin, to thee,
For thou comest well to chase my foes from hence.
　　Mou. The king himself is come in person hither;
Dear aunt, descend, and gratulate his highness.
　　Cou. How may I entertain his majesty,
To shew my duty, and his dignity?   [*Exit, from above.*

　　Flourish. Enter King EDWARD, WARWICK, ARTOIS, *and others.*

　　Edw. What, are the stealing foxes fled and gone,
Before we could uncouple at their heels?
　　War. They are, my liege; but, with a cheerful cry,
Hot hounds, and hardy, chase them at the heels.

　　　　　　Re-enter Countess, *attended.*

　　Edw. This is the countess, Warwick, is it not?
　　War. Even she, my liege; whose beauty tyrant fear,
As a may-blossom with pernitious winds,
Hath sully'd, wither'd, overcast, and done.

Edw. Hath she been fairer, Warwick, than she is?
War. My gracious king, fair is she not at all,
If that herself were by to stain herself,
As I have seen her when she was herself.
  Edw. What strange enchantment lurk'd in those her eyes,
When they excell'd this excellence they have,
That now their dim decline hath power to draw
My subject eyes from piercing majesty,
To gaze on her with doting admiration?
  Cou. In duty lower than the ground I kneel,
And for my dull knees bow my feeling heart,
To witness my obedience to your highness;
With many millions of a subject's thanks
For this your royal presence, whose approach
Hath driven war and danger from my gate.
  Edw. Lady, stand up: I come to bring thee peace,
However thereby I have purchasèd war.
  Cou. No war to you, my liege; the Scots are gone,
And gallop home toward Scotland with their haste.
  Edw. Lest yielding here I pine in shameful love,
Come, we'll pursue the Scots;—Artois, away.
  Cou. A little while, my gracious sovereign, stay,
And let the power of a mighty king
Honour our roof; my husband in the wars,
When he shall hear it, will triumph for joy:
Then, dear my liege, now niggard not thy state;
Being at the wall, enter our homely gate.
  Edw. Pardon me, countess, I will come no near;
I dream'd to-night of treason, and I fear.
  Cou. Far from this place let ugly treason lie!
  Edw. [*aside*] No farther off, than her conspiring eye;
Which shoots infected poison in my heart,
Beyond repulse of wit, or cure of art.
Now in the sun alone it doth not lie,
With light to take light from a mortal eye;
For here two day-stars, that mine eyes would see,
More than the sun, steal mine own light from me.

Contemplative desire! desire to be
In contemplation, that may master thee!—
Warwick, Artois, to horse, and let's away.
   Cou. What might I speak, to make my sovereign stay?
   Edw. What needs a tongue to such a speaking eye,
That more persuades than winning oratory?
   Cou. Let not thy presence, like the April sun,
Flatter our earth, and suddenly be done.
More happy do not make our outward wall,
Than thou wilt grace our inward house withal.
Our house, my liege, is like a country swain,
Whose habit rude, and manners blunt and plain,
Presageth nought; yet inly beautify'd
With bounty's riches, and fair hidden pride:
For, where the golden ore doth bury'd lie,
The ground, undeck'd with nature's tapestry,
Seems barren, sere, unfertil, fruitless, dry;
And where the upper turf of earth doth boast
His pied perfumes, and party-colour'd cost,
Delve there, and find this issue, and their pride,
To spring from ordure, and corruption's side.
But, to make up my all too long compare,—
These raggèd walls no testimony are
What is within; but, like a cloak, doth hide,
From weather's waste, the undergarnish'd pride.
More gracious than my terms can let thee be,
Intreat thyself to stay a while with me.
   Edw. [*aside*] As wise as fair; What fond fit can be heard,
When wisdom keeps the gate as beauty's guard?—
Countess, albeit my business urgeth me,
It shall attend, while I attend on thee.—
Come on, my lords, here will I host to-night.

ACT II.

SCENE I. *Roxborough. Gardens of the castle.*

Enter LODOWICK.

Lod. I might perceive his eye in her eye lost,
His ear to drink her sweet tongue's utterance;
'And changing passion, like inconstant clouds,—
That, rack'd upon the carriage of the winds,
Increase, and die,—in his disturbèd cheeks.
Lo, when she blush'd, even then did he look pale;
As if her cheeks, by some enchanted power,
Attracted had the cherry blood from his:
Anon, with reverent fear when she grew pale,
His cheeks put on their scarlet ornaments;
But no more like her oriental red,
Than brick to coral, or live things to dead.
Why did he then thus counterfeit her looks?
If she did blush, 'twas tender modest shame,
Being in the sacred presence of a king;
If he did blush, 'twas red immodest shame,
To vail his eyes amiss, being a king:
If she look'd pale, 'twas silly woman's fear,
To bear herself in presence of a king;
If he look'd pale, it was with guilty fear,
To dote amiss, being a mighty king:
Then, Scottish wars, farewell; I fear, 'twill prove
A ling'ring English siege of peevish love.
Here comes his highness, walking all alone.

Enter King EDWARD.

Edw. She is grown more fairer far since I came hither;
Her voice more silver every word than other,
Her wit more fluent: What a strange discourse
Unfolded she, of David, and his Scots?
Even thus, quoth she, he spake,—and then spoke broad,
With epithets and accents of the Scots;

But somewhat better than the Scot could speak:
And thus, quoth she,—and answer'd then herself;
For who could speak like her? but she herself
Breathes from the wall an angel's note from heaven
Of sweet defiance to her barbarous foes.
When she would talk of peace, methinks, her tongue
Commanded war to prison; when of war,
It waken'd Cæsar from his Roman grave,
To hear war beautify'd by her discourse.
Wisdom is foolishness, but in her tongue;
Beauty a slander, but in her fair face:
There is no summer, but in her cheerful looks;
Nor frosty winter, but in her disdain.
I cannot blame the Scots, that did besiege her,
For she is all the treasure of our land;
But call them cowards, that they ran away,
Having so rich and fair a cause to stay.—
Art thou there, Lodowick? give me ink and paper.

 Lod. I will, my sovereign.
 Edw. And bid the lords hold on their play at chess,
For we will walk and meditate alone.
 Lod. I will, my liege.   [*Exit Lodowick.*
 Edw. This fellow is well read in poetry,
And hath a lusty and persuasive spirit:
I will acquaint him with my passion;
Which he shall shadow with a veil of lawn,
Through which the queen of beauty's queens shall see
Herself the ground of my infirmity.—

   Re-enter LODOWICK.

Hast thou pen, ink, and paper ready, Lodowick?
 Lod. Ready, my liege.
 Edw. Then in the summer arbour sit by me,
Make it our council-house, or cabinet;
Since green our thoughts, green be the conventicle,
Where we will ease us by disburd'ning them.
Now, Lodowick, invocate some golden muse,

To bring thee hither an enchanted pen,
That may, for sighs, set down true sighs indeed;
Talking of grief, to make thee ready groan;
And, when thou writ'st of tears, encouch the word,
Before, and after, with such sweet laments,
That it may raise drops in a Tartar's eye,
And make a flint heart Scythian pitiful:
For so much moving hath a poet's pen;
Then, if thou be a poet, move thou so,
And be enrichèd by thy sovereign's love.
For, if the touch of sweet concordant strings
Could force attendance in the ears of hell;
How much more shall the strains of poet's wit
Beguile, and ravish, soft and humane minds?
   Lod. To whom, my lord, shall I direct my stile?
   Edw. To one that shames the fair, and sots the wise;
Whose body, as an abstract, or a brief,
Contains each general virtue in the world:
Better than beautiful,—thou must begin;
Devise for fair a fairer word than fair;
And every ornament, that thou wouldst praise,
Fly it a pitch above the soar of praise:
For flattery fear thou not to be convicted;
For, were thy admiration ten times more,
Ten times ten thousand more the worth exceeds,
Of that thou art to praise, thy praise's worth.
Begin, I will to contemplate the while:
Forget not to set down, how passionate,
How heart-sick, and how full of languishment,
Her beauty makes me.
   Lod.   Write I to a woman?
   Edw. What beauty else could triumph over me;
Or who, but women, do our love-lays greet?
What, think'st thou I did bid thee praise a horse?
   Lod. Of what condition or estate she is,
'Twere requisite that I should know, my lord.
   Edw. Of such estate, that hers is as a throne,

And my estate the footstool where she treads:
Then mayst thou judge what her condition is,
By the proportion of her mightiness.
Write on, while I peruse her in my thoughts.—
Her voice to music, or the nightingale:—
To music every summer-leaping swain
Compares his sun-burnt lover when she speaks:
And why should I speak of the nightingale?
The nightingale sings of adulterate wrong;
And that, compar'd, is too satirical:
For sin, though sin, would not be so esteem'd;
But, rather, virtue sin, sin virtue deem'd.
Her hair, far softer than the silk-worm's twist,
Like to a flattering glass, doth make more fair
The yellow amber: Like a flattering glass
Comes in too soon; for, writing of her eyes,
I'll say, that like a glass they catch the sun,
And thence the hot reflection doth rebound
Against my breast, and burns my heart within.
Ah, what a world of descant makes my soul
Upon this voluntary ground of love!—
Come, Lodowick, hast thou turn'd thy ink to gold?
If not, write but in letters capital
My mistress' name,
And it will gild thy paper: Read, lord, read,
Fill thou the empty hollows of mine ears
With the sweet hearing of thy poetry.

   Lod. I have not to a period brought her praise.

   Edw. Her praise is as my love, both infinite,
Which apprehend such violent extremes,
That they disdain an ending period.
Her beauty hath no match, but my affection;
Hers more than most, mine most, and more than more:
Hers more to praise, than tell the sea by drops;
Nay, more, than drop the massy earth by sands,
And, sand by sand, print them in memory:
Then wherefore talk'st thou of a period,

To that which craves unended admiration?
Read, let us hear.
  Lod. "More fair, and chaste, than is the queen of
    shades,"—
  Edw. That line hath two faults, gross and palpable:
Compar'st thou her to the pale queen of night,
Who, being set in dark, seems therefore light?
What is she, when the sun lifts up his head,
But like a fading taper, dim and dead?
My love shall brave the eye of heaven at noon,
And, being unmask'd, outshine the golden sun.
  Lod. What is the other fault, my sovereign lord?
  Edw. Read o'er the line again.
  Lod. "More fair, and chaste,"—
  Edw. I did not bid thee talk of chastity,
To ransack so the treasure of her mind;
For I had rather have her chas'd, than chaste.
Out with the moon-line, I will none of it,
And let me have her liken'd to the sun:
Say, she hath thrice more splendor than the sun,
That her perfection emulates the sun,
That she breeds sweets as plenteous as the sun,
That she doth thaw cold winter like the sun,
That she doth cheer fresh summer like the sun,
That she doth dazzle gazers like the sun:
And, in this application to the sun,
Bid her be free and general as the sun;
Who smiles upon the basest weed that grows,
As lovingly as on the fragrant rose.
Let's see what follows that same moon-light line.
  Lod. "More fair, and chaste, than is the queen of shades;
More bold in constancy"—
  Edw. In constancy! than who?
  Lod.—"than Judith was."
  Edw. O monstrous line! Put in the next a sword,
And I shall woo her to cut off my head.
Blot, blot, good Lodowick! Let us hear the next.

KING EDWARD III.

Lod. There's all that yet is done.
Edw. I thank thee then, thou hast done little ill;
But what is done, is passing passing ill.
No, let the captain talk of boist'rous war;
The prisoner, of immurèd dark constraint;
The sick man best sets down the pangs of death;
The man that starves, the sweetness of a feast;
The frozen soul, the benefit of fire;
And every grief, his happy opposite:
Love cannot sound well, but in lovers' tongues;
Give me the pen and paper, I will write.—

Enter Countess.

But, soft, here comes the treasure of my spirit.—
Lodowick, thou know'st not how to draw a battle;
These wings, these flankers, and these squadrons
Argue in thee defective discipline:
Thou shouldst have plac'd this here, this other here.
 Cou. Pardon my boldness, my thrice gracious lord;
Let my intrusion here be call'd my duty,
That comes to see my sovereign how he fares.
 Edw. Go, draw the same, I tell thee in what form.
 Lod. I go. [*Exit Lodowick.*
 Cou. Sorry I am to see my liege so sad:
What may thy subject do, to drive from thee
Thy gloomy consort, sullen melancholy?
 Edw. Ah, lady, I am blunt, and cannot strew
The flowers of solace in a ground of shame:—
Since I came hither, countess, I am wrong'd.
 Cou. Now, God forbid, that any in my house
Should think my sovereign wrong! Thrice gentle king,
Acquaint me with your cause of discontent.
 Edw. How near then shall I be to remedy?
 Cou. As near, my liege, as all my woman's power
Can pawn itself to buy thy remedy.
 Edw. If thou speak'st true, then have I my redress:

Shakespeare, Doubtful Plays. 2

Engage thy power to redeem my joys,
And I am joyful, countess; else, I die.
 Cou. I will, my liege.
 Edw.   Swear, countess, that thou wilt.
 Cou. By heaven, I will.
 Edw. Then take thyself a little way aside;
And tell thyself a king doth dote on thee:
Say, that within thy power it doth lie,
To make him happy; and that thou hast sworn
To give me all the joy within thy power:
Do this, and tell me when I shall be happy.
 Cou. All this is done, my thrice dread sovereign:
That power of love, that I have power to give,
Thou hast with all devout obedience;
Employ me how thou wilt in proof thereof.
 Edw. Thou hear'st me say that I do dote on thee.
 Cou. If on my beauty, take it if thou canst;
Though little, I do prize it ten times less:
If on my virtue, take it if thou canst;
For virtue's store by giving doth augment:
Be it on what it will, that I can give,
And thou canst take away, inherit it.
 Edw. It is thy beauty that I would enjoy.
 Cou. O, were it painted, I would wipe it off,
And dispossess myself, to give it thee:
But, sovereign, it is solder'd to my life;
Take one, and both; for, like an humble shadow,
It haunts the sunshine of my summer's life.
 Edw. But thou mayst lend it me, to sport withal.
 Cou. As easy may my intellectual soul
Be lent away, and yet my body live,
As lend my body, palace to my soul,
Away from her, and yet retain my soul.
My body is her bower, her court, her abbey,
And she an angel, pure, divine, unspotted;
If I should lend her house, my lord, to thee,
I kill my poor soul, and my poor soul me.

Edw. Didst thou not swear, to give me what I would?
Cou. I did, my liege; so, what you would, I could.
Edw. I wish no more of thee, than thou mayst give:
Nor beg I do not, but I rather buy,
That is, thy love; and, for that love of thine,
In rich exchange, I tender to thee mine.
Cou. But that your lips were sacred, o my lord,
You would prophane the holy name of love:
That love, you offer me, you cannot give;
For Cæsar owes that tribute to his queen:
That love, you beg of me, I cannot give;
For Sarah owes that duty to her lord.
He, that doth clip, or counterfeit, your stamp,
Shall die, my lord: And will your sacred self
Commit high treason against the King of heaven,
To stamp his image in forbidden metal,
Forgetting your allegiance, and your oath?
In violating marriage sacred law,
You break a greater honour than yourself:
To be a king, is of a younger house,
Than to be marry'd; your progenitor,
Sole-reigning Adam on the universe,
By God was honour'd for a marry'd man,
But not by him anointed for a king.
It is a penalty, to break your statutes,
Though not enacted by your highness' hand:
How much more, to infringe the holy act
Made by the mouth of God, seal'd with his hand?
I know, my sovereign—in my husband's love,
Who now doth loyal service in his wars—
Doth but to try the wife of Salisbury,
Whether she will hear a wanton's tale, or no;
Lest being therein guilty by my stay,
From that, not from my liege, I turn away.
[*Exit Countess.*
Edw. Whether is her beauty by her words divine;
Or are her words sweet chaplains to her beauty?

Like as the wind doth beautify a sail,
And as a sail becomes the unseen wind,
So do her words her beauty, beauty words.
O, that I were a hony-gathering bee,
To bear the comb of virtue from his flower;
And not a poison-sucking envious spider,
To turn the vice I take to deadly venom!
Religion is austere, and beauty gentle;
Too strict a guardian for so fair a ward.
O, that she were, as is the air, to me!
Why, so she is; for, when I would embrace her,
This do I, and catch nothing but myself.
I must enjoy her; for I cannot beat,
With reason, and reproof, fond love away.

Enter WARWICK.

Here comes her father: I will work with him,
To bear my colours in this field of love.
   War. How is it, that my sovereign is so sad?
May I with pardon know your highness' grief,
And that my old endeavour will remove it,
It shall not cumber long your majesty.
   Edw. A kind and voluntary gift thou proffer'st,
That I was forward to have begg'd of thee.
But, o thou world, great nurse of flattery,
Why dost thou tip men's tongues with golden words,
And peize their deeds with weight of heavy lead,
That fair performance cannot follow promise?
O, that a man might hold the heart's close book;
And choke the lavish tongue, when it doth utter
The breath of falsehood not character'd there!
   War. Far be it from the honour of my age,
That I should owe bright gold, and render lead!
Age is a cynic, not a flatterer:
I say again, that, if I knew your grief,
And that by me it may be lessenèd,
My proper harm should buy your highness' good.

Edw. These are the vulgar tenders of false men,
That never pay the duty of their words.
Thou wilt not stick to swear what thou hast said;
But, when thou know'st my grief's condition,
This rash-disgorgèd vomit of thy word
Thou wilt eat up again, and leave me helpless.
  War. By heaven, I will not; though your majesty
Did bid me run upon your sword, and die.
  Edw. Say, that my grief is no way med'cinable,
But by the loss and bruising of thine honour?
  War. If nothing but that loss may vantage you,
I would account that loss my vantage too.
  Edw. Think'st, that thou canst unswear thy oath again?
  War. I cannot; nor I would not, if I could.
  Edw. But, if thou dost, what shall I say to thee?
  War. What may be said to any perjur'd villain,
That breaks the sacred warrant of an oath.
  Edw. What wilt thou say to one that breaks an oath?
  War. That he hath broke his faith with God and man,
And from them both stands excommunicate.
  Edw. What office were it, to suggest a man
To break a lawful and religious vow?
  War. An office for the devil, not for man.
  Edw. That devil's office must thou do for me;
Or break thy oath, or cancel all the bonds
Of love, and duty, 'twixt thyself and me.
And therefore, Warwick, if thou art thyself,
The lord and master of thy word and oath,
Go to thy daughter; and, in my behalf,
Command her, woo her, win her any ways,
To be my mistress, and my secret love.
I will not stand to hear thee make reply;
Thy oath break hers, or let thy sovereign die.
                                       [*Exit Edward.*
  War. O doting king! O detestable office!
Well may I tempt myself to wrong myself,
When he hath sworn me by the name of God,

To break a vow made by the name of God.
What if I swear by this right hand of mine,
To cut this right hand off? the better way
Were, to prophane the idol, than confound it:
But neither will I do; I'll keep my oath,
And to my daughter make a recantation
Of all the virtue I have preach'd to her:
I'll say, she must forget her husband Salisbury,
If she remember, to embrace the king;
I'll say, an oath may easily be broken,
But not so easily pardon'd, being broken;
I'll say, it is true charity to love,
But not true love to be so charitable;
I'll say, his greatness may bear out the shame,
But not his kingdom can buy out the sin;
I'll say, it is my duty to persuade,
But not her honesty to give consent.

Enter Countess.

See, where she comes: Was never father, had,
Against his child, an embassage so bad.
 Cou. My lord and father, I have sought for you:
My mother and the peers importune you,
To keep in presence of his majesty,
And do your best to make his highness merry.
 War. [*aside*] How shall I enter in this graceless errand?
I must not call her child; for where's the father
That will, in such a suit, seduce his child?
Then, Wife of Salisbury,—shall I so begin?
No, he's my friend; and where is found the friend,
That will do friendship such endamagement?—
Neither my daughter, nor my dear friend's wife.
I am not Warwick, as thou think'st I am,
But an attorney from the court of hell;
That thus have hous'd my spirit in his form,
To do a message to thee from the king.
The mighty king of England dotes on thee:

He, that hath power to take away thy life,
Hath power to take thine honour; then consent
To pawn thine honour, rather than thy life:
Honour is often lost, and got again;
But life, once gone, hath no recovery.
The sun, that withers hay, doth nourish grass;
The king, that would distain thee, will advance thee.
The poets write, that great Achilles' spear
Could heal the wound it made: the moral is,
What mighty men misdo, they can amend.
The lion doth become his bloody jaws,
And grace his foragement, by being mild
When vassal fear lies trembling at his feet.
The king will in his glory hide thy shame;
And those, that gaze on him to find out thee,
Will lose their eyesight, looking in the sun.
What can one drop of poison harm the sea,
Whose hugy vastures can digest the ill,
And make it lose his operation?
The king's great name will temper thy misdeeds,
And give the bitter potion of reproach
A sugar'd sweet and most delicious taste:
Besides, it is no harm, to do the thing
Which without shame could not be left undone.
Thus have I, in his majesty's behalf,
Apparel'd sin in virtuous sentences,
And dwell upon thy answer in his suit.

Cou. Unnatural besiege! Woe me, unhappy,
To have escap'd the danger of my foes,
And to be ten times worse environ'd by friends!
Hath he no means to stain my honest blood,
But to corrupt the author of my blood,
To be his scandalous and vile solicitor?
No marvel, though the branches be infected,
When poison hath encompassèd the root:
No marvel, though the leprous infant die,
When the stern dam envenometh the dug.

Why, then, give sin a passport to offend,
And youth the dangerous rein of liberty:
Blot out the strict forbidding of the law;
And cancel every canon that prescribes
A shame for shame, or penance for offence.
No, let me die, if his too boist'rous will
Will have it so, before I will consent
To be an actor in his graceless lust.

War. Why, now thou speak'st as I would have thee speak:
And mark how I unsay my words again.
An honourable grave is more esteem'd
Than the polluted closet of a king:
The greater man, the greater is the thing,
Be it good, or bad, that he shall undertake:
An unreputed mote, flying in the sun,
Presents a greater substance than it is:
The freshest summer's day doth soonest taint
The loathed carrion that it seems to kiss:
Deep are the blows made with a mighty axe:
That sin doth ten times aggravate itself
That is committed in a holy place:
An evil deed, done by authority,
Is sin and subornation: Deck an ape
In tissue, and the beauty of the robe
Adds but the greater scorn unto the beast.
A spacious field of reasons could I urge,
Between his glory, daughter, and thy shame:
That poison shows worst in a golden cup;
Dark night seems darker by the lightning flash;
Lilies, that fester, smell far worse than weeds;
And every glory that inclines to sin,
The shame is treble by the opposite.
So leave I, with my blessing in thy bosom;
Which then convert to a most heavy curse,
When thou convert'st from honour's golden name
To the black faction of bed-blotting shame!

[*Exit.*

Cou. I'll follow thee: And, when my mind turns so,
My body sink my soul in endless woe! [*Exit.*

    Scene II. *The same. A room in the castle.*
    Enter Derby, *and* Audley, *meeting.*
Der. Thrice noble Audley, well encounter'd here:
How is it with our sovereign, and his peers?
  Awd. 'Tis full a fortnight, since I saw his highness,
What time he sent me forth to muster men;
Which I accordingly have done, and bring them hither
In fair array before his majesty.
What news, my lord of Derby, from the emperor?
  Der. As good as we desire: the emperor
Hath yielded to his highness friendly aid;
And makes our king lieutenant general,
In all his lands and large dominions:
Then via for the spacious bounds of France!
  Aud. What, doth his highness leap to hear these news?
  Der. I have not yet found time to open them;
The king is in his closet, malecontent,
For what, I know not, but he gave in charge,
Till after dinner, none should interrupt him:
The countess Salisbury, and her father Warwick,
Artois, and all, look underneath the brows.
  Aud. Undoubtedly, then something is amiss.
                            [*Trumpet within.*
  Der. The trumpets sound; the king is now abroad.
    Enter Edward.
  Aud. Here comes his highness.
  Der. Befall my sovereign all my sovereign's wish!
  Edw. Ah, that thou wert a witch, to make it so!
  Der. The emperor greeteth you: [*Presenting letters.*
  Edw. [*aside*] 'Would it were the countess.
  Der. And hath accorded to your highness' suit.
  Edw. [*Aside*] Thou liest, she hath not; but I would, she had!
  Aud. All love, and duty, to my lord the king!

Edw. [*Aside*] Well, all but one is none:—What news with
  you?
  Aud. I have, my liege, levy'd those horse and foot,
According to your charge, and brought them hither.
  Edw. Then let those foot trudge hence upon those horse,
According to our discharge, and be gone.—
Derby, I'll look upon the countess' mind
Anon.
  Der. The countess' mind, my liege?
  Edw. I mean the emperor: Leave me alone.
  Aud. What's in his mind?
  Der.   Let's leave him to his humour.
            [*Exeunt Derby and Audley.*
  Edw. Thus from the heart's abundance speaks the tongue;
Countess for emperor: And, indeed, why not?
She is as imperator over me;
And I to her
Am as a kneeling vassal, that observes
The pleasure, or displeasure, of her eye.—

            Enter LODOWICK.

What says the more than Cleopatra's match
To Cæsar now?
  Lod. That yet, my liege, ere night
She will resolve your majesty.   [*Drum within.*
  Edw. What drum is this, that thunders forth this march,
To start the tender Cupid in my bosom?
Poor sheep-skin, how it brawls with him that beateth it!
Go, break the thundring parchment bottom out,
And I will teach it to conduct sweet lines
Unto the bosom of a heavenly nymph:
For I will use it as my writing-paper;
And so reduce him, from a scolding drum,
To be the herald, and dear counsel-bearer,
Betwixt a goddess and a mighty king.
Go, bid the drummer learn to touch the lute,
Or hang him in the braces of his drum;

For now we think it an uncivil thing,
To trouble heaven with such harsh resounds:
Away.—   [*Exit Lodowick.*
The quarrel, that I have, requires no arms,
But these of mine; and these shall meet my foe
In a deep march of penetrable groans:
My eyes shall be my arrows; and my sighs
Shall serve me as the vantage of the wind,
To whirl away my sweet'st artillery:
Ah but, alas, she wins the sun of me,
For that is she herself; and thence it comes,
That poets term the wanton warrior, blind;
But love hath eyes as judgment to his steps,
Till too much lov'd glory dazzles them.—

Re-enter LODOWICK.

How now?
    Lod. My liege, the drum, that struck the lusty march,
Stands with Prince Edward, your thrice valiant son.

Enter PRINCE. LODOWICK *retires to the door.*

    Edw. [*aside*] I see the boy. O, how his mother's face,
Moulded in his, corrects my stray'd desire,
And rates my heart, and chides my thievish eye;
Who, being rich enough in seeing her,
Yet seeks elsewhere: and basest theft is that
Which cannot check itself on poverty.—
Now, boy, what news?
    Pri. I have assembled, my dear lord and father,
The choicest buds of all our English blood,
For our affairs to France; and here we come,
To take direction from your majesty.
    Edw. [*aside*] Still do I see in him delineate
His mother's visage; those his eyes are hers,
Who, looking wistly on me, make me blush;
For faults against themselves give evidence:
Lust is a fire; and men, like lanthorns, show
Light lust within themselves, even through themselves.

Away, loose silks of wavering vanity!
Shall the large limit of fair Britany
By me be overthrown? and shall I not
Master this little mansion of myself?
Give me an armour of eternal steel;
I go to conquer kings: and shall I then
Subdue myself, and be my enemy's friend?
It must not be. — Come, boy, forward, advance!
Let's with our colours sweep the air of France.
    Lod. My liege, the countess, with a smiling cheer,
Desires access unto your majesty.
                      [*Advancing from the door, and whispering him.*
    Edw. Why, there it goes! that very smile of hers
Hath ransom'd captive France; and set the king,
The dauphin, and the peers, at liberty. —
Go, leave me, Ned, and revel with thy friends. [*Exit Prince.*
[*Aside*] Thy mother is but black; and thou, like her,
Dost put into my mind how foul she is. —
Go, fetch the countess hither in thy hand,
And let her chase away those winter clouds;
For she gives beauty both to heaven and earth.
                                [*Exit Lodowick.*
The sin is more, to hack and hew poor men,
Than to embrace, in an unlawful bed,
The register of all fair rarities
Since leathern Adam till this youngest hour.

        Re-enter LODOWICK, *with the* Countess.

Go, Lodowick, put thy hand into my purse,
Play, spend, give, riot, waste; do what thou wilt,
So thou wilt hence a while, and leave me here.
                                [*Exit Lodowick.*
Now, my soul's playfellow! and art thou come,
To speak the more than heavenly word of yea,
To my objection in thy beauteous love?
    Cou. My father on his blessing hath commanded —
    Edw. That thou shalt yield to me.

Cou. Ay, dear my liege, your due.
Edw. And that, my dearest love, can be no less
Than right for right, and tender love for love.
Cou. Than wrong for wrong, and endless hate for hate.—
But,—sith I see your majesty so bent,
That my unwillingness, my husband's love,
Your high estate, nor no respect respected
Can be my help, but that your mightiness
Will overbear and awe these dear regards,—
I bind my discontent to my content,
And, what I would not, I'll compell I will;
Provided that yourself remove those lets
That stand between your highness' love and mine.
Edw. Name them, fair countess, and, by heaven, I will.
Cou. It is their lives, that stand between our love,
That I would have chok'd up, my sovereign.
Edw. Whose lives, my lady?
Cou. My thrice loving liege,
Your queen, and Salisbury my wedded husband;
Who living have that title in our love,
That we cannot bestow but by their death.
Edw. Thy opposition is beyond our law.
Cou. And so is your desire: If the law
Can hinder you to execute the one,
Let it forbid you to attempt the other:
I cannot think you love me as you say,
Unless you do make good what you have sworn.
Edw. No more; thy husband and the queen shall die.
Fairer thou art by far than Hero was;
Beardless Leander not so strong as I:
He swom an easy current for his love;
But I will, through a helly spout of blood,
Arrive at Sestos where my Hero lies.
Cou. Nay, you'll do more; you'll make the river too,
With their heart-bloods that keep our love asunder,
Of which, my husband, and your wife, are twain.
Edw. Thy beauty makes them guilty of their death,

And gives in evidence, that they shall die;
Upon which verdict, I, their judge, condemn them.
    Cou. O perjur'd beauty! more corrupted judge!
When, to the great star-chamber o'er our heads,
The universal sessions calls to count
This packing evil, we both shall tremble for it.
    Edw. What says my fair love? is she resolute?
    Cou. Resolv'd to be dissolv'd; and, therefore, this,—
Keep but thy word, great king, and I am thine.
Stand where thou dost, I'll part a little from thee,
And see how I will yield me to thy hands.
    [*Turning suddenly upon him, and showing two daggers.*
Here by my side do hang my wedding knives:
Take thou the one, and with it kill thy queen,
And learn by me to find her where she lies;
And with this other I'll dispatch my love,
Which now lies fast asleep within my heart:
When they are gone, then I'll consent to love.
Stir not, lascivious king, to hinder me;
My resolution is more nimbler far,
Than thy prevention can be in my rescue,
And, if thou stir, I strike: therefore stand still,
And hear the choice that I will put thee to:
Either swear to leave thy most unholy suit,
And never henceforth to solicit me;
Or else, by heaven [*kneeling*], this sharp-pointed knife
Shall stain thy earth with that which thou wouldst stain,
My poor chaste blood. Swear, Edward, swear,
Or I will strike, and die, before thee here.
    Edw. Even by that Power I swear, that gives me now
The power to be ashamèd of myself,
I never mean to part my lips again
In any word that tends to such a suit.
Arise, true English lady; whom our isle
May better boast of, than e'er Roman might
Of her, whose ransack'd treasury hath task'd
The vain endeavour of so many pens:

Arise; and be my fault thy honour's fame,
Which after-ages shall enrich thee with.
I am awakèd from this idle dream;—
Warwick, my son, Derby, Artois, and Audley,
Brave warriors all, where are you all this while?

Enter Prince *and* Lords.

Warwick, I make thee warden of the north:—
You, prince of Wales, and Audley, straight to sea;
Scour to New-haven; some, there stay for me:—
Myself, Artois, and Derby, will through Flanders,
To greet our friends there, and to crave their aid:
This night will scarce suffice me, to discover
My folly's siege against a faithful lover;
For, ere the sun shall gild the eastern sky,
We'll wake him with our martial harmony. [*Exeunt.*

ACT III.

SCENE I. *Flanders. The French camp.*

Enter King JOHN *of France;* his two sons, CHARLES Duke
of Normandy, *and* PHILIP; Duke of LORRAIN, *and
others.*

Joh. Here, till our navy, of a thousand sail,
Have made a breakfast to our foe by sea,
Let us encamp, to wait their happy speed.—
Lorrain, what readiness is Edward in?
How hast thou heard that he provided is
Of martial furniture for this exploit?

Lor. To lay aside unnecessary soothing,
And not to spend the time in circumstance,
'Tis bruited for a certainty, my lord,
That he's exceeding strongly fortify'd;
His subjects flock as willingly to war,
As if unto a triumph they were led.

Cha. England was wont to harbour malecontents,

Blood-thirsty and seditious Catilines,
Spend-thrifts, and such as gape for nothing else
But change and alteration of the state;
And is it possible, that they are now
So loyal in themselves?

Lor. All but the Scot; who solemnly protests,
As heretofore I have inform'd his grace,
Never to sheath his sword, or take a truce.

Joh. Ah, that's the anchorage of some better hope!
But, on the other side; to think what friends
King Edward hath retain'd in Netherland,
Among those ever-bibbing epicures,
Those frothy Dutchmen, puff'd with double beer,
That drink and swill in every place they come,
Doth not a little aggravate mine ire:
Besides, we hear, the emperor conjoins,
And stalls him in his own authority:
But, all the mightier that their number is,
The greater glory reaps the victory.
Some friends have we, beside domestic power;
The stern Polonian, and the warlike Dane,
The king of Bohemia, and of Sicily,
Are all become confederates with us,
And, as I think, are marching hither apace.

[*Drum within.*

But, soft, I hear the music of their drums,
By which I guess that their approach is near.

Enter BOHEMIA, *and Forces; and Aid of Danes, Poles, and Muscovites.*

Boh. King John of France, as league, and neighbourhood
Requires, when friends are any way distress'd,
I come to aid thee with my country's force.

Pol. And from great Moscow, fearful to the Turk,
And lofty Poland, nurse of hardy men,
I bring these servitors to fight for thee,
Who willingly will venture in thy cause.

Joh. Welcome, Bohemian king; and welcome, all:
This your great kindness I will not forget;
Beside your plentiful rewards in crowns,
That from our treasury ye shall receive:
There comes a hare-brain'd nation, deck'd in pride,
The spoil of whom will be a treble gain.—
And now my hope is full, my joy complete:
At sea, we are as puissant as the force
Of Agamemnon in the haven of Troy;
By land, with Xerxes we compare of strength,
Whose soldiers drank up rivers in their thirst:
Then, Bayard-like, blind over-weening Ned,
To reach at our imperial diadem,
Is, either to be swallow'd of the waves,
Or hack'd apieces when thou comest ashore.

Enter a Mariner.

Mar. Near to the coast I have descry'd, my lord,
As I was busy in my watchful charge,
The proud armado of King Edward's ships:
Which, at the first, far off when I did ken,
Seem'd as it were a grove of wither'd pines;
But, drawing near, their glorious bright aspect,
Their streaming ensigns wrought of colour'd silk,
Like to a meadow full of sundry flowers,
Adorns the naked bosom of the earth:
Majestical the order of their course,
Figuring the hornèd circle of the moon:
On the top-gallant of the admiral,
And likewise all the handmaids of his train,
The arms of England and of France united
Are quarter'd equally by herald's art.
Thus, tightly carry'd with a merry gale,
They plough the ocean hitherward amain.

Joh. Dare he already crop the flower-de-luce?
I hope, the honey being gather'd thence,

He, with the spider, afterward approach'd,
Shall suck forth deadly venom from the leaves.—
But where's our navy? how are they prepar'd
To wing themselves against this flight of ravens?

Mar. They, having knowledge brought them by the
 scouts,
Did break from anchor straight; and, puff'd with rage,
No otherwise than were their sails with wind,
Made forth; as when the empty eagle flies,
To satisfy his hungry griping maw.

Joh. There's for thy news. Return unto thy bark;
And, if thou 'scape the bloody stroke of war,
And do survive the conflict, come again,
And let us hear the manner of the fight.— *[Exit Mariner.*
Mean space, my lords, 'tis best we be dispers'd
To several places, lest they chance to land:
First, you, my lord, with your Bohemian troops,
Shall pitch your battles on the lower hand;
My eldest son, the Duke of Normandy,
Together with this aid of Muscovites,
Shall climb the higher ground another way;
Here in the middle coast, betwixt you both,
Philip, my youngest boy, and I will lodge.
So, lords, be gone, and look unto your charge;
You stand for France, an empire fair and large.—
 [Exeunt Cha., Lor., Bohemia, and Forces.
Now tell me, Philip, what is thy conceit,
Touching the challenge that the English make?

Phi. I say, my lord, claim Edward what he can,
And bring he ne'er so plain a pedigree,
'Tis you are in possession of the crown,
And that's the surest point of all the law:
But, were it not; yet, ere he should prevail,
I'll make a conduit of my dearest blood,
Or chase those straggling upstarts home again.

Joh. Well said, young Philip! Call for bread and wine,

That we may cheer our stomachs with repast,
To look our foes more sternly in the face.
    [*A table and provisions brought in; King and his
    son set down to it. Ordnance afar off.*
Now is begun the heavy day at sea.
Fight, Frenchmen, fight; be like the field of bears,
When they defend their younglings in their caves!
Steer, angry Nemesis, the happy helm;
That, with the sulphur battles of your rage,
The English fleet may be dispers'd, and sunk!
          [*Ordnance again.*

 Phi. O, father, how this echoing cannon shot,
Like sweetest harmony, digests my cates!

 Joh. Now, boy, thou hear'st what thundering terror 'tis.
To buckle for a kingdom's sovereignty:
The earth, with giddy trembling when it shakes,
Or when the exhalations of the air
Break in extremity of lightning flash,
Affrights not more, than kings, when they dispose
To show the rancour of their high-swoln hearts.
          [*Retreat heard.*
Retreat is sounded; one side hath the worse:
O, if it be the French!—Sweet fortune, turn;
And, in thy turning, change the froward winds,
That, with advantage of a favouring sky,
Our men may vanquish, and the other fly!

      Enter Mariner.

My heart misgives:—Say, mirror of pale death,
To whom belongs the honour of this day?
Relate, I pray thee, if thy breath will serve,
The sad discourse of this discomfiture.

 Mar. I will, my lord.
My gracious sovereign, France hath ta'n the foil,
And boasting Edward triumphs with success.
These iron-hearted navies,
When last I was reporter to your grace,

Both full of angry spleen, of hope, and fear,
Hasting to meet each other in the face,
At last conjoin'd; and by their admiral
Our admiral encounter'd many shot:
By this, the other, that beheld these twain
Give earnest penny of a further wreck,
Like fiery dragons took their haughty flight;
And, likewise meeting, from their smoky wombs
Sent many grim embassadors of death.
Then 'gan the day to turn to gloomy night;
And darkness did as well enclose the quick,
As those that were but newly reft of life:
No leisure serv'd for friends to bid farewell;
And, if it had, the hideous noise was such,
As each to other seem'd deaf, and dumb:
Purple the sea; whose channel fill'd as fast
With streaming gore, that from the maimèd fell,
As did her gushing moisture break into
The cranny'd clefturcs of the through-shot planks:
Here flew a head, dissever'd from the trunk;
There mangled arms, and legs, were toss'd aloft;
As when a whirlwind takes the summer dust,
And scatters it in middle of the air:
Then might ye see the reeling vessels split,
And tottering sink into the ruthless flood,
Until their lofty tops were seen no more.
All shifts were try'd, both for defence and hurt:
And now the effect of valour, and of fear,
Of resolution, and of cowardice,
Were lively pictur'd; how the one for fame,
The other by compulsion lay'd about:
Much did the Nonparcille, that brave ship;
So did the black-snake of Boulogne, than which
A bonnier vessel never yet spred sail:
But all in vain; both sun, the wind and tide,
Revolted all unto our foemen's side,
That we perforce were fain to give them way,

And they are landed: Thus my tale is done;
We have untimely lost, and they have won.
   Joh. Then rests there nothing, but, with present speed,
To join our several forces all in one,
And bid them battle, ere they range too far.—
Come, gentle Philip, let us hence depart;
This soldier's words have pierc'd thy father's heart.

           SCENE II. *Picardy. Fields near Cressy.*
   Enter A Frenchman, *meeting certain others, a* Woman *and
two* Children, *laden with household-stuff, as removing.*
   First F. Well met, my masters: How now? what's the news?
And wherefore are you laden thus with stuff?
What, is it quarter-day, that you remove,
And carry bag and baggage too?
   Sec. F. Quarter-day? ay, and quartering day, I fear:
Have you not heard the news that flies abroad?
   First F. What news?
   Third F. How the French navy is destroy'd at sea.
And that the English army is arriv'd.
   First F. What then?
   Sec. F. What then, quoth you? why, is't not time to fly,
When enemy and destruction is so nigh?
   First F. Content thee, man; they are far enough from hence;
And will be met, I warrant you, to their cost,
Before they break so far into the realm.
   Sec. F. Ay, so the grass-hopper doth spend the time
In mirthful jollity, till winter come;
And then too late he would redeem his time,
When frozen cold hath nipp'd his careless head.
He, that no sooner will provide a cloak,
Than when he sees it doth begin to rain,
May, peradventure, for his negligence,
Be throughly wash'd when he suspects it not.
We, that have charge, and such a train as this,
Must look in time to look for them and us,
Lest, when we would, we cannot be reliev'd.

First F. Belike, you then despair of all success,
And think your country will be subjugate.
   Third F. We cannot tell; 'tis good, to fear the worst.
   First F. Yet rather fight, than, like unnatural sons,
Forsake your loving parents in distress.
   Sec. F. Tush, they, that have already taken arms,
Are many fearful millions, in respect
Of that small handful of our enemies:
But 'tis a rightful quarrel must prevail;
Edward is son unto our late king's sister,
Where John Valois is three degrees remov'd.
   Wom. Besides, there goes a prophesy abroad,
Publish'd by one that was a friar once,
Whose oracles have many times prov'd true;
And now he says, "The time will shortly come,
When as a lion, rous̀ed in the west,
Shall carry hence the flower-de-luce of France:"
These, I can tell ye, and such like surmises
Strike many Frenchmen cold unto the heart.

            Enter another Frenchman, *hastily.*

   Fourth F. Fly, countrymen, and citizens of France!
Sweet-flow'ring peace, the root of happy life,
Is quite abandon'd and expuls'd the land:
Instead of whom, ransack-constraining war
Sits raven-like upon your houses' tops;
Slaughter and mischief walk within your streets,
And, unrestrain'd, make havoc as they pass:
The form whereof even now myself beheld,
Now, upon this fair mountain, whence I came.
For so far off as I direct mine eyes,
I might perceive five cities all on fire,
Corn-fields, and vineyards, burning like an oven;
And, as the reeking vapour in the wind
Turned aside, I likewise might discern
The poor inhabitants, escap'd the flame,
Fell numberless upon the soldiers' pikes·

Three ways these dreadful ministers of wrath
Do tread the measures of their tragic march;
Upon the right hand comes the conquering king,
Upon the left his hot unbridled son,
And in the midst our nation's glittering host;
All which, though distant, yet conspire in one
To leave a desolation where they come.
Fly, therefore, citizens, if you be wise,
Seek out some habitation further off:
Here if you stay, your wives will be abus'd,
Your treasure shar'd before your weeping eyes;
Shelter yourselves, for now the storm doth rise;
Away, away! methinks, I hear their drums:—
Ah, wretched France, I greatly fear thy fall;
Thy glory shaketh like a tottering wall. [*Exeunt.*

SCENE III. *The same.*

Drums. Enter King EDWARD, *marching;* DERBY, *&c., and Forces, and* GOBIN DE GREY.

Edw. Where is the Frenchman, by whose cunning guidance
We found the shallow of this river Somme,
And had direction how to pass the sea?
Gob. Here, my good lord.
Edw. How art thou call'd? thy name?
Gob. Gobin de Grey, if please your excellence.
Edw. Then, Gobin, for the service thou hast done,
We here enlarge and give thee liberty;
And, for a recompence, beside this good,
Thou shalt receive five hundred marks in gold.—
I know not how, we should have met our son;
Whom now in heart I wish I might behold.

Enter ARTOIS.

Art. Good news, my lord; the prince is hard at hand,
And with him comes lord Audley, and the rest,
Whom since our landing we could never meet.

Drums. Enter Prince, Audley, *and Forces.*

Edw. Welcome, fair prince! How hast thou sped, my son,
Since thy arrival on the coast of France?
  Pri. Successfully, I thank the gracious heavens:
Some of their strongest cities we have won,
As Harfleur, Lo, Crotage, and Carentan;
And others wasted; leaving at our heels
A wide apparent field, and beaten path,
For solitariness to progress in:
Yet, those that would submit, we kindly pardon'd;
But who in scorn refus'd our proffer'd peace,
Indur'd the penalty of sharp revenge.
  Edw. Ah, France, why shouldst thou be thus obstinate
Against the kind embracement of thy friends?
How gently had we thought to touch thy breast,
And set our foot upon thy tender mould,
But that, in froward and disdainful pride,
Thou, like a skittish and untamèd colt,
Dost start aside, and strike us with thy heels?—
But tell me, Ned, in all thy warlike course
Hast thou not seen the usurping king of France?
  Pri. Yes, my good lord, and not two hours ago,
With full an hundred thousand fighting men,
Upon the one side o' the river's bank,
I on the other; with his multitudes
I fear'd he would have cropp'd our smaller power:
But, happily, perceiving your approach,
He hath withdrawn himself to Cressy plains;
Where, as it seemeth by his good array,
He means to bid us battle presently.
  Edw. He shall be welcome, that's the thing we crave.

  Drums. Enter King John; Charles, *and* Philip, *his sons;*
    Bohemia, Lorrain, *&c., and Forces.*

  Joh. Edward, know, that John, the true king of France,—
Musing thou shouldst encroach upon his land,
And, in thy tyrannous proceeding, slay

His faithful subjects, and subvert his towns,—
Spits in thy face; and in this manner following
Upbraids thee with thine arrogant intrusion.
First, I condemn thee for a fugitive,
A thievish pirate, and a needy mate;
One, that hath either no abiding place,
Or else, inhabiting some barren soil,
Where neither herb or fruitful grain is had,
Dost altogether live by pilfering:
Next,—insomuch thou hast infring'd thy faith,
Broke league and solemn covenant made with me,—
I hold thee for a false pernitious wretch:
And last of all,—although I scorn to cope
With one such an inferior to myself;
Yet, in respect thy thirst is all for gold,
Thy labour rather to be fear'd than lov'd,—
To satisfy thy lust in either part,
Here am I come; and with me I have brought
Exceeding store of treasure, pearl, and coin.
Leave therefore now to persecute the weak;
And, armed ent'ring conflict with the arm'd,
Let it be seen, 'mongst other petty thefts,
How thou canst win this pillage manfully.

Edw. If gall, or wormwood, have a pleasant taste,
Then is thy salutation honey-sweet:
But as the one hath no such property,
So is the other most satirical.
Yet wot how I regard thy worthless taunts;—
If thou have utter'd them to soil my fame,
Or dim the reputation of my birth,
Know, that thy wolfish barking cannot hurt:
If slily to insinuate with the world,
And with a strumpet's artificial line
To paint thy vitious and deformèd cause,
Be well assur'd, the counterfeit will fade,
And in the end thy foul defects be seen:
But if thou didst it to provoke me on,—

As who should say, I were but timorous,
Or, coldly negligent, did need a spur,—
Bethink thyself, how slack I was at sea;
How, since my landing, I have won no towns,
Enter'd no further but upon the coast,
And there have ever since securely slept.
But if I have been otherways employ'd,
Imagine, Valois, whether I intend
To skirmish, not for pillage, but for the crown
Which thou dost wear; and that I vow to have,
Or one of us shall fall into his grave.

 Pri. Look not for cross invectives at our hands,
Or railing execrations of despite:
Let creeping serpents, hid in hollow banks,
Sting with their tongues; we have remorseless swords,
And they shall plead for us, and our affairs.
Yet thus much, briefly, by my father's leave:
As all the immodest poison of thy throat
Is scandalous and most notorious lies,
And our pretended quarrel truly just,
So end the battle when we meet to-day;
May either of us prosper and prevail,
Or, luckless curst, receive eternal shame!

 Edw. That needs no further question; and, I know,
His conscience witnesseth, it is my right.—
Therefore, Valois, say, wilt thou yet resign,
Before the sickle 's thrust into the corn,
Or that enkindled fury turn to flame?

 Joh. Edward, I know what right thou hast in France;
And ere I basely will resign my crown,
This champion field shall be a pool of blood,
And all our prospect as a slaughter-house.

 Pri. Ay, that approves thee, tyrant, what thou art:
No father, king, or shepherd of thy realm;
But one, that tears her entrails with thy hands,
And, like a thirsty tiger, suck'st her blood.

Aud. You peers of France, why do you follow him
That is so prodigal to spend your lives?
 Cha. Whom should they follow, aged impotent,
But he that is their true-born sovereign?
 Edw. Upbraid'st thou him, because within his face
Time hath engrav'd deep characters of age?
Know, these grave scholars of experience,
Like stiff-grown oaks, will stand immoveable,
When whirlwinds quickly turn up younger trees.
 Der. Was ever any of thy father's house
King, but thyself, before this present time?
Edward's great linage, by the mother's side,
Five hundred years hath held the scepter up:—
Judge then, conspirators, by this descent,
Which is the true-born sovereign, this, or that.
 Pri. Good father, range your battles, prate no more;
These English fain would spend the time in words,
That, night approaching, they might 'scape unfought.
 Joh. Lords, and my loving subjects, now 's the time,
That your intended force must bide the touch:
Therefore, my friends, consider this in brief,—
He, that you fight for, is your natural king;
He, against whom you fight, a foreigner:
He, that you fight for, rules in clemency,
And reins you with a mild and gentle bit;
He, against whom you fight, if he prevail,
Will straight enthrone himself in tyranny,
Make slaves of you, and, with a heavy hand,
Curtail and curb your sweetest liberty.
Then, to protect your country, and your king,
Let but the haughty courage of your hearts
Answer the number of your able hands,
And we shall quickly chase these fugitives.
For what's this Edward, but a belly-god,
A tender and lascivious wantonness,
That t'other day was almost dead for love?
And what, I pray you, is his goodly guard?

Such as, but scant them of their chines of beef,
And take away their downy feather-beds,
And, presently, they are as resty-stiff
As 'twere a many over-ridden jades.
Then, Frenchmen, scorn that such should be your lords,
And rather bind ye them in captive bands.
  Fre. Vive le roi! God save king John of France!
  Joh. Now on this plain of Cressy spread yourselves,—
And, Edward, when thou dar'st, begin the fight.
  [*Exeunt King John, Cha. Phi. Lor. Boh. and Forces.*
  Edw. We presently will meet thee, John of France:—
And, English lords, let us resolve the day,
Either to clear us of that scandalous crime,
Or be entombèd in our innocence.—
And, Ned, because this battle is the first
That ever yet thou fought'st in pitchèd field,
As ancient custom is of martialists,
To dub thee with the type of chivalry,
In solemn manner we will give thee arms:—
Come, therefore, heralds, orderly bring forth
A strong attirement for the prince my son.—

  *Flourish. Enter four Heralds, bringing a coat-armour, a
   helmet, a lance, and a shield:* First Herald *delivers the
   armour to* King Edward; *who, putting it on his son.*

Edward Plantagenet, in the name of God,
As with this armour I impall thy breast,
So be thy noble unrelenting heart
Wall'd in with flint of matchless fortitude,
That never base affections enter there;
Fight and be valiant, conquer where thou comest!—
Now follow, lords, and do him honour too.
  Der. [*Receiving the helmet from the second Herald.*
Edward Plantagenet, prince of Wales,
As I do set this helmet on thy head,
Wherewith the chamber of thy brain is fenc'd,
So may thy temples, with Bellona's hand,

Be still adorn'd with laurel victory;
Fight and be valiant, conquer where thou comest!
   Aud. [*Receiving the lance from the third Herald.*
Edward Plantagenet, prince of Wales,
Receive this lance, into thy manlike hand;
Use it in fashion of a brazen pen,
To draw forth bloody stratagems in France,
And print thy valiant deeds in honour's book;
Fight and be valiant, conquer where thou comest!
   Art. [*Receiving the shield from the fourth Herald.*
Edward Plantagenet, prince of Wales,
Hold, take this target, wear it on thy arm;
And may the view thereof, like Perseus' shield,
Astonish and transform thy gazing foes
To senseless images of meager death;
Fight and be valiant, conquer where thou comest!
   Edw. Now wants there nought but knighthood; which, deferr'd,
We leave, till thou hast won it in the field.
   Pri. My gracious father, and ye forward peers,
This honour, you have done me, animates
And cheers my green yet-scarce-appearing strength
With comfortable good-presaging signs;
No otherwise than did old Jacob's words,
When as he breath'd his blessings on his sons:
These hallow'd gifts of yours when I prophane,
Or use them not to glory of my God,
To patronage the fatherless, and poor,
Or for the benefit of England's peace,
Be numb my joints! wax feeble both mine arms!
Wither my heart! that, like a sapless tree,
I may remain the map of infamy.
   Edw. Then thus our steeled battles shall be rang'd;—
The leading of the vaward, Ned, is thine;
To dignify whose lusty spirit the more,
We temper it with Audley's gravity;
That, courage and experience join'd in one,

Your manage may be second unto none:
For the main battles, I will guide myself;
And, Derby, in the rearward march behind.
That orderly dispos'd, and set in 'ray,
Let us to horse; and God grant us the day!

Scene IV. *The same.*

Alarums, as of a battle join'd. Enter a many Frenchmen, flying; Prince, and English, pursuing; and Exeunt: then Enter King John, *and* Lorrain.

Joh. O Lorrain, say, what mean our men to fly?
Our number is far greater than our foes.
Lor. The garrison of Genoeses, my lord,
That came from Paris, weary with their march,
Grudging to be so suddenly employ'd,
No sooner in the fore-front took their place,
But, straight retiring, so dismay'd the rest,
As likewise they betook themselves to flight;
In which, for haste to make a safe escape,
More in the clust'ring throng are press'd to death,
Than by the enemy, a thousand fold.
Joh. O hapless fortune! Let us yet assay
If we can counsel some of them to stay.   [*Exeunt.*

Scene V. *The same.*

Drums. Enter King Edward, *and* Audley.

Edw. Lord Audley, whiles our son is in the chase,
Withdraw your powers unto this little hill,
And here a season let us breathe ourselves.
Aud. I will, my lord.   [*Exit Audley. Retreat.*
Edw. Just-dooming heaven, whose secret providence
To our gross judgment is unscrutable,
How are we bound to praise thy wondrous works,
That hast this day giv'n way unto the right,
And made the wicked stumble at themselves?

Enter Artois, *hastily.*

Art. Rescue, king Edward! rescue for thy son!
Edw. Rescue, Artois? what, is he prisoner?
Or, else, by violence fell beside his horse?
Art. Neither; my lord; but narrowly beset
With turning Frenchmen, whom he did pursue,
As 'tis impossible that he should escape,
Except your highness presently descend.
Edw. Tut, let him fight; we gave him arms to-day,
And he is labouring for a knighthood, man.

Enter Derby, *hastily.*

Der. The prince, my lord, the prince! O, succour him;
He's close encompass'd with a world of odds!
Edw. Then will he win a world of honour too,
If he by valour can redeem him thence:
If not, what remedy? we have more sons
Than one, to comfort our declining age.

Re-enter Audley, *hastily.*

Aud. Renownèd Edward, give me leave, I pray,
To lead my soldiers where I may relieve
Your grace's son, in danger to be slain.
The snares of French, like emmets on a bank,
Muster about him; whilst he, lion-like,
Entangled in the net of their assaults,
Franticly rends, and bites the woven toil:
But all in vain, he cannot free himself.
Edw. Audley, content; I will not have a man,
On pain of death, sent forth to succour him:
This is the day ordain'd by destiny
To season his green courage with those thoughts,
That, if he breathe out Nestor's years on earth,
Will make him savour still of this exploit.
Der. Ah! but he shall not live to see those days.
Edw. Why, then his epitaph is lasting praise.
Aud. Yet, good my lord, 'tis too much wilfulness,
To let his blood be spilt, that may be sav'd.

Edw. Exclaim no more; for none of you can tell,
Whether a borrow'd aid will serve, or no;
Perhaps, he is already slain, or ta'en:
And dare a falcon when she's in her flight,
And ever after she'll be haggard-like:
Let Edward be deliver'd by our hands,
And still, in danger, he'll expect the like;
But if himself himself redeem from thence,
He will have vanquish'd, cheerful, death and fear,
And ever after dread their force no more,
Than if they were but babes, or captive slaves.
 Aud. O cruel father!—Farewell, Edward, then!
 Der. Farewell, sweet prince, the hope of chivalry!
 Art. O, would my life might ransom him from death!
 Edw. But, soft; methinks, I hear [*Retreat sounded.*
The dismal charge of trumpets' loud retreat:
All are not slain, I hope, that went with him;
Some will return with tidings, good, or bad.

 Flourish. Enter Prince EDWARD *in triumph, bearing in his hand his shivered lance; his sword, and battered armour, borne before him, and the body of the King of* BOHEMIA, *wrapped in the colours: Lords run and embrace him.*

 Aud. O joyful sight! victorious Edward lives!
 Der. Welcome, brave prince!
 Edw.   Welcome, Plantagenet! [*Embracing him.*
 Pri. First having done my duty, as beseem'd.
      [*Kneels, and kisses his father's hand.*
Lords, I regreet you all with hearty thanks.
And now, behold,—after my winter's toil,
My painful voyage on the boist'rous sea
Of war's devouring gulphs and steely rocks,—
I bring my fraught unto the wished port,
My summer's hope, my travel's sweet reward:
And here, with humble duty, I present
This sacrifice, this first fruit of my sword,
Cropp'd and cut down even at the gate of death,

The king of Bohemia, father, whom I slew;
Whose thousands had intrench'd me round about,
And lay as thick upon my batter'd crest,
As on an anvil, with their pond'rous glaives:
Yet marble courage still did underprop;
And when my weary arms, with often blows,—
Like the continual-lab'ring woodman's axe,
That is enjoin'd to fell a load of oaks,—
Began to falter, straight I would remember
My gifts you gave me, and my zealous vow,
And then new courage made me fresh again;
That, in despite, I carv'd my passage forth,
And put the multitude to speedy flight.
Lo, thus hath Edward's hand fill'd your request,
And done, I hope, the duty of a knight.

Edw. Ay, well thou hast deserv'd a knighthood, Ned!
And, therefore, with thy sword, yet recking warm
    [*Receiving it from the soldier who bore it, and*
      laying it on the kneeling Prince.
With blood of those that fought to be thy bane,
Arise, prince Edward, trusty knight at arms:
This day thou hast confounded me with joy,
And prov'd thyself fit heir unto a king.

Pri. Here is a note, my gracious lord, of those
That in this conflict of our foes were slain:
Eleven princes of esteem; fourscore
Barons; a hundred and twenty knights;
And thirty thousand common soldiers;
And, of our men, a thousand.

Edw. Our God be prais'd! Now, John of France, I hope,
Thou know'st king Edward for no wantonness,
No love-sick cockney; nor his soldiers, jades.—
But which way is the fearful king escap'd?

Pri. Towards Poitiers, noble father, and his sons.

Edw. Ned, thou, and Audley, shall pursue them still;
Myself, and Derby, will to Calais straight,
And there begirt that haven-town with siege:

Now lies it on an upshot; therefore strike,
And wistly follow while the game's on foot.
What picture 's this?   [*Pointing to the colours.*
   Pri.   A pelican, my lord,
Wounding her bosom with her crookèd beak,
That so her nest of young ones may be fed
With drops of blood that issue from her heart;
The motto, "Sic et vos, And so should you."
                    [*Flourish. Exeunt in triumph.*

ACT IV.

SCENE I. *Bretagne. Camp of the English; Salisbury's tent.*

Forces under the Earl *of* SALISBURY. *Enter* SALISBURY; *to him, the* Earl *of* MONTFORT, *attended, a coronet in his hand.*

   Mon. My lord of Salisbury, since by your aid
Mine enemy Sir Charles of Blois is slain,
And I again am quietly possess'd
In Bretagne's dukedom, know, that I resolve,
For this kind furtherance of your king, and you,
To swear allegiance to his majesty:
In sign whereof, receive this coronet,
Bear it unto him; and, withal, my oath,
Never to be but Edward's faithful friend.
   Sal. I take it, Montfort: Thus, I hope, ere long
The whole dominions of the realm of France
Will be surrender'd to his conquering hand.
                    [*Exeunt Montfort, and Train.*
Now, if I knew but safely how to pass,
I would at Calais gladly meet his grace,
Whither, I am by letters certify'd,
That he intends to have his host remov'd.
It shall be so: this policy will serve:—
Ho, who's within? Bring Villiers to me.—

Enter VILLIERS.

Villiers, thou know'st, thou art my prisoner,
And that I might, for ransom, if I would,
Require of thee an hundred thousand franks,
Or else retain and keep thee captive still:
But so it is, that for a smaller charge
Thou mayst be quit, an if thou wilt thyself;
And this it is, Procure me but a passport
Of Charles the duke of Normandy, that I,
Without restraint, may have recourse to Calais
Through all the countries where he hath to do,
(Which thou mayst easily obtain, I think,
By reason I have often heard thee say,
He and thyself were students once together)
And then thou shalt be set at liberty.
How say'st thou? wilt thou undertake to do it?
 Vil. I will, my lord; but I must speak with him.
 Sal. Why, so thou shalt; take horse, and post from hence:
Only, before thou go'st, swear by thy faith,
That, if thou canst not compass my desire,
Thou wilt return my prisoner back again;
And that shall be sufficient warrant for thee.
 Vil. To that condition I agree, my lord,
And will unfeignèdly perform the same.
 Sal. Farewell, Villiers.— [*Exit Villiers.*
This once I mean to try a Frenchman's faith.

SCENE II. *Picardy. The English camp before Calais.*

Enter King EDWARD, *and* DERBY, *with Soldiers.*

 Edw. Since they refuse our proffer'd league, my lord,
And will not ope their gates, and let us in,
We will intrench ourselves on every side,
That neither victuals, nor supply of men,
May come to succour this accursèd town;
Famine shall combat where our swords are stopp'd.
 Der. The promis'd aid, that made them stand aloof,

Is now retir'd, and gone another way;
It will repent them of their stubborn will.

Enter some poor Frenchmen.

But what are these poor ragged slaves, my lord?
    Edw. Ask what they are; it seems, they come from Calais.
    Der. You wretched patterns of despair and woe,
What are ye? living men; or gliding ghosts,
Crept from your graves to walk upon the earth?
    First Fre. No ghosts, my lord, but men that breathe a life
Far worse than is the quiet sleep of death:
We are distressèd poor inhabitants,
That long have been diseased, sick, and lame;
And now, because we are not fit to serve,
The captain of the town hath thrust us forth,
That so expence of victuals may be sav'd.
    Edw. A charitable deed, and worthy praise.—
But how do you imagine then to speed?
We are your enemies; in such a case
We can no less but put you to the sword,
Since, when we proffer'd truce, it was refus'd.
    First Fre. An if your grace no otherwise vouchsafe,
As welcome death is unto us as life.
    Edw. Poor silly men, much wrong'd, and more dis-
                                                tress'd I—
Go, Derby, go, and see they be reliev'd;
Command that victuals be appointed them,
And give to every one five crowns apiece:—
                        [*Exeunt Derby, and Frenchmen.*
The lion scorns to touch the yielding prey;
And Edward's sword must flesh itself in such
As wilful stubbornness hath made perverse.—

Enter the Lord Percy, *from England.*

Lord Percy! welcome: What's the news in England?
    Per. The queen, my lord, commends her to your grace;
And from her highness, and the lord vice-gerent,

I bring this happy tidings of success:
David of Scotland, lately up in arms,
(Thinking, belike, he soonest should prevail,
Your highness being absent from the realm)
Is, by the faithful service of your peers,
And painful travel of the queen herself,
That, big with child, was every day in arms,
Vanquish'd, subdu'd, and taken prisoner.

   Edw. Thanks, Percy, for thy news, with all my heart!
What was he, took him prisoner in the field?

   Per. A squire, my lord; John Copland is his name:
Who since, entreated by her majesty,
Denies to make surrender of his prize
To any but unto your grace alone;
Whereat the queen is grievously displeas'd.

   Edw. Well, then we'll have a pursuivant dispatch'd,
To summon Copland hither out of hand,
And with him he shall bring his prisoner king.

   Per. The queen's, my lord, herself by this at sea;
And purposeth, as soon as wind will serve,
To land at Calais, and to visit you.

   Edw. She shall be welcome; and, to wait her coming,
I'll pitch my tent near to the sandy shore.

           Enter a French Captain.

   Cap. The burgesses of Calais, mighty king,
Have, by a council, willingly decreed
To yield the town, and castle, to your hands;
Upon condition, it will please your grace
To grant them benefit of life, and goods.

   Edw. They will so! then, belike, they may command,
Dispose, elect, and govern as they list.
No, sirrah, tell them, since they did refuse
Our princely clemency at first proclaim'd,
They shall not have it now, although they would;
I will accept of nought but fire and sword,
Except, within these two days, six of them,

That are the wealthiest merchants in the town,
Come naked, all but for their linen shirts,
With each a halter hang'd about his neck,
And prostrate yield, themselves, upon their knees,
To be afflicted, hang'd, or what I please;
And so you may inform their masterships.
        [Exeunt Edward, and Percy.
 Cap. Why, this it is to trust a broken staff.
Had we not been persuaded, John our king
Would with his army have reliev'd the town,
We had not stood upon defiance so:
But now 'tis past that no man can recall;
And better some do go to wreck, than all.   *[Exit.*

   Scene III. *Poitou. Fields near Poitiers.*
  The French camp; Tent of the Duke of Normandy.

    Enter Charles, *and* Villiers.

 Cha. I wonder, Villiers, thou shouldst importune me
For one that is our deadly enemy.
 Vil. Not for his sake, my gracious lord, so much
Am I become an earnest advocate,
As that thereby my ransom will be quit.
 Cha. Thy ransom, man! why, need'st thou talk of that?
Art thou not free? and are not all occasions,
That happen for advantage on our foes,
To be accepted of, and stood upon?
 Vil. No, good my lord, except the same be just;
For profit must with honour be commix'd,
Or else our actions are but scandalous:
But, letting pass these intricate objections,
Will 't please your highness to subscribe, or no?
 Cha. Villiers, I will not, nor I cannot do it;
Salisbury shall not have his will so much,
To claim a passport how it please himself.
 Vil. Why, then I know the extremity, my lord,
I must return to prison whence I came.

Cha. Return! I hope, thou wilt not, Villiers:
What bird, that hath escap'd the fowler's gin,
Will not be ware how she's ensnar'd again?
Or, what is he, so senseless, and secure,
That, having hardly pass'd a dangerous gulph,
Will put himself in peril there again?
　Vil. Ah, but it is mine oath, my gracious lord,
Which I in conscience may not violate,
Or else a kingdom should not draw me hence.
　Cha. Thine oath! why, that doth bind thee to abide:
Hast thou not sworn obedience to thy prince?
　Vil. In all things that uprightly he commands:
But either to persuade, or threaten me,
Not to perform the covenant of my word,
Is lawless, and I need not to obey.
　Cha. Why, is it lawful for a man to kill,
And not, to break a promise with his foe?
　Vil. To kill, my lord, when war is once proclaim'd,
So that our quarrel be for wrongs receiv'd,
No doubt, is lawfully permitted us:
But, in an oath, we must be well advis'd
How we do swear; and, when we once have sworn,
Not to infringe it, though we die therefore:
Therefore, my lord, as willing I return,
As if I were to fly to paradise.　　　　　　　[*Going.*
　Cha. Stay, my Villiers; thy honourable mind
Deserves to be eternally admir'd.
Thy suit shall be no longer thus deferr'd;
Give me the paper, I'll subscribe to it:
　　　　　　　　　　　　[*Signs, and gives it back.*
And, where tofore I lov'd thee as Villiers,
Hereafter I'll embrace thee as myself;
Stay, and be still in favour with thy lord.
　Vil. I humbly thank your grace: I must dispatch,
And send this passport first unto the earl,
And then I will attend your highness' pleasure.
　　　　　　　　　　　　　　　　　[*Exit Villiers.*

Cha. Do so, Villiers;—And Charles, when he hath need,
Be such his soldiers, howsoe'er he speed!

Enter King JOHN.

Joh. Come, Charles, and arm thee; Edward is entrapp'd,
The prince of Wales is fall'n into our hands,
And we have compass'd him, he cannot 'scape.
  Cha. But will your highness fight to-day?
  Joh. What else, my son? he's scarce eight thousand
    strong,
And we are threescore thousand at the least.
  Cha. I have a prophesy, my gracious lord,
Wherein is written, what success is like
To happen us in this outrageous war;
It was deliver'd me at Cressy field,
By one that is an aged hermit there.   [*Reads.*
  "When feather'd fowl shall make thine army tremble,
    And flint stones rise, and break the battle 'ray,
  Then think on him that doth not now dissemble;
    For that shall be the hapless dreadful day:
  Yet, in the end, thy foot thou shalt advance
  As far in England, as thy foe in France."
  Joh. By this it seems we shall be fortunate:
For as it is impossible, that stones
Should ever rise, and break the battle 'ray;
Or airy fowl make men in arms to quake;
So is it like, we shall not be subdu'd:
Or, say this might be true, yet, in the end,
Since he doth promise, we shall drive him hence,
And forage their country, as they have done ours;
By this revenge that loss will seem the less.
But all are frivolous fancies, toys, and dreams:
Once, we are sure we have ensnar'd the son,
Catch we the father after how we can.   [*Exeunt.*

SCENE IV. *The same. The English camp.*

Enter Prince EDWARD, AUDLEY, *and* others.

Pri. Audley, the arms of death embrace us round,
And comfort have we none, save that to die,
We pay sour earnest for a sweeter life.
At Cressy field our clouds of warlike smoke
Chok'd up those French moths, and dissever'd them:
But now their multitudes of millions hide,
Masking as 'twere, the beauteous burning sun;
Leaving no hope to us, but sullen dark,
And eyeless terror of all-ending night.

Aud. This sudden, mighty, and expedient head,
That they have made, fair prince, is wonderful.
Before us in the valley lies the king,
Vantag'd with all that heaven and earth can yield;
His party stronger battled than our whole:
His son, the braving duke of Normandy,
Hath trimm'd the mountain on our right hand up
In shining plate, that now the aspiring hill
Shows like a silver quarry, or an orb;
Aloft the which, the banners, bannerets,
And new-replenish'd pendants, cuff the air,
And beat the winds, that, for their gaudiness,
Struggles to kiss them: on our left hand lies
Philip, the younger issue of the king,
Coating the other hill in such array,
That all his gilded upright pikes do seem
Strait trees of gold, the pendant streamers, leaves;
And their device of antique heraldry,
Quarter'd in colours seeming sundry fruits,
Makes it the orchard of the Hesperides:
Behind us too the hill doth bear his height,
(For, like a half-moon, op'ning but one way,
It rounds us in) there at our backs are lodg'd
The fatal cross-bows; and the battle there
Is govern'd by the rough Chatillion.

Then thus it stands,—The valley for our flight
The king binds in; the hills on either hand
Are proudly royalized by his sons;
And on the hill behind stands certain death,
In pay and service with Chatillion.
  Pri. Death's name is much more mighty than his deeds;—
Thy parcelling this power hath made it more.
As many sands as these my hands can hold,
Are but my handful of so many sands;
Then, all the world,—and call it but a power,—
Easily ta'en up, and quickly thrown away:
But, if I stand to count them sand by sand,
The number would confound my memory,
And make a thousand millions of a task,
Which, briefly, is no more, indeed, than one.
These quarters, squadrons, and these regiments,
Before, behind us, and on either hand,
Are but a power: When we name a man,
His hand, his foot, his head, have several strengths;
And being all but one self instant strength,
Why, all this many, Audley, is but one,
And we can call it all but one man's strength.
He, that hath far to go, tells it by miles;
If he should tell the steps, it kills his heart:
The drops are infinite, that make a flood;
And yet, thou know'st, we call it but a rain.
There is but one France, and one king of France,
That France hath no more kings; and that same king
Hath but the puissant legion of one king;
And we have one: Then apprehend no odds;
For one to one is fair equality.—

Enter a Herald.

What tidings, messenger? be plain, and brief.
  Her. The king of France, my sovereign lord and master,
Greets thus by me his foe the prince of Wales:
If thou call forth an hundred men of name,

Of lords, knights, squires, and English gentlemen,
And with thyself and those kneel at his feet,
He straight will fold his bloody colours up,
And ransom shall redeem lives forfeited:
If not, this day shall drink more English blood
Than e'er was bury'd in your British earth.
What is the answer to his proffer'd mercy?
   Pri. This heaven, that covers France, contains the mercy
That draws from me submissive orisons;
That such base breath should vanish from my lips,
To urge the plea of mercy to a man,
The Lord forbid! Return, and tell thy king,
My tongue is made of steel, and it shall beg
My mercy on his coward burgonet;
Tell him, my colours are as red as his,
My men as bold, our English arms as strong,
Return him my defiance in his face.
   Her. I go.   [*Exit Herald.*
                Enter another Herald.
   Pri. What news with thee?
   Her. The duke of Normandy, my lord and master,
Pitying thy youth is so engirt with peril,
By me hath sent a nimble-jointed jennet,
As swift as ever yet thou didst bestride,
And therewithal he counsels thee to fly;
Else, death himself hath sworn, that thou shalt die.
   Pri. Back with the beast unto the beast that sent him;
Tell him, I cannot sit a coward's horse:
Bid him to-day bestride the jade himself;
For I will stain my horse quite o'er with blood,
And double-gild my spurs, but I will catch him;
So tell the carping boy, and get thee gone.   [*Exit Herald.*
                Enter another Herald.
   Her. Edward of Wales, Philip, the second son
To the most mighty christian king of France,
Seeing thy body's living date expir'd,

All full of charity and christian love,
Commends this book, full fraught with prayers,
To thy fair hand, and, for thy hour of life,
Intreats thee that thou meditate therein,
And arm thy soul for her long journey towards.
Thus have I done his bidding, and return.

Pri. Herald of Philip, greet thy lord from me;
All good, that he can send, I can receive:
But think'st thou not, the unadvised boy
Hath wrong'd himself, in thus far tend'ring me?
Haply, he cannot pray without the book;
I think him no divine extemporal:
Then render back this common-place of prayer,
To do himself good in adversity;
Besides, he knows not my sin's quality,
And therefore knows no prayers for my avail;
Ere night his prayer may be, to pray to God
To put it in my heart to hear his prayer;
So tell the courtly wanton, and be gone.

Her. I go. *[Exit Herald.*

Pri. How confident their strength and number makes
 them!—
Now, Audley, sound those silver wings of thine,
And let those milk-white messengers of time
Show thy time's learning in this dangerous time;
Thyself art bruis'd and bit with many broils,
And stratagems forepast with iron pens
Are texted in thine honourable face;
Thou art a marry'd man in this distress,
But danger wooes me as a blushing maid:
Teach me an answer to this perilous time.

Aud. To die is all as common, as to live;
The one in choice, the other holds in chace:
For, from the instant we begin to live,
We do pursue and hunt the time to die:
First bud we, then we blow, and after seed;
Then, presently, we fall; and, as a shade

Follows the body, so we follow death.
If then we hunt for death, why do we fear it?
Or, if we fear it, why do we follow it?
If we do fear, with fear we do but aid
The thing we fear to seize on us the sooner:
If we fear not, then no resolvèd proffer
Can overthrow the limit of our fate:
For, whether ripe, or rotten, drop we shall,
As we do draw the lottery of our doom.

   Pri. Ah, good old man, a thousand thousand armours
These words of thine have buckled on my back:
Ah, what an idiot hast thou made of life,
To seek the thing it fears! and how disgrac'd
The imperial victory of murd'ring death!
Since all the lives his conquering arrows strike
Seek him, and he not them, to shame his glory.
I will not give a penny for a life,
Nor half a halfpenny to shun grim death;
Since for to live is but to seek to die,
And dying but beginning of new life:
Let come the hour when He that rules it will!
To live, or die, I hold indifferent.   *[Exeunt.*

    Scene V. *The same. The French camp.*

    Enter King John, *and* Charles.

   Joh. A sudden darkness hath defac'd the sky,
The winds are crept into their caves for fear,
The leaves move not, the wood is hush'd and still,
The birds cease singing, and the wand'ring brooks
Murmur no wonted greeting to their shores;
Silence attends some wonder, and expecteth
That heaven should pronounce some prophesy:
Whence, or from whom, proceeds this silence, Charles?

   Cha. Our men, with open mouths, and staring eyes,
Look on each other, as they did attend
Each other's words, and yet no creature speaks;

A tongue-ty'd fear hath made a midnight hour,
And speeches sleep through all the waking regions.
   Joh. But now the pompous sun, in all his pride,
Look'd through his golden coach upon the world,
And, on a sudden, hath he hid himself;
That now the under earth is as a grave,
Dark, deadly, silent, and uncomfortable.
                         [*A clamour of ravens heard.*
Hark! what a deadly outcry do I hear!
   Cha. Here comes my brother Philip.
   Joh.   All dismay'd:—

            Enter Philip.

What fearful words are those thy looks presage?
   Phi. A flight, a flight!
   Joh. Coward, what flight? thou liest, there needs no
        flight.
   Phi. A flight!
   Joh. Awake thy craven powers, and tell on
The very substance of that fear indeed,
Which is so gastly printed in thy face:
What is the matter?
   Phi.   A flight of ugly ravens
Do croak and hover o'er our soldiers' heads,
And keep in triangles, and corner'd squares,
Right as our forces are embattled;
With their approach there came this sudden fog,
Which now hath hid the airy floor of heaven,
And made at noon a night unnatural
Upon the quaking and dismayèd world:
In brief, our soldiers have let fall their arms,
And stand like metamorphos'd images,
Bloodless and pale, one gazing on another.
   Joh. Ay, now I call to mind the prophesy;
But I must give no entrance to a fear.—
Return, and hearten up those yielding souls;
Tell them, the ravens, seeing them in arms,—

So many fair against a famish'd few,—
Come but to dine upon their handy-work,
And prey upon the carrion that they kill:
For when we see a horse lay'd down to die,
Although he be not dead, the ravenous birds
Sit watching the departure of his life;
Even so these ravens, for the carcases
Of those poor English, that are mark'd to die,
Hover about, and, if they cry to us,
'Tis but for meat that we must kill for them.
Away, and comfort up my soldiers,
And sound the trumpets; and at once dispatch
This little business of a silly fraud. [*Exit Philip.*

Noise within. Enter a French Captain, *with* Salisbury, *prisoner.*

Cap. Behold, my liege, this knight, and forty more,—
Of whom the better part are slain and fled,—
With all endeavour sought to break our ranks,
And make their way to the encompass'd prince;
Dispose of him as please your majesty.
Joh. Go, and the next bough, soldier, that thou see'st,
Disgrace it with his body presently:
For I do hold a tree in France too good
To be the gallows of an English thief.
Sal. My lord of Normandy, I have your pass
And warrant for my safety through this land.
Cha. Villiers procur'd it for thee, did he not?
Sal. He did.
Cha. And it is current, thou shalt freely pass.
Joh. Ay, freely to the gallows to be hang'd,
Without denial, or impediment:—
Away with him.
Cha. I hope, your highness will not so disgrace me,
And dash the virtue of my seal at arms:
He hath my never-broken name to show,
Character'd with this princely hand of mine;

And rather let me leave to be a prince,
Than break the stable verdict of a prince:
I do beseech you, let him pass in quiet.

   Joh. Thou and thy word lie both in my command;
What canst thou promise, that I cannot break?
Which of these twain is greater infamy,
To disobey thy father, or thyself?
Thy word, nor no man's, may exceed his power;
Nor that same man doth never break his word,
That keeps it to the utmost of his power:
The breach of faith dwells in the soul's consent;
Which if thyself without consent do break,
Thou art not chargèd with the breach of faith.—
Go, hang him; for thy licence lies in me:
And my constraint stands the excuse for thee.

   Cha. What, am I not a soldier in my word?
Then, arms adieu, and let them fight that list:
Shall I not give my girdle from my waist,
But with a guardian I shall be control'd,
To say, I may not give my things away?
Upon my soul, had Edward prince of Wales,
Engag'd his word, writ down his noble hand,
For all your knights to pass his father's land,
The royal king, to grace his warlike son,
Would not alone safe-conduct give to them,
But with all bounty feasted them and theirs.

   Joh. Dwell'st thou on precedents? Then be it so.—
Say, Englishman, of what degree thou art?

   Sal. An earl in England, though a prisoner here;
And those, that know me, call me Salisbury.

   Joh. Then, Salisbury, say, whither thou art bound?

   Sal. To Calais, where my liege, king Edward, is.

   Joh. To Calais, Salisbury? Then to Calais pack;
And bid the king prepare a noble grave,
To put his princely son, black Edward, in.
And as thou travel'st westward from this place,
Some two leagues hence there is a lofty hill,

Whose top seems topless, for the embracing sky
Doth hide his high head in her azure bosom;
Unto whose tall top when thy foot attains,
Look back upon the humble vale below,
(Humble of late, but now made proud with arms)
And thence behold the wretched prince of Wales,
Hoop'd with a band of iron round about.
After which sight, to Calais spur amain,
And say, the prince was smother'd, and not slain:
And tell the king, this is not all his ill;
For I will greet him, ere he thinks I will.
Away, be gone; The smoke but of our shot
Will choke our foes, though bullets hit them not.

SCENE VI. *The same. A part of the field of battle.*
Alarums, as of a battle join'd, skirmishings.

Enter Prince EDWARD, *and* ARTOIS.

Art. How fares your grace? are you not shot, my lord?
Pri. No, dear Artois; but chok'd with dust and smoke,
And stepp'd aside for breath and fresher air.
Art. Breathe then, and to 't again: the amasèd French
Are quite distract with gazing on the crows;
And, were our quivers full of shafts again,
Your grace should see a glorious day of this:—
O, for more arrows, lord! that is our want.
Pri. Courage, Artois! a fig for feather'd shafts,
When feather'd fowls do bandy on our side!
What need we fight, and sweat, and keep a coil,
When railing crows outscold our adversaries?
Up, up, Artois! the ground itself is arm'd:
Fire-containing flint; command our bows
To hurl away their pretty-colour'd yew,
And to 't with stones: Away, Artois, away;
My soul doth prophesy we win the day. [*Exeunt.*

Alarums, and Parties skirmishing.

Enter King JOHN.

Joh. Our multitudes are in themselves confounded,
Dismayèd, and distraught; swift-starting fear
Hath buzz'd a cold dismay through all our army,
And every petty disadvantage prompts
The fear-possessèd abject soul to fly:
Myself, whose spirit is steel to their dull lead,
(What with recalling of the prophesy,
And that our native stones from English arms
Rebel against us) find myself attainted
With strong surprize of weak and yielding fear.

Enter CHARLES.

Cha. Fly, father, fly! the French do kill the French;
Some, that would stand, let drive at some that fly:
Our drums strike nothing but discouragement,
Our trumpets sound dishonour and retire;
The spirit of fear, that feareth nought but death,
Cowardly works confusion on itself.

Enter PHILIP.

Phi. Pluck out your eyes, and see not this days' shame!
An arm hath beat an army; one poor David
Hath with a stone foil'd twenty stout Goliaths:
Some twenty naked starvelings, with small flints,
Have driven back a puissant host of men,
Array'd and fenc'd in all accomplements.

Joh. Mordieu, they quoit at us, and kill us up;
No less than forty thousand wicked elders
Have forty lean slaves this day ston'd to death.

Cha. O, that I were some other countryman!
This day hath set derision on the French;
And all the world will blurt and scorn at us.

Joh. What, is there no hope left?

Phi. No hope, but death, to bury up our shame.

Joh. Make up once more with me; the twentieth part

Of those that live, are men enough to quail
The feeble handful on the adverse part.
   Cha. Then charge again: if heaven be not oppos'd,
We cannot lose the day.
   Joh.   On, on; away.   [*Exeunt.*

     Alarums, &c. Enter AUDLEY, *wounded, and two
          Esquires, his rescuers.*

   First E. How fares my lord?
   Aud.   E'en as a man may do,
That dines at such a bloody feast as this.
   Sec. E. I hope, my lord, that is no mortal scar.
   Aud. No matter, if it be; the count is cast,
And, in the worst, ends but a mortal man.
Good friends, convey me to the princely Edward,
That, in the crimson bravery of my blood,
I may become him with saluting him;
I'll smile, and tell him, that this open scar
Doth end the harvest of his Audley's war.   [*Exeunt.*
         Other alarums; afterwards, a retreat.

     SCENE VII. *The same. The English camp.*

Flourish. Enter Prince EDWARD, *in triumph, leading prisoners,*
   King JOHN, *and his son* Charles; *and* Officers, Soldiers,
   &c., *with ensigns spred.*

   Pri. Now, John in France, and lately John of France,
Thy bloody ensigns are my captive colours;
And you, high-vaunting Charles of Normandy,
That once to-day sent me a horse to fly,
Are now the subjects of my clemency.
Fie, lords! is't not a shame, that English boys,
Whose early days are yet not worth a beard,
Should in the bosom of your kingdom thus,
One against twenty, beat you up together?
   Joh. Thy fortune, not thy force, hath conquer'd us.
   Pri. An argument, that heaven aids the right.—

Enter ARTOIS, *with* PHILIP.

See, see, Artois doth bring along with him
The late good counsel-giver to my soul!—
Welcome, Artois;—and welcome, Philip, too:
Who now, of you, or I, have need to pray?
Now is the proverb verify'd in you,
Too bright a morning breeds a louring day.—

Enter AUDLEY, *led by the* two Esquires.

But, say, what grim discouragement comes here!
Alas, what thousand armèd men of France
Have writ that note of death in Audley's face?—
Speak, thou that woo'st death with thy careless smile,
And look'st so merrily upon thy grave
As if thou wert enamour'd on thine end,
What hungry sword hath so bereav'd thy face,
And lopp'd a true friend from my loving soul?

Aud. O prince, thy sweet bemoaning speech to me
Is as a mournful knell to one dead-sick.

Pri. Dear Audley, if my tongue ring out thy end,
My arms shall be thy grave: What may I do,
To win thy life, or to revenge thy death?
If thou wilt drink the blood of captive kings,—
Or, that it were restorative, command
A health of king's blood, and I'll drink to thee:
If honour may dispense for thee with death,
The never-dying honour of this day
Share wholly, Audley, to thyself, and live.

Aud. Victorious prince,—that thou art so, behold
A Cæsar's fame in kings' captivity,—
If I could hold dim death but at a bay,
Till I did see my liege thy royal father,
My soul should yield this castle of my flesh,
This mangled tribute, with all willingness,
To darkness, consummation, dust, and worms.

Pri. Cheerly, bold man! thy soul is all too proud,
To yield her city for one little breach;

She'ld be divorcèd from her earthly spouse
By the soft temper of a Frenchman's sword?
Lo, to repair thy life, I give to thee
Three thousand marks a year in English land.

Aud. I take thy gift, to pay the debts I owe:
These two poor squires redeem'd me from the French,
With lusty and dear hazard of their lives;
What thou hast given to me, I give to them;
And, as thou lov'st me, prince, lay thy consent
To this bequeath in my last testament.

Pri. Renownèd Audley, live, and have from me
This gift twice doubled, to these squires, and thee:
But, live, or die, what thou hast given away,
To these, and theirs, shall lasting freedom stay.—
Come, gentlemen, I'll see my friend bestow'd
Within an easy litter; then we'll march
Proudly toward Calais, with triumphant pace,
Unto my royal father, and there bring
The tribute of my wars, fair France's king.

ACT V.

SCENE I. *Picardy. The English camp before Calais.*

Enter King EDWARD, *with* PHILIPPA *his Queen, and* DERBY;
  Officers, Soldiers, &c.

Edw. No more, queen Philippe, pacify yourself;
Copland, except he can excuse his fault,
Shall find displeasure written in our looks.—
And now unto this proud resisting town:
Soldiers, assault; I will no longer stay,
To be deluded by their false delays;
Put all to sword, and make the spoil your own.

Trumpets sound to arms. Enter, from the town, six Citizens, in their shirts, and bare-footed, with halters about their necks.

Cit. Mercy, king Edward! mercy, gracious lord!
Edw. Contemptuous villains! call ye now for truce?
Mine ears are stopp'd against your bootless cries:—
Sound, drums; [*Alarum*] draw, threat'ning swords!
First C. Ah, noble prince,
Take pity on this town, and hear us, mighty king!
We claim the promise that your highness made;
The two days' respite is not yet expir'd,
And we are come, with willingness, to bear
What torturing death, or punishment, you please,
So that the trembling multitude be sav'd.
Edw. My promise? well, I do confess as much:
But I requir'd the chiefest citizens,
And men of most account, that should submit;
You, peradventure, are but servile grooms,
Or some felonious robbers on the sea,
Whom, apprehended, law would execute,
Albeit severity lay dead in us:
No, no, ye cannot overreach us thus.
Sec. C. The sun, dread lord, that in the western fall
Beholds us now low brought through misery,
Did in the orient purple of the morn
Salute our coming forth, when we were known;
Or may our portion be with damnèd fiends.
Edw. If it be so, then let our covenant stand,
We take possession of the town in peace:
But, for yourselves, look you for no remorse;
But, as imperial justice hath decreed,
Your bodies shall be dragg'd about these walls,
And after feel the stroke of quartering steel:
This is your doom;—Go, soldiers, see it done.
Que. Ah, be more mild unto these yielding men!
It is a glorious thing, to 'stablish peace;
And kings approach the nearest unto God,
By giving life and safety unto men:
As thou intendest to be king of France,
So let her people live to call thee king;

For what the sword cuts down, or fire hath spoil'd,
Is held in reputation none of ours.
   Edw. Although experience teach us this is true,
That peaceful quietness brings most delight
When most of all abuses are control'd,
Yet, insomuch it shall be known, that we
As well can master our affections,
As conquer other by the dint of sword,
Philippe, prevail; we yield to thy request;
These men shall live to boast of clemency,—
And, tyranny, strike terror to thyself.
   Cit. Long live your highness! happy be your reign!
   Edw. Go, get you hence, return unto the town;
And if this kindness hath deserv'd your love,
Learn then to reverence Edward as your king.—
                             [Exeunt Citizens.
Now, might we hear of our affairs abroad,
We would, till gloomy winter were o'erspent,
Dispose our men in garrison a while.
But who comes here?

          Enter COPLAND, *and* King David.

   Der. Copland, my lord, and David king of Scots.
   Edw. Is this the proud presumptuous squire o'the north,
That would not yield his prisoner to my queen?
   Cop. I am, my liege, a northern squire, indeed,
But neither proud nor insolent, I trust.
   Edw. What mov'd thee then, to be so obstinate
To contradict our royal queen's desire?
   Cop. No wilful disobedience, mighty lord,
But my desert, and public law of arms:
I took the king myself in single fight;
And, like a soldier, would be loth to lose
The least preeminence that I had won:
And Copland, straight, upon your highness' charge,
Is come to France, and, with a lowly mind,
Doth vail the bonnet of his victory.

Receive, dread lord, the custom of my fraught,
The wealthy tribute of my labouring hands;
Which should long since have been surrender'd up,
Had but your gracious self been there in place.

Que. But, Copland, thou didst scorn the king's command,
Neglecting our commission in his name.

Cop. His name I reverence, but his person more;
His name shall keep me in allegiance still,
But to his person I will bend my knee.

Edw. I pray thee, Philippe, let displeasure pass;
This man doth please me, and I like his words:
For what is he, that will attempt high deeds,
And lose the glory that ensues the same?
All rivers have recourse unto the sea;
And Copland's faith, relation to his king.—
Kneel therefore down; now rise, king Edward's knight:
And, to maintain thy state, I freely give
Five hundred marks a year to thee and thine.—

Enter SALISBURY.

Welcome, lord Salisbury: what news from Bretagne?

Sal. This, mighty king: the country we have won:
And John de Montfort, regent of that place,
Presents your highness with this coronet,
Protesting true allegiance to your grace.

Edw. We thank thee for thy service, valiant earl;
Challenge our favour, for we owe it thee.

Sal. But now, my lord, as this is joyful news,
So must my voice be tragical again,
And I must sing of doleful accidents.

Edw. What, have our men the overthrow at Poitiers?
Or is my son beset with too much odds?

Sal. He was, my lord: and as my worthless self,
With forty other serviceable knights,
Under safe-conduct of the dauphin's seal,
Did travel that way, finding him distress'd,
A troop of lances met us on the way,

Surpris'd, and brought us prisoners to the king;
Who, proud of this, and eager of revenge,
Commanded straight to cut off all our heads:
And surely we had dy'd, but that the duke,
More full of honour than his angry sire,
Procur'd our quick deliverance from thence:
But, ere we went, Salute your king, quoth he,
Bid him provide a funeral for his son,
To-day our sword shall cut his thread of life;
And, sooner than he thinks, we'll be with him,
To quittance those displeasures he hath done:
This said, we pass'd, not daring to reply;
Our hearts were dead, our looks diffus'd and wan.
Wand'ring, at last we climb'd unto a hill;
From whence, although our grief were much before,
Yet now to see the occasion with our eyes
Did thrice so much encrease our heaviness:
For there, my lord, O, there we did descry
Down in a valley how both armies lay.
The French had cast their trenches like a ring;
And every barricado's open front
Was thick emboss'd with brazen ordinance:
Here stood a battle of ten thousand horse;
There twice as many pikes, in quadrant wise:
Here cross-bows, arm'd with deadly-wounding darts:
And in the midst, like to a slender point
Within the compass of the horizon,—
As 'twere a rising bubble in the sea,
A hazel-wand amidst a wood of pines,—
Or as a bear fast chain'd unto a stake,
Stood famous Edward, still expecting when
Those dogs of France would fasten on his flesh.
Anon, the death-procuring knell begins:
Off go the cannons, that, with trembling noise,
Did shake the very mountain where we stood;
Then sound the trumpets' clangors in the air,
The battles join: and, when we could no more

Discern the difference 'twixt the friend and foe,
(So intricate the dark confusion was)
Away we turn'd our watry eyes, with sighs
As black as powder fuming into smoke.
And thus, I fear, unhappy have I told
The most untimely tale of Edward's fall.

 Que. Ah me! is this my welcome into France?
Is this the comfort, that I look'd to have,
When I should meet with my belovèd son?
Sweet Ned, I would, thy mother in the sea
Had been prevented of this mortal grief!

 Edw. Content thee, Philippe; 'tis not tears, will serve
To call him back, if he be taken hence:
Comfort thyself, as I do, gentle queen,
With hope of sharp, unheard-of, dire revenge.—
He bids me to provide his funeral;
And so I will: but all the peers in France
Shall mourners be, and weep out bloody tears,
Until their empty veins be dry and sere:
The pillars of his hearse shall be their bones;
The mould that covers him, their cities' ashes;
His knell, the groaning cries of dying men;
And, in the stead of tapers on his tomb,
An hundred fifty towers shall burning blaze,
While we bewail our valiant son's decease.

   Flourish of trumpets within. Enter a Herald.

 Her. Rejoice, my lord; ascend the imperial throne!
The mighty and redoubted prince of Wales,
Great servitor to bloody Mars in arms,
The Frenchman's terror, and his country's fame,
Triumphant rideth like a Roman peer:
And, lowly at his stirrup, comes afoot
King John of France, together with his son,
In captive bonds; whose diadem he brings,
To crown thee with, and to proclaim thee king.

Edw. Away with mourning, Philippe, wipe thine eyes;—
Sound, trumpets, welcome in Plantagenet!

A loud flourish. Enter Prince, AUDLEY, ARTOIS,
with King JOHN, *and* PHILIP.

As things, long lost, when they are found again,
So doth my son rejoice his father's heart,
For whom, even now, my soul was much perplex'd!
 [*Running to the Prince, and embracing him.*
Que. Be this a token to express my joy,
 [*Kissing him.*
For inward passions will not let me speak.
 Pri. My gracious father, here receive the gift,
 [*Presenting him with King John's crown.*
This wreath of conquest, and reward of war,
Got with as mickle peril of our lives,
As e'er was thing of price before this day;
Install your highness in your proper right:
And, herewithal, I render to your hands
These prisoners, chief occasion of our strife.
 Edw. So, John of France, I see, you keep your word
You promis'd to be sooner with ourself
Than we did think for, and 'tis so indeed:
But, had you done at first as now you do,
How many civil towns had stood untouch'd,
That now are turn'd to ragged heaps of stones?
How many people's lives might you have sav'd,
That are untimely sunk into their graves?
 Joh. Edward, recount not things irrevocable;
Tell me what ransom thou requir'st to have?
 Edw. Thy ransom, John, hereafter shall be known
But first to England thou must cross the seas,
To see what entertainment it affords;
Howe'er it falls, it cannot be so bad
As ours hath been since we arriv'd in France.
 Joh. Accursèd man! of this I was foretold,
But did misconstrue what the prophet told.

Pri. Now, father, this petition Edward makes:
To Thee, [*kneels*] whose grace hath been his strongest shield,
That, as thy pleasure chose me for the man
To be the instrument to show thy power,
So thou wilt grant, that many princes more,
Bred and brought up within that little isle,
May still be famous for like victories!—
And, for my part, the bloody scars I bear,
The weary nights that I have watch'd in field,
The dangerous conflicts I have often had,
The fearful menaces were proffer'd me,
The heat, and cold, and what else might displease,
I wish were now redoubled twenty-fold;
So that hereafter ages, when they read
The painful traffic of my tender youth,
Might thereby be enflam'd with such resolve,
As not the territories of France alone,
But likewise Spain, Turkey, and what countries else
That justly would provoke fair England's ire,
Might, at their presence, tremble, and retire!

Edw. Here, English lords, we do proclaim a rest,
And interceasing of our painful arms:
Sheathe up your swords, refresh your weary limbs,
Peruse your spoils; and, after we have breath'd
A day or two within this haven town,
God willing, then for England we'll be shipp'd;
Where, in a happy hour, I trust, we shall
Arrive, three kings, two princes, and a queen.
                    [*Flourish. Exeunt omnes.*

THE LIFE AND DEATH
OF
THOMAS LORD CROMWELL.

DRAMATIS PERSONÆ.

DUKE OF NORFOLK.
DUKE OF SUFFOLK.
EARL OF BEDFORD.
CARDINAL WOLSEY.
GARDINER, Bishop of Winchester.
SIR THOMAS MORE.
SIR CHRISTOPHER HALES.
SIR RALPH SADLER.
SIR RICHARD RADCLIFF.
OLD CROMWELL, a Blacksmith of Putney.
THOMAS CROMWELL, his son.
BANISTER,
BOWSER,   } English Merchants.
NEWTON,
CROSBY,
BAGOT, a Money-broker.
FRESCOBALD, a Florentine Merchant.
The Governor of the English Factory at Antwerp.
Governor and other States of Bologna.
Master of an Hotel in Bologna.
SEELY, a Publican of Hounslow.
Lieutenant of the Tower.
YOUNG CROMWELL, the son of Thomas.
HODGE, WILL, and TOM; old Cromwell's servants.
Two Citizens.
Mrs. BANISTER.
JOAN, wife to Seely.

Two Witnesses, a Sergeant-at-arms, a Herald, a Hangman, a Post, Messengers, Officers, Ushers, and Attendants.

SCENE—*partly in London, and the adjoining district; partly in Antwerp and Bologna.*

ACT I.

SCENE I. *Putney. The entrance of a Smith's shop.*

Enter HODGE, WILL, *and* TOM.

Hodge. Come, masters, I think it be past five o'clock; is it not time we were at work? my old master he'll be stirring anon.

Will. I cannot tell whether my old master will be stirring or no; but I am sure I can hardly take my afternoon's nap, for my young Master Thomas. He keeps such a coil in his study, with the sun, and the moon, and the seven stars, that I do verily think he'll read out his wits.

Hodge. He skill of the stars! There's goodman Car of Fulham (he that carried us to the strong ale, where goody Trundel had her maid got with child), O, he knows the stars; he'll tickle you Charles's wain in nine degrees: that same man will tell goody Trundel when her ale shall miscarry, only by the stars.

Tom. Ay! that's a great virtue indeed; I think Thomas be nobody in comparison to him.

Will. Well, masters, come; shall we to our hammers?

Hodge. Ay, content: first let's take our morning's draught, and then to work roundly.

Tom. Ay, agreed. Go in, Hodge. [*Exeunt.*

SCENE II. *The same.*

Enter young CROMWELL.

Crom. Good morrow, morn; I do salute thy brightness.
The night seems tedious to my troubled soul,
Whose black obscurity breeds in my mind
A thousand sundry cogitations:
And now Aurora with a lively dye
Adds comfort to my spirit, that mounts on high;
Too high indeed, my state being so mean.
My study, like a mineral of gold,
Makes my heart proud, wherein my hope's enroll'd:
My books are all the wealth I do possess,
And unto them I have engag'd my heart.
O, learning, how divine thou seem'st to me,
Within whose arms is all felicity!
[*The smiths beat with their hammers, within.*
Peace with your hammers! leave your knocking there!

You do disturb my study and my rest:
Leave off, I say: you mad me with the noise.

Enter Hodge, Will, *and* Tom, *from within.*

Hodge. Why, how now, Master Thomas? how now? will you not let us work for you?

Crom. You fret my heart with making of this noise.

Hodge. How, fret your heart? ay, but Thomas, you'll fret your father's purse, if you let us from working.

Tom. Ay, this 'tis for him to make him a gentleman. Shall we leave work for your musing? that's well, i' faith. But here comes my old master now.

Enter old Cromwell.

Old Crom. You idle knaves, what are you loit'ring now?
No hammers, talking, and my work to do!
What, not a heat among your work to-day?

Hodge. Marry, Sir, your son Thomas will not let us work at all.

Old Crom. Why, knave, I say, have I thus cark'd and car'd,
And all to keep thee like a gentleman;
And dost thou let my servants at their work,
That sweat for thee, knave, labour thus for thee?

Crom. Father, their hammers do offend my study.

Old Crom. Out of my doors, knave, if thou lik'st it not.
I cry you mercy; are your ears so fine?
I tell thee, knave, these get when I do sleep;
I will not have my anvil stand for thee.

Crom. There's money, father; I will pay your men.
 [*Throws money among them.*

Old Crom. Have I thus brought thee up unto my cost,
In hope that one day thou'dst relieve my age;
And art thou now so lavish of thy coin,
To scatter it among these idle knaves?

Crom. Father, be patient, and content yourself:
The time will come I shall hold gold as trash:

And here, I speak with a presaging soul,
I'll build a palace where this cottage stands,
As fine as is King Henry's house at Sheen.

Old Crom. You build a house? you knave, you'll be a beggar!
Now, afore God, all is but cast away,
That is bestow'd upon this thriftless lad!
Well, had I bound him to some honest trade,
This had not been; but 'twas his mother's doing,
To send him to the university.
How? build a house where now this cottage stands,
As fair as that at Sheen?—They shall not hear me. [*Aside.*
A good boy, Tom; I con thee thank, Tom;
Well said, Tom; gramercy, Tom.—
In to your work, knaves; hence, thou saucy boy.
            [*Exeunt all but young Cromwell.*

Crom. Why should my birth keep down my mounting
            spirit?
Are not all creatures subject unto time,
To time, who doth abuse the cheated world,
And fills it full of hodge-podge bastardy?
There's legions now of beggars on the earth,
That their original did spring from kings;
And many monarchs now, whose fathers were
The riff-raff of their age: for time and fortune
Wears out a noble train to beggary;
And from the dunghill minions do advance
To state and mark in this admiring world.
This is but course, which, in the name of fate,
Is seen as often as it whirls about.
The river Thames, that by our door doth pass,
His first beginning is but small and shallow;
Yet, keeping on his course, grows to a sea.
And likewise Wolsey, the wonder of our age,
His birth as mean as mine, a butcher's son;
Now who within this land a greater man?
Then, Cromwell, cheer thee up, and tell thy soul,
That thou mayst live to flourish and control.

Enter old CROMWELL.

Old Crom. Tom Cromwell; what, Tom, I say.
Crom. Do you call, Sir?
Old Crom. Here is Master Bowser come to know if you have despatched his petition for the lords of the council, or no.
Crom. Father, I have; please you to call him in.
Old Crom. That's well said, Tom; a good lad, Tom.

Enter BOWSER.

Bow. Now, Master Cromwell, have you despatched this petition?
Crom. I have, Sir; here it is: please you peruse it.
Bow. It shall not need; we'll read it as we go
By water.
And, Master Cromwell, I have made a motion
May do you good, an if you like of it.
Our secretary at Antwerp, Sir, is dead,
And now the merchants there have sent to me,
For to provide a man fit for the place:
Now I do know none fitter than yourself,
If it stand with your liking, Master Cromwell.
Crom. With all my heart, Sir; and I much am bound
In love and duty for your kindness shown.
Old Crom. Body of me, Tom, make haste, lest somebody get between thee and honour, Tom.—I thank you, good Master Bowser, I thank you for my boy: I thank you always, I thank you most heartily, Sir: ho, a cup of beer here for Master Bowser.
Bow. It shall not need, Sir.—Master Cromwell, will you go?
Crom. I will attend you, Sir.
Old Crom. Farewell, Tom: God bless thee, Tom! God speed thee, good Tom! [*Exeunt.*

SCENE III. *London. A street before* FRESCOBALD'S *house.*

Enter BAGOT.

Bag. I hope this day is fatal unto some,
And by their loss must Bagot seek to gain.
This is the lodge of Master Frescobald,
A liberal merchant, and a Florentine;
To whom Banister owes a thousand pound.
A merchant-bankrupt, whose father was my master.
What do I care for pity or regard?
He once was wealthy, but be now is fallen;
And I this morning have got him arrested
At suit of this same Master Frescobald;
And by this means shall I be sure of coin,
For doing this same good to him unknown:
And in good time see where the merchant comes.

Enter FRESCOBALD.

Good morrow to kind Master Frescobald.
 Fres. Good morrow to yourself, good Master Bagot;
And what's the news, you are so early stirring?
It is for gain, I make no doubt of that.
 Bag. 'Tis for the love, Sir, that I bear to you.
When did you see your debtor Banister?
 Fres. I promise you I have not seen the man
This two months day: his poverty is such,
As I do think he shuns to see his friends.
 Bag. Why then assure yourself to see him straight,
For at your suit I have arrested him,
And here they will be with him presently.
 Fres. Arrest him at my suit? you were to blame.
I know the man's misfortunes to be such,
As he's not able for to pay the debt;
And were it known to some, he were undone.
 Bag. This is your pitiful heart to think it so;
But you are much deceiv'd in Banister.
Why, such as he will break for fashion's sake,

And unto those they owe a thousand pound,
Pay scarce a hundred. O, Sir, beware of him.
The man is lewdly given to dice and drabs;
Spends all he hath in harlots' companies;
It is no mercy for to pity him.
I speak the truth of him, for nothing else,
But for the kindness that I bear to you.

   Fres. If it be so, he hath deceiv'd me much;
And to deal strictly with such a one as he,
Is better sure than too much lenity.
But here is Master Banister himself,
And with him, as I take it, are the officers.

     Enter BANISTER, *his* Wife *and two* Officers.

   Ban. O, Master Frescobald, you have undone me:
My state was well-nigh overthrown before,
Now altogether downcast by your means.

   Mrs. Ban. O, Master Frescobald, pity my husband's case,
He is a man hath liv'd as well as any,
Till envious fortune and the ravenous sea
Did rob, disrobe, and spoil us of our own.

   Fres. Mistress Banister, I envy not your husband,
Nor willingly would I have us'd him thus:
But that I hear he is so lewdly given,
Haunts wicked company, and hath enough
To pay his debts, yet will not own thereof.

   Ban. This is that damn'd broker, that same Bagot,
Whom I have often from my trencher fed:
Ungrateful villain, for to use me thus!

   Bag. What I have said to him is naught but truth.

   Mrs. Ban. What thou hast said springs from an envious
           heart:
O! cannibal, that doth eat men alive!
But here, upon my knee, believe me, Sir
(And what I speak, so help me God, is true),
We scarce have meat to feed our little babes,
Most of our plate is in that broker's hand:

Which, had we money to defray our debts,
O think, we would not 'bide that penury.
Be merciful, kind Master Frescobald;
My husband, children, and myself will eat
But one meal a day; the other will we keep,
And sell, as part to pay the debt we owe you.
If ever tears did pierce a tender mind,
Be pitiful; let me some favour find.

 Fres. Go to, I see thou art an envious man.— [*To Bagot.*
Good Mistress Banister, kneel not to me;
I pray rise up; you shall have your desire.
Hold, officers; be gone; there's for your pains.—
You know you owe to me a thousand pound: [*To Banister.*
Here, take my hand; if e'er God make you able,
And place you in your former state again,
Pay me; but yet, if still your fortune frown,
Upon my faith, I'll never ask a crown.
I never yet did wrong to men in thrall,
For God doth know what to myself may fall.

 Ban. This unexpected favour, undeserved,
Doth make my heart bleed inwardly with joy.
Ne'er may aught prosper with me as my own,
If I forget this kindness you have shown.

 Mrs. Ban. My children in their prayers, both night and day,
For your good fortune and success shall pray.

 Fres. I thank you both; I pray go dine with me.
Within these three days, if God give me leave,
I will to Florence, to my native home.—
Hold, Bagot, there's a portague to drink,
Although you ill deserv'd it by your merit.
Give not such cruel scope unto your heart;
Be sure the ill you do will be requited:
Remember what I say, Bagot: farewell.—
Come, Master Banister, you shall with me;
My fare's but simple, but welcome heartily.
       [*Exeunt all but Bagot.*

Bag. A plague go with you! would you had eat your
             last!
Is this the thanks I have for all my pains?
Confusion light upon you all for me!
Where he had wont to give a score of crowns,
Doth he now foist me with a portague?
Well, I will be reveng'd upon this Banister.
I'll to his creditors; buy all the debts he owes,
As seeming that I do it for good will;
I 'm sure to have them at an easy rate:
And when 'tis done, in Christendom he stays not,
But I will make his heart to ache with sorrow.
And if that Banister become my debtor,
By heaven and earth, I'll make his plague the greater.
                                                    [*Exit.*

ACT II.

Enter CHORUS.

Cho. Now, gentlemen, imagine that young Cromwell
In Antwerp's lieger for the English merchants;
And Banister, to shun this Bagot's hate,
Hearing that he hath got some of his debts,
Is fled to Antwerp, with his wife and children;
Which Bagot hearing, is gone after them,
And thither sends his bills of debt before,
To be reveng'd on wretched Banister.
What doth fall out, with patience sit and see,
A just requital of false treachery.   [*Exit.*

SCENE I. *Antwerp.*

CROMWELL *discovered in his study, sitting at a table, on which
         are placed money-bags and books of account.*

Crom. Thus far my reckoning doth go straight and even.
But, Cromwell, this same plodding fits not thee;
Thy mind is altogether set on travel,

And not to live thus cloister'd like a nun.
It is not this same trash that I regard:
Experience is the jewel of my heart.

Enter a Post.

Post. I pray, Sir, are you ready to despatch me?
Crom. Yes; here's those sums of money you must carry.
You go so far as Frankfort, do you not?
Post. I do, Sir.
Crom. Well, pr'ythee, then, make all the haste thou canst;
For there be certain English gentlemen
Are bound for Venice, and may haply want,
An if that you should linger by the way:
But in the hope that you will make good speed,
There are two angels, to buy you spurs and wands.
Post. I thank you, Sir, this will add wings, indeed.
  [*Exit Post.*
Crom. Gold is of power to make an eagle's speed.

Enter Mistress Banister.

What gentlewoman is this that grieves so much?
It seems she doth address herself to me.
Mrs. Ban. God save you, Sir. Pray, is your name Master Cromwell?
Crom. My name is Thomas Cromwell, gentlewoman.
Mrs. Ban. Know you one Bagot, Sir, that's come to Antwerp?
Crom. No, trust me, I ne'er saw the man; but here
Are bills of debt I have receiv'd against
One Banister, a merchant fallen into decay.
Mrs. Ban. Into decay indeed, 'long of that wretch.
I am the wife to woful Banister,
And by that bloody villain am pursu'd,
From London, here to Antwerp, where my husband
Lies in the governor's hands; and God of heaven
He only knows how he will deal with him.
Now, Sir, your heart is fram'd of milder temper;

Be merciful to a distressèd soul,
And God no doubt will treble bless your gain.
  Crom. Good Mistress Banister, what I can, I will,
In anything that lies within my power.
  Mrs. Ban. O speak to Bagot, that same wicked wretch:
An angel's voice may move a damnèd devil.
  Crom. Why is he come to Antwerp, as you hear?
  Mrs. Ban. I heard he landed some two hours since.
  Crom. Well, Mistress Banister, assure yourself,
I will speak to Bagot in your behalf,
And win him to all the pity that I can.
Meantime, to comfort you in your distress,
Receive these angels to relieve your need;
And be assur'd, that what I can effect,
To do you good, no way I will neglect.
  Mrs. Ban. That mighty God that knows each mortal's heart,
Keep you from trouble, sorrow, grief, and smart.
            [*Exit Mistress Banister.*
  Crom. Thanks, courteous woman, for thy hearty prayer.
It grieves my soul to see her misery:
But we that live under the work of fate,
May hope the best, yet know not to what state
Our stars and destinies have us assign'd;
Fickle is Fortune, and her face is blind.   [*Exit.*

SCENE II. *A street in Antwerp.*

Enter BAGOT.

  Bag. So, all goes well; it is as I would have it.
Banister, he is with the governor,
And shortly shall have gyves upon his heels.
It glads my heart to think upon the slave;
I hope to have his body rot in prison,
And after hear his wife to hang herself,
And all his children die for want of food.
The jewels I have brought with me to Antwerp

Are reckon'd to be worth five thousand pound;
Which scarcely stood me in three hundred pound.
I bought them at an easy kind of rate;
I care not much which way they came by them,
That sold them me; it comes not near my heart:
And lest they should be stolen (as sure they are),
I thought it meet to sell them here in Antwerp;
And so have left them in the governor's hand,
Who offers me within two hundred pound
Of all my price: but now no more of that.—
I must go see an if my bills be safe,
The which I sent before to Master Cromwell;
That if the wind should keep me on the sea,
He might arrest him here before I came:
And in good time, see where he is.

     Enter CROMWELL.

God save you, Sir.
 Crom. And you.—Pray, pardon me, I know you not.
 Bag. It may be so, Sir; but my name is Bagot;
The man that sent to you the bills of debt.
 Crom. O, you're the man that pursues Banister.
Here are the bills of debt you sent to me;
As for the man, you best know where he is.
It is reported you 've a flinty heart,
A mind that will not stoop to any pity.
An eye that knows not how to shed a tear,
A hand that's always open for reward.
But, Master Bagot, would you be rul'd by me,
You should turn all these to the contrary:
Your heart should still have feeling of remorse,
Your mind, according to your state, be liberal
To those that stand in need and in distress;
Your hand to help them that do sink in want,
Rather than with your poise to hold them down:
For every ill turn show yourself more kind;
Thus should I do; pardon, I speak my mind.

Bag. Ay, Sir, you speak to hear what I would say;
But you must live, I know, as well as I.
I know this place to be extortionous;
And 'tis not for a man to keep safe here,
But he must lie, cog with his dearest friend,
And as for pity, scorn it; hate all conscience:—
But yet I do commend your wit in this,
To make a show of what I hope you are not;
But I commend you, and it is well done:
This is the only way to bring you gain.
Crom. Gain? I had rather chain me to an oar,
And, like a slave, there toil out all my life,
Before I'd live so base a slave as thou.
I, like an hypocrite, to make a show
Of seeming virtue, and a devil within!
No, Bagot; if thy conscience were as clear,
Poor Banister ne'er had been troubled here.
Bag. Nay, Master Cromwell, be not angry, Sir,
I know full well that you are no such man;
But if your conscience were as white as snow,
It will be thought that you are otherwise.
Crom. Will it be thought that I am otherwise?
Let them that think so, know they are deceiv'd.
Shall Cromwell live to have his faith misconstru'd?
Antwerp, for all the wealth within thy town,
I will not stay here full two hours longer.—
As good luck serves, my accounts are all made even;
Therefore I'll straight unto the treasurer.
Bagot, I know you'll to the governor:
Commend me to him; say I 'm bound to travel,
To see the fruitful parts of Italy;
And as you ever bore a Christian mind,
Let Banister some favour of you find.
Bag. For your sake, Sir; I'll help him all I can—
To starve his heart out ere he gets a groat;   [*Aside.*
So, Master Cromwell, do I take my leave,
For I must straight unto the governor.

Crom. Farewell, Sir; pray remember what I've said.
[*Exit Bagot.*
No, Cromwell, no; thy heart was ne'er so base,
To live by falsehood, or by brokery.
But it falls out well;—I little it repent;
Hereafter time in travel shall be spent.

Enter HODGE.

Hodge. Your son Thomas, quoth you! I have been Thomass'd. I had thought it had been no such matter to ha' gone by water; for at Putney, I'll go you to Parish-Garden for twopence; sit as still as may be, without any wagging or jolting in my guts, in a little boat too: here, we were scarce four miles in the great green water, but I, thinking to go to my afternoon's nuncheon, as 'twas my manner at home, felt a kind of rising in my guts. At last, one of the sailors spying of me—"Be of good cheer," says he; "set down thy victuals, and up with it; thou hast nothing but an eel in thy belly." Well, to't went I, and to my victuals went the sailors; and thinking me to be a man of better experience than any in the ship, asked me what wood the ship was made of: they all swore I told them as right as if I had been acquainted with the carpenter that made it. At last we grew near land, and I grew villanous hungry, and went to my bag. The devil a bit there was, the sailors had tickled me; yet I cannot blame them: it was a part of kindness; for I in kindness told them what wood the ship was made of, and they in kindness eat up my victuals: as indeed one good turn asketh another. Well, would I could find my master Thomas in this Dutch town! he might put some English beer into my belly.

Crom. What, Hodge, my father's man! by my hand, welcome. How doth my father? what's the news at home?

Hodge. Master Thomas, O God! Master Thomas, your hand, glove and all. This is to give you to understand, that your father is in health, and Alice Downing here hath sent you a nutmeg, and Bess Make-water a race of ginger; my fellows, Will and Tom, hath between them sent you a dozen

of points; and goodman Toll, of the Goat, a pair of mittens:
myself came in person; and this is all the news.

Crom. Gramercy, good Hodge, and thou art welcome
to me,
But in as ill a time thou comest as may be;
For I am travelling into Italy.
What say'st thou, Hodge? wilt thou bear me company?

Hodge. Will I bear thee company, Tom? what tell'st me
of Italy? Were it to the farthest part of Flanders, I would
go with thee, Tom: I am thine in all weal and woe; thine own
to command. What, Tom! I have passed the rigorous waves
of Neptune's blasts. I tell you, Thomas, I have been in danger
of the floods; and when I have seen Boreas begin to play the
ruffian with us, then would I down on my knees, and call
upon Vulcan.

Crom. And why upon him?

Hodge. Because, as this same fellow Neptune is god of
the seas, so Vulcan is lord over the smiths; and therefore I,
being a smith, thought his godhead would have some care
yet of me.

Crom. A good conceit: but tell me, hast thou din'd yet?

Hodge. Thomas, to speak the truth, not a bit yet, I.

Crom. Come, go with me, thou shalt have cheer, good store;
And farewell, Antwerp, if I come no more.

Hodge. I follow thee, sweet Tom, I follow thee.
[*Exeunt.*

SCENE III. *Another street in the same.*

Enter *the* Governor *of the English Factory*, BAGOT, MR. *and*
MRS. BANISTER, *and two* Officers.

Gov. Is Cromwell gone, then, say you, Master Bagot?
On what dislike, I pray you? what was the cause?

Bag. To tell you true, a wild brain of his own;
Such youth as he can't see when they are well.
He is all bent to travel (that's his reason),
And doth not love to eat his bread at home.

Gov. Well, good fortune with him, if the man be gone.
We hardly shall find such a one as he,
To fit our turns, his dealings were so honest.
But now, Sir, for your jewels that I have—
What do you say? what, will you take my price?
    Bag. O, Sir, you offer too much under foot.
    Gov. 'Tis but two hundred pound between us, man,
What's that in payment of five thousand pound?
    Bag. Two hundred pound! by'r lady, Sir, 'tis great;
Before I got so much, it made me sweat.
    Gov. Well, Master Bagot, I'll proffer you fairly.
You see this merchant, Master Banister,
Is going now to prison at your suit;
His substance all is gone: what would you have?
Yet, in regard I knew the man of wealth
(Never dishonest dealing, but such mishaps
Have fallen on him, may light on me or you),
There is two hundred pound between us two;
We will divide the same: I'll give you one,
On that condition you will set him free.
His state is nothing; that you see yourself;
And where naught is, the king must lose his right.
    Bag. O Sir, you speak out of your love; but know
'Tis foolish love, Sir, sure, to pity him.
Therefore content yourself; this is my mind;
To do him good I will not bate a penny.
    Ban. This is my comfort, though thou dost no good,
A mighty ebb follows a mighty flood.
    Mrs. Ban. O thou base wretch, whom we have fostered,
Even as a serpent, for to poison us!
If God did ever right a woman's wrong,
To that same God I bend and bow my heart,
To let his heavy wrath fall on thy head,
By whom my hopes and joys are butcherèd.
    Bag. Alas, fond woman! I pr'ythee pray thy worst;
The fox fares better still when he is curst.

Enter Bowser.

Gov. Master Bowser! you are welcome, Sir, from England.
What's the best news? and how do all our friends?
  Bow. They are all well, and do commend them to you.
There's letters from your brother and your son:
So, fare you well, Sir; I must take my leave,
My haste and business doth require it so.
  Gov. Before you dine, Sir? What, go you out of town?
  Bow. I' faith unless I hear some news in town,
I must away; there is no remedy.
  Gov. Master Bowser, what is your business? may I know
    it?
  Bow. You may so, Sir, and so shall all the city.
The king of late hath had his treasury robb'd,
And of the choicest jewels that he had:
The value of them was seven thousand pound.
The fellow that did steal these jewels is hang'd,
And did confess that for three hundred pound
He sold them to one Bagot dwelling in London.
Now Bagot's fled, and, as we hear, to Antwerp;
And hither am I come to seek him out;
And they that first can tell me of his news,
Shall have a hundred pound for their reward.
  Ban. How just is God to right the innocent!
  Gov. Master Bowser, you come in happy time:
Here is the villain Bagot that you seek,
And all those jewels have I in my hands:
Here, officers, look to him, hold him fast.
  Bag. The devil ow'd me a shame, and now hath paid it.
  Bow. Is this that Bagot? Fellows, bear him hence;
We will not now stand here for his reply.
Lade him with irons; we will have him tried
In England, where his villanies are known.
  Bag. Mischief, confusion, light upon you all!
O hang me, drown me, let me kill myself;
Let go my arms, let me run quick to hell.

Bow. Away; bear him away; stop the slave's mouth.
            [*Exeunt Officers and Bagot.*
Mrs. Ban. Thy works are infinite, great God of heaven.
Gov. I heard this Bagot was a wealthy fellow.
Bow. He was indeed; for when his goods were seiz'd,
Of jewels, coin, and plate, within his house
Was found the value of five thousand pound;
His furniture worth fully half so much;
Which being all distrained for the king,
He frankly gave it to the Antwerp merchants;
And they again, out of their bounteous mind,
Have to a brother of their company,
A man decay'd by fortune of the seas,
Given Bagot's wealth, to set him up again,
And keep it for him; his name is Banister.
    Gov. Good Master Bowser, with this happy news
You have reviv'd two from the gates of death:
This is that Banister, and this his wife.
    Bow. Sir, I am glad my fortune is so good
To bring such tidings as may comfort you.
    Ban. You have given life unto a man deem'd dead;
For by these news my life is newly bred.
    Mrs. Ban. Thanks to my God, next to my sovereign king;
And last to you, that these good news do bring.
    Gov. The hundred pound I must receive, as due
For finding Bagot, I freely give to you.
    Bow. And, Master Banister, if so you please,
I'll bear you company, when you cross the seas.
    Ban. If it please you, Sir;—my company is but mean:
Stands with your liking, I will wait on you.
    Gov. I'm glad that all things do accord so well.
Come, Master Bowser, let us in to dinner;
And, Mistress Banister, be merry, woman.
Come, after sorrow now let's cheer your spirit;
Knaves have their due, and you but what you merit.
                            [*Exeunt*

ACT III.

SCENE I. *The principal bridge at Florence.*

Enter CROMWELL *and* HODGE *in their shirts, and without hats.*

Hodge. Call you this seeing of fashions? marry, would I had stayed at Putney still. O, Master Thomas, we are spoiled, we are gone.

Crom. Content thee, man; this is but fortune.

Hodge. Fortune! a plague of this fortune, it makes me go wet-shod; the rogues would not leave me a shoe to my feet.
For my hose,
They scorn'd them with their heels:
But for my doublet and hat,
O Lord, they embrac'd me,
And unlac'd me,
And took away my clothes,
And so disgrac'd me.

Crom. Well, Hodge, what remedy? What shift shall we make now?

Hodge. Nay, I know not. For begging I am naught; for stealing, worse. By my troth, I must even fall to my old trade, to the hammer and the horse-heels again:—But now the worst is, I am not acquainted with the humour of the horses in this country; whether they are not coltish, given much to kicking, or no: for when I have one leg in my hand, if he should up and lay t'other on my chaps, I were gone; there lay I, there lay Hodge.

Crom. Hodge, I believe thou must work for us both.

Hodge. O, Master Thomas, have not I told you of this? Have not I many a time and often said, "Tom, or Master Thomas, learn to make a horse-shoe, it will be your own another day:" this was not regarded.—Hark you, Thomas! what do you call the fellows that robbed us?

Crom. The banditti.

Hodge. The banditti, do you call them? I know not what they are called here, but I am sure we call them plain thieves

in England. O, Tom, that we were now at Putney, at the ale
there!
 Crom. Content thee, man: here set up these two bills;
And let us keep our standing on the bridge.
The fashion of this country is such,
If any stranger be oppress'd with want,
To write the manner of his misery;
And such as are disposèd to succour him,
         [*Hodge sets up the bills.*
Will do it. What, Hodge, hast thou set them up?
 Hodge. Ay, they are up; God send some to read them;
and not only to read them, but also to look on us; and not
altogether look on us, but to relieve us. O, cold, cold, cold!
    [*Cromwell stands at one end of the bridge, and
     Hodge at the other.*

      Enter FRESCOBALD.

 Fres. [*reads the bills*]. What's here?
Two Englishmen, and robb'd by the banditti!
One of them seems to be a gentleman.
'Tis pity that his fortune was so hard,
To fall into the desperate hands of thieves:
I'll question him of what estate he is.
God save you, Sir. Are you an Englishman?
 Crom. I am, Sir, a distressèd Englishman.
 Fres. And what are you, my friend?
 Hodge. Who, I Sir? by my troth, I do not know myself
what I am now; but, Sir, I was a smith, Sir, a poor farrier,
of Putney. That's my master, Sir, yonder; I was robbed for
his sake, Sir.
 Fres. I see you have been met by the banditti,
And therefore need not ask how you came thus.
But, Frescobald, why dost thou question them
Of their estate, and not relieve their need?
Sir, the coin I have about me is not much:
There's sixteen ducats for to clothe yourselves,

There's sixteen more to buy your diet with,
And there's sixteen to pay for your horse-hire.
'Tis all the wealth, you see, my purse possesses;
But, if you please for to inquire me out,
You shall not want for aught that I can do.
My name is Frescobald, a Florence merchant,
A man that always lov'd your nation much.

Crom. This unexpected favour at your hands,
Which God doth know, if e'er I shall requite.—
Necessity makes me to take your bounty,
And for your gold can yield you naught but thanks.
Your charity hath help'd me from despair;
Your name shall still be in my hearty prayer.

Fres. It is not worth such thanks: come to my house;
Your want shall better be reliev'd than thus.

Crom. I pray, excuse me; this shall well suffice,
To bear my charges to Bolognia,
Whereas a noble earl is much distress'd:
An Englishman, Russell tho earl of Bedford,
Is by the French king sold unto his death.
It may fall out, that I may do him good;
To save his life, I'll hazard my heart-blood.
Therefore, kind Sir, thanks for your liberal gift;
I must be gone to aid him, there's no shift.

Fres. I'll be no hinderer to so good an act.
Heaven prosper you in that you go about!
If fortune bring you this way back again,
Pray let me see you: so I take my leave;
All good a man can wish, I do bequeath.   [*Exit Frescobald.*

Crom. All good that God doth send light on your head!
There's few such men within our climate bred.
How say you, Hodge? is not this good fortune?

Hodge. How say you? I'll tell you what, Master Thomas;
if all men be of this gentleman's mind, let's keep our standings upon this bridge; we shall get more here, with begging, in one day, than I shall with making horse-shoes in a whole year.

Crom. No, Hodge, we must be gone unto Bolognia,
There to relieve the noble earl of Bedford:
Where, if I fail not in my policy,
I shall deceive their subtle treachery.

Hodge. Nay, I'll follow you. God bless us from the thieving banditti again.   [*Exeunt.*

SCENE II. *Bolognia. A room in an hotel.*

Enter BEDFORD *and* Host.

Bed. Am I betray'd? was Bedford born to die
By such base slaves, in such a place as this?
Have I escap'd so many times in France,
So many battles have I overpass'd,
And made the French skir, when they heard my name;
And am I now betray'd unto my death?
Some of their hearts' blood first shall pay for it.

Host. They do desire, my lord, to speak with you.

Bed. The traitors do desire to have my blood;
But by my birth, my honour, and my name,
By all my hopes, my life shall cost them dear.
Open the door; I'll venture out upon them,
And if I must die, then I'll die with honour.

Host. Alas, my lord, that is a desperate course:
They have begirt you round about the house.
Their meaning is, to take you prisoner,
And so to send your body unto France.

Bed. First shall the ocean be as dry as sand,
Before alive they send me unto France.
I'll have my body first bor'd like a sieve,
And die as Hector, 'gainst the Myrmidons,
Ere France shall boast Bedford 's their prisoner.
O! treacherous France! that, 'gainst the law of arms,
Hath here betray'd thine enemy to death.
But be assur'd, my blood shall be reveng'd
Upon the best lives that remain in France.

Enter a Servant.

Stand back, or else thou run'st upon thy death.
　Ser. Pardon, my lord; I come to tell your honour,
That they have hir'd a Neapolitan,
Who by his oratory hath promis'd them,
Without the shedding of one drop of blood,
Into their hands safe to deliver you;
And therefore craves none but himself may enter,
And a poor swain that attends upon him.
　Bed. A Neapolitan? bid him come in.　　[*Exit Servant.*
Were he as cunning in his eloquence
As Cicero, the famous man of Rome,
His words would be as chaff against the wind.
Sweet-tongued Ulysses, that made Ajax mad,
Were he, and his tongue in this speaker's head,
Alive, he wins me not; then 'tis no conquest dead.

Enter CROMWELL, *in a Neapolitan habit, and* HODGE.

　Crom. Sir, are you the master of the house?
　Host. I am, Sir.
　Crom. By this same token you must leave this place,
And leave none but the carl and I together,
And this my peasant here to tend on us.
　Host. With all my heart: God grant you do some good.
　　　　　　　[*Exit Host. Cromwell shuts the door.*
　Bed. Now, Sir, what is your will with me?
　Crom. Intends your honour not to yield yourself?
　Bed. No, goodman goose, not while my sword doth last.
Is this your eloquence for to persuade me?
　Crom. My lord, my eloquence is for to save you:
I am not, as you judge, a Neapolitan,
But Cromwell, your servant, and an Englishman.
　Bed. How! Cromwell? not my farrier's son?
　Crom. The same, Sir; and am come to succour you.
　Hodge. Yes, faith, Sir; and I am Hodge, your poor smith:
many a time and oft have I shod your dapple-grey.
　Bed. And what avails it me that thou art here?

7*

Crom. It may avail, if you'll be rul'd by me.
My lord, you know, the men of Mantua
And these Bolognians are at deadly strife;
And they, my lord, both love and honour you.
Could you but get out of the Mantua port,
Then were you safe, despite of all their force.

Bed. Tut, man, thou talk'st of things impossible;
Dost thou not see that we are round beset?
How then is't possible we should escape?

Crom. By force we cannot, but by policy.
Put on the apparel here that Hodge doth wear,
And give him yours: The states, they know you not
(For, as I think, they never saw your face);
And at a watch-word must I call them in,
And will desire that we two safe may pass
To Mantua, where I'll say my business lies.
How doth your honour like of this device?

Bed. O, wondrous good.—But wilt thou venture, Hodge?

Hodge. Will I?
    O noble lord,
    I do accord,
   In any thing I can:
    And do agree,
    To set thee free,
   Do Fortune what she can.

Bed. Come then, and change we our apparel straight.

Crom. Go, Hodge; make haste, lest they should chance
 to call.

Hodge. I warrant you I'll fit him with a suit.
       [*Exeunt Bedford and Hodge.*

Crom. Heavens grant this policy doth take success,
And that the earl may safely 'scape away!
And yet it grieves me for this simple wretch,
For fear lest they should offer him violence:
But of two evils, 'tis best to shun the greatest;
And better is it that he live in thrall,
Than such a noble earl as this should fall.

Their stubborn hearts, it may be, will relent,
Since he is gone to whom their hate is bent.

Re-enter BEDFORD *and* HODGE.

My lord, have you despatch'd?

Bed. How dost thou like us, Cromwell? is it well?

Crom. O, my good lord, excellent.—Hodge, how dost feel thyself?

Hodge. How do I feel myself? why, as a nobleman should do. O, how I feel honour come creeping on! My nobility is wonderful melancholy: is it not most gentlemanlike to be melancholy?

Bed. Yes, Hodge: now go, and sit down in the study, and take state upon thee.

Hodge. I warrant you, my lord; let me alone to take state upon me: But hark, my lord, do you feel nothing bite about you?

Bed. No, trust me, Hodge.

Hodge. Ay, they know they want their old pasture. 'Tis a strange thing of this vermin, they dare not meddle with nobility.

Crom. Go take thy place, Hodge; I will call them in. Now all is done:—Enter, an if you please.

Enter the Governor *and other* States *and* Citizens *of Bolognia, and* Officers *with halberds.*

Gov. What, have you won him? will he yield himself?

Crom. I have, an't please you; and the quiet earl
Doth yield himself to be dispos'd by you.

Gov. Give him the money that we promis'd him:
So let him go, whither it please himself.

Crom. My business, Sir, lies unto Mantua;
Please you to give me a safe conduct thither.

Gov. Go, and conduct him to the Mantua port,
And see him safe deliver'd presently.

[*Exeunt Cromwell, Bedford, and an Officer.*

Go draw the curtains, let us see the earl:—

[*An Attendant opens the curtains.*]

O, he is writing; stand apart awhile.

Hodge [*reads*]. *Fellow William, I am not as I have been; I went from you a smith, I write to you as a lord. I am, at this present writing, among the Polonian sausages. I do commend my lordship to Ralph and to Roger, to Bridget and to Dorothy, and so to all the youth of Putney.*

Gov. Sure these are the names of English noblemen, Some of his special friends, to whom he writes:—

[*Hodge sounds a note.*]

But stay, he doth address himself to sing.

[*Hodge sings a song.*]

My lord, I am glad you are so frolic and so blithe:
Believe me, noble lord, if you knew all,
You'd change your merry vein to sudden sorrow.

Hodge. I change my merry vein? no, thou Polonian, no;
I am a lord, and therefore let me go.
I do defy thee and thy sausages;
Therefore stand off, and come not near my honour.

Gov. My lord, this jesting cannot serve your turn.

Hodge. Dost think, thou black Polonian beast,
That I do flout, do gibe, or jest?
No, no, thou beer-pot, know that I,
A noble earl, a lord par-dy— [*A trumpet sounds.*]

Gov. What means this trumpet's sound?

Enter a Messenger.

Cit. One is come from the states of Mantua.

Gov. What would you with us? speak, thou man of Mantua.

Mes. Men of Bolognia, this my message is;
To let you know the noble earl of Bedford
Is safe within the town of Mantua,
And wills you send the peasant that you have,
Who hath deceiv'd your expectation:
Or else the states of Mantua have vow'd,

They will recall the truce that they have made;
And not a man shall stir from forth your town,
That shall return, unless you send him back.

Gov. O this misfortune, how it mads my heart!
The Neapolitan hath beguil'd us all.
Hence with this fool. What shall we do with him,
The earl being gone? a plague upon it all!

Hodge. No, I'll assure you, I am no earl, but a smith, Sir; one Hodge, a smith at Putney, Sir; one that hath gulled you, that hath bored you, Sir.

Gov. Away with him; take hence the fool you came for.

Hodge. Ay, Sir, and I'll leave the greater fool with you.

Mes. Farewell, Bolognians.—Come, friend, along with me.

Hodge. My friend, afore; my lordship will follow thee.
[*Exeunt Hodge and Messenger.*

Gov. Well, Mantua, since by thee the earl is lost,
Within few days I hope to see thee crost.
[*Exeunt Governor, States, Attendants, &c.*

Enter Chorus.

Cho. Thus far you see how Cromwell's fortune pass'd.
The earl of Bedford, being safe in Mantua,
Desires Cromwell's company into France,
To make requital for his courtesy;
But Cromwell doth deny the earl his suit,
And tells him of those parts he meant to see,
He had not yet set footing on the land;
And so directly takes his way to Spain;
The earl to France; and so they both do part.
Now let your thoughts, as swift as is the wind,
Skip some few years that Cromwell spent in travel;
And now imagine him to be in England,
Servant unto the Master of the Rolls;
Where in short time he there began to flourish:
An hour shall show you what few years did nourish. [*Exit.*

SCENE III. *London. A room in* SIR CHRISTOPHER
HALES' *house.*

Music plays; then a banquet is brought in. Enter SIR CHRISTOPHER HALES, CROMWELL, *and two* Servants.

Hales. Come, Sirs, be careful of your master's credit;
And as our bounty now exceeds the figure
Of common entertainment, so do you,
With looks as free as is your master's soul,
Give formal welcome to the thronged tables,
That shall receive the cardinal's followers,
And the attendants of the great Lord Chancellor.
But, Cromwell, all my care depends on thee:
Thou art a man differing from vulgar form,
And by how much thy spirit's rank'd 'bove these,
In rules of art, by so much it shines brighter
By travel, whose observance pleads thy merit,
In a most learn'd, yet unaffected spirit.
Good Cromwell, cast an eye of fair regard
'Bout all my house; and what this ruder flesh,
Through ignorance, or wine, do miscreate,
Salve thou with courtesy. If welcome want,
Full bowls and ample banquets will seem scant.

Crom. Sir, as to whatsoever lies in me,
Assure you, I will show my utmost duty.

Hales. About it, then; the lords will straight be here.
[*Exit Cromwell.*
Cromwell, thou hast those parts would rather suit
The service of the state than of my house:
I look upon thee with a loving eye,
That one day will prefer thy destiny.

Enter a Servant.

Ser. Sir, the lords be at hand.

Hales. They are welcome; bid Cromwell straight attend us,
And look you all things be in readiness.
[*Exit Servant.*

The music plays. Enter Cardinal WOLSEY, SIR THOMAS MORE, GARDINER; CROMWELL, *and* Attendants.

Wol. O, Sir Christopher,
You are too liberal. What! a banquet, too?

Hales. My lords, if words could show the ample welcome
That my free heart affords you, I could then
Become a prater; but I now must deal
Like a feast-politician with your lordships;
Defer your welcome till the banquet end,
That it may then salve our defect of fare:
Yet welcome now, and all that tend on you.

Wol. Our thanks to the kind Master of the Rolls.
Come and sit down; sit down, Sir Thomas More.
'Tis strange, how that we and the Spaniard differ;
Their dinner is our banquet after dinner,
And they are men of active disposition.
By this I gather that, by their sparing meat,
Their bodies are more fitter for the wars;
And if that famine chance to pinch their maws,
Being us'd to fast, it breeds in them less pain.

Hales. Fill me some wine; I'll answer Cardinal Wolsey.
My lord, we English are of more free souls,
Than hunger-starv'd and ill-complexion'd Spaniards.
They that are rich in Spain spare belly-food,
To deck their backs with an Italian hood,
And silks of Seville; and the poorest snake
That feeds on lemons, pilchards, and ne'er heated
His palate with sweet flesh, will bear a case
More fat and gallant than his starvèd face.
Pride, the Inquisition, and this belly-evil,
Are, in my judgment, Spain's three-headed devil.

More. Indeed it is a plague unto their nation,
Who stagger after in blind imitation.

Hales. My lords, with welcome, I present your lordships
A solemn health.

More. I love healths well; but whenas healths do bring

Pain to the head, and body's surfeiting,
Then cease I healths:
Nay, spill not, friend; for though the drops be small,
Yet have they force to force men to the wall.

Wol. Sir Christopher, is that your man?

Hales. An't like
Your grace, he is a scholar, and a linguist;
One that hath travellèd through many parts
Of Christendom, my lord.

Wol. My friend, come nearer; have you been a traveller?

Crom. My lord,
I 've added to my knowledge the Low Countries,
With France, Spain, Germany, and Italy;
And though small gain of profit I did find,
Yet it did please my eye, content my mind.

Wol. What do you think then of the several states
And princes' courts as you have travellèd?

Crom. My lord, no court with England may compare,
Neither for state, nor civil government.
Lust dwells in France, in Italy, and Spain,
From the poor peasant to the prince's train.
In Germany and Holland, riot serves;
And he that most can drink, most he deserves.
England I praise not, for I here was born,
But sure she laughs the others unto scorn.

Wol. My lord, there dwells within that spirit more
Than can be discern'd by the outward eye:—
Sir Christopher, will you part with your man?

Hales. I 've sought to proffer him unto your lordship;
And now I see he hath preferr'd himself.

Wol. What is thy name?

Crom. Cromwell, my lord.

Wol. Then, Cromwell, here we make thee solicitor
Of our causes, and nearest, next ourself:
Gardiner, give you kind welcome to the man.

[*Gardiner embraces him.*

More. O, my lord cardinal, you 're a royal winner,

Have got a man, besides your bounteous dinner.
Well, my good knight, pray that we come no more:
If we come often, thou mayst shut thy door.
 Wol. Sir Christopher, hadst thou given me half thy lands,
Thou couldst not have pleased me so much as with
This man of thine. My infant thoughts do spell,
Shortly his fortune shall be lifted higher;
True industry doth kindle honour's fire:
And so, kind Master of the Rolls, farewell.
 Hales. Cromwell, farewell.
 Crom. Cromwell takes leave of you,
That ne'er will leave to love and honour you.
[*Exeunt. The music plays as they go out.*

ACT IV.

Enter Chorus.

 Cho. Now Cromwell's highest fortunes do begin.
Wolsey, that lov'd him as he did his life,
Committed all his treasure to his hands,
Wolsey is dead; and Gardiner, his man,
Is now created bishop of Winchester.
Pardon if we omit all Wolsey's life,
Because our play depends on Cromwell's death.
Now sit, and see his highest state of all,
His height of rising, and his sudden fall.
Pardon the errors are already past,
And live in hope the best doth come at last.
My hope upon your favour doth depend,
And looks to have your liking ere the end. [*Exit.*

SCENE I. *London. A public walk.*

Enter GARDINER Bishop of WINCHESTER, *the Dukes of* NORFOLK *and of* SUFFOLK, SIR THOMAS MORE, SIR CHRISTOPHER HALES, *and* CROMWELL.

 Nor. Master Cromwell, since Cardinal Wolsey's death,
His majesty is given to understand

There's certain bills and writings in your hand,
That much concern the present state of England.
My lord of Winchester, is it not so?
   Gar. My lord of Norfolk, we two were whilom fellows:
And Master Cromwell, though our master's love
Did bind us, while his love was to the king,
It is no boot now to deny those things,
Which may be prejudicial to the state:
And though that God hath rais'd my fortune higher
Than any way I look'd for, or deserv'd,
Yet may my life no longer with me dwell,
Than I prove true unto my sovereign!
What say you, Master Cromwell? Speak, have you
Those writings, ay, or no?
   Crom.   Here are the writings:
And on my knees I give them up unto
The worthy dukes of Suffolk, and of Norfolk.
He was my master, and each virtuous part
That liv'd in him, I tender'd with my heart;
But what his head complotted 'gainst the state,
My country's love commands me that to hate.
His sudden death I grieve for, not his fall,
Because he sought to work my country's thrall.
   Suf. Cromwell, the king shall hear of this thy duty;
Who, I assure myself, will well reward thee.
My lord, let's go unto his majesty,
And show these writings which he longs to see.
                           [*Exeunt Norfolk and Suffolk.*

          Enter BEDFORD, *hastily.*

   Bed. How now, who is this? Cromwell? By my soul,
Welcome to England: thou once didst save my life;
Didst thou not, Cromwell?
   Crom. If I did so, 'tis greater glory for me
That you remember it, than for myself
Now vainly to report it.
   Bed. Well, Cromwell, now's the time for gratitude:

I shall commend thee to my sovereign.
Cheer up thyself, for I will raise thy state:
A Russell yet was never found ingrate.   [*Exit.*

Hales. O how uncertain is the wheel of fate!
Who lately greater than the cardinal,
For fear and love? and now who lower lies?
Gay honours are but Fortune's flatteries;
And whom this day pride and promotion swell,
To-morrow envy and ambition quell.

More. Who sees the cobweb tangle the poor fly
May boldly say, the wretch's death is nigh.

Gard. I knew his state and proud ambition
Were too, too violent to last o'erlong.

Hales. Who soars too near the sun with golden wings,
Melts them; to ruin his own fortune brings.

Enter the Duke of SUFFOLK.

Suf. Cromwell, kneel down, and, in King Henry's name,
Arise Sir Thomas;—thus begins thy fame.

Enter the Duke of NORFOLK.

Nor. Cromwell, the gracious majesty of England,
For the good liking he conceives of thee,
Makes thee the master of the jewel-house,
Chief secretary to himself, and withal
Creates thee one of his highness' privy-council.

Enter the Earl of BEDFORD.

Bed. Where is Sir Thomas Cromwell? is he knighted?
Suf. He is, my lord.
Bed. Then, to add honour to
His name, the king creates him the lord-keeper
Of his privy seal, and master of the rolls,
Which you, Sir Christopher, do now enjoy:
The king determines higher place for you.

Crom. My lords,
These honours are too high for my desert.

More. O content thee, man; who would not choose it?
Yet thou art wise in seeming to refuse it.
   Gard. Here's honours, titles, and promotions:
I fear this climbing will have sudden fall.   [*Aside.*
   Nor. Then come, my lords; let's all together bring
This new-made counsellor to England's king.
                            [*Exeunt all but Gardiner.*
   Gard. But Gardiner means his glory shall be dimm'd.
Shall Cromwell live a greater man than I?
My envy with his honour now is bred:
I hope to shorten Cromwell by the head.   [*Exit.*

SCENE II. *London. A street before* CROMWELL'S *house.*

Enter FRESCOBALD.

   Fres. O Frescobald, what shall become of thee?
Where shalt thou go, or which way shalt thou turn?
Fortune, that turns her too inconstant wheel,
Hath drown'd thy wealth and riches in the sea.
All parts abroad wherever I have been
Grow weary of me, and deny me succour.
My debtors, they that should relieve my want,
Forswear my money, say they owe me none;
They know my state too mean to bear out law:
And here in London, where I oft have been,
And have done good to many a wretched man,
I 'm now most wretched and despis'd myself.
In vain it is more of their hearts to try;
Be patient, therefore, lay thee down and die.   [*Lies down.*

Enter SEELY *and* JOAN.

   Seely. Come, Joan, come; let's see what he'll do for us
now. I wis we have done for him, when many a time and
often he might have gone a-hungry to bed.
   Joan. Alas, man, now he is made a lord, he'll never look
upon us; he'll fulfil the old proverb, *Set beggars a horseback
and they'll ride*—A well-a-day for my cow! such as he hath

made us come behind-hand; we had never pawned our cow else to pay our rent.

Seely. Well, Joan, he'll come this way; and by God's dickers I'll tell him roundly of it, an if he were ten lords: a' shall know that I had not my cheese and my bacon for nothing.

Joan. Do you remember, husband, how he would mouch up my cheese-cakes? He hath forgot this now; but now we'll remember him.

Seely. Ay, we shall have now three flaps with a fox-tail: but i' faith I'll jibber a joint, but I'll tell him his own.—Stay, who comes here? O, stand up, here he comes; stand up.

Enter HODGE *with a tipstaff;* CROMWELL, *with the mace carried before him; the Dukes of* NORFOLK *and* SUFFOLK, *and Attendants.*

Hodge. Come; away with these beggars here. Rise up, sirrah; come out, good people; run afore there, ho.

[*Frescobald rises, and stands at a distance.*

Seely. Ay, we are kicked away, now we come for our own; the time hath been, he would ha' looked more friendly upon us: And you, Hodge, we know you well enough, though you are so fine.

Crom. Come hither, sirrah:—Stay, what men are these? My honest host of Hounslow, and his wife? I owe thee money, father, do I not?

Seely. Ay, by the body of me, dost thou. Would thou wouldst pay me: good four pound it is; I hav't o' the post at home.

Crom. I know 'tis true. Sirrah, give him ten angels:— And look your wife and you do stay to dinner; And while you live, I freely give to you Four pound a year, for the four pound I ow'd you.

Seely. Art not changed? Art old Tom still? Now God bless thee, good Lord Tom. Home, Joan, home; I'll dine with my Lord Tom to-day, and thou shalt come next week. Fetch my cow; home, Joan, home.

Joan. Now God bless thee, my good Lord Tom; I'll fetch my cow presently. [*Exit Joan.*

Enter GARDINER.

Crom. Sirrah, go to yon stronger; tell him, I
Desire him stay to dinner: I must speak
With him. [*To Hodge.*

Gard. My lord of Norfolk, see you this same bubble?
That's a mere puff? but mark the end, my lord;
But mark the end.

Nor. I promise you, I like not something he hath done:
But let that pass; the king doth love him well.

Crom. Good morrow to my lord of Winchester: I know
You bear me hard about the abbey lands.

Gard. Have I not reason, when religion's wrong'd?
You had no colour for what you have done.

Crom. Yes, the abolishing of Antichrist,
And of his popish order, from our realm.
I am no enemy to religion;
But what is done, it is for England's good.
What did they serve for, but to feed a sort
Of lazy abbots and of full-fed friars?
They neither plough nor sow, and yet they reap
The fat of all the land, and suck the poor.
Look, what was theirs is in King Henry's hands;
His wealth before lay in the abbey lands.

Gard. Indeed these things you have alleg'd, my lord;
When, God doth know, the infant yet unborn
Will curse the time the abbeys were pull'd down:
I pray now where is hospitality?
Where now may poor distressed people go,
For to relieve their need, or rest their bones,
When weary travel doth oppress their limbs?
And where religious men should take them in,
Shall now be kept back with a mastiff dog;
And thousand thousand——

Nor. O my lord, no more:
Things past redress 'tis bootless to complain.
Crom. What, shall we to the convocation-house?
Nor. We'll follow you, my lord; pray, lead the way.

Enter old CROMWELL, *in the dress of a farmer.*

Old Crom. How! one Cromwell made lord keeper, since I left Putney, and dwelt in Yorkshire? I never heard better news: I'll see that Cromwell, or it shall go hard.
Crom. My agèd father here! State set aside,
Father, upon my knee I crave your blessing.
One of my servants, go, and have him in;
At better leisure will we talk with him.
Old Crom. Now if I die, how happy were the day!
To see this comfort rains forth showers of joy.
[*Exeunt old Cromwell and Servant.*
Nor. This duty in him shows a kind of grace. [*Aside.*
Crom. Go on before, for time draws on apace.
[*Exeunt all but Frescobald.*
Fres. I wonder what this lord would have with me,
His man so strictly gave me charge to stay:
I never did offend him, to my knowledge.
Well, good or bad, I mean to bide it all;
Worse than I am now, never can befall.

Enter BANISTER *and his* Wife.

Ban. Come, wife,
I take it to be almost dinner time;
For Master Newton and Master Crosby sent
To me last night, they would come dine with me,
And take their bond in. Pray thee, hie thee home,
And see that all things be in readiness.
Mrs. Ban. They shall be welcome, husband; I'll go before:
But is not that man Master Frescobald?
[*She runs and embraces him.*
Ban. O heavens! it is kind Master Frescobald:
Say, Sir, what hap hath brought you to this pass?

Fres. The same that brought you to your misery.
Ban. Why would you not acquaint me with your state?
Is Banister, your poor friend, then forgot,
Whose goods, whose love, whose life and all is yours?
Fres. I thought your usage would be as the rest,
That had more kindness at my hands than you,
Yet look'd askance when as they saw me poor.
Mrs. Ban. If Banister would bear so base a heart,
I ne'er would look my husband in the face,
But hate him as I would a cockatrice.
Ban. And well thou mightst, should Banister so deal.
Since that I saw you, Sir, my state is mended;
And for the thousand pound I owe to you,
I have it ready for you, Sir, at home:
And though I grieve your fortune is so bad,
Yet that my hap's to help you makes me glad.
And now, Sir, will it please you walk with me?
Fres. Not yet I cannot, for the lord chancellor
Hath here commanded me to wait on him:
For what, I know not; pray God it be for good.
Ban. Never make doubt of that; I'll warrant you,
He is as kind and noble a gentleman,
As ever did possess the place he hath.
Mrs. Ban. Sir, my brother is his steward: if you please,
We'll go along and bear you company;
I know we shall not want for welcome there.
Fres. With all my heart, but what's become of Bagot?
Ban. He is hang'd for buying jewels of the king's.
Fres. A just reward for one so impious.
The time draws on, Sir, will you go along?
Ban. I'll follow you, kind Master Frescobald. [*Exeunt.*

SCENE III. *The same. Another street.*

Enter NEWTON *and* CROSBY.

New. Now, Master Crosby, I see you have a care
To keep your word, in payment of your money.

Cros. By my faith, I have reason on a bond:
Three thousand pound is far too much to forfeit;
And yet I doubt not Master Banister.
　New. By my faith, Sir, your sum is more than mine;
And yet I am not much behind you too,
Considering that to-day I paid at court.
　Cros. Mass, and 'tis well remember'd: what 's the reason
That the Lord Cromwell's men wear such long skirts
Upon their coats? they reach down to their hams.
　New. I will resolve you, Sir; and thus it is:
The bishop of Winchester, that loves not Cromwell
(As great men are envied as well as less),
A while ago there was a jar between them;
And it was brought to my Lord Cromwell's ear
That Bishop Gardiner would sit on his skirts:
Upon which word he made his men long blue coats,
And in the court wore one of them himself;
And meeting with the bishop, quoth he, "My lord,
Here's skirts enough now for your grace to sit on;"
Which vex'd the bishop to the very heart.
This is the reason why they wear long coats.
　Cros. 'Tis always seen, and mark it for a rule,
That one great man will envy still another;
But 'tis a thing that nothing concerns me:—
What, shall we now to Master Banister's?
　New. Ay, come, we'll pay him royally for our dinner.
　　　　　　　　　　　　　　　　　　　　　[*Exeunt.*

Scene IV. *The same. A room in* Cromwell's *house.*

Enter the Usher, *and the* Sewer. *Several* Servants *cross the stage with dishes in their hands.*

　Ush. Uncover there, gentlemen.

Enter Cromwell, Bedford, Suffolk, *old* Cromwell, Fres-
　　cobald, Seely, *and* Attendants.

　Crom. My noble lords of Suffolk and of Bedford,

Your honours are welcome to poor Cromwell's house.
Where is my father? nay, be cover'd, father;
Although that duty to these noblemen
Doth challenge it, yet I'll make bold with them.
Your head doth bear the calendar of care.
What! Cromwell cover'd, and his father bare?
It must not be—Now, Sir, to you: is not
Your name Frescobald, and a Florentine?
  Fres. My name was Frescobald, till cruel fate
Did rob me of my name, and of my state.
  Crom. What fortune brought you to this country now?
  Fres. All other parts have left me succourless,
Save only this. Because of debts I have,
I hope to gain, for to relieve my want.
  Crom. Did you not once, upon your Florence bridge,
Help a distress'd man, robb'd by the banditti?
His name was Cromwell.
  Fres.   I never made my brain
A calendar of any good I did:
I always lov'd this nation with my heart.
  Crom. I am that Cromwell that you there reliev'd.
Sixteen ducats you gave me for to clothe me,
Sixteen to bear my charges by the way,
And sixteen more I had for my horse-hire.
There be those several sums justly return'd:
Yet 'twere injustice, serving at my need,
For to repay thee without interest:
Therefore receive of me these several bags:
In each of them there are four hundred marks:
And bring to me the names of all your debtors;
And if they will not see you paid, I will.
O, God forbid that I should see him fall,
That help'd me in my greatest need of all.
Here stands my father, that first gave me life;
Alas, what duty is too much for him?
This man in time of need did save my life;
I therefore cannot do too much for him.

By this old man I oftentimes was fed,
Else might I have gone supperless to bed.
Such kindness have I had of these three men,
That Cromwell no way can repay again.
Now in to dinner, for we stay too long;
And to good stomachs is no greater wrong. [*Exeunt.*

SCENE V. *The same. A room in the* Bishop of WINCHESTER'S *house.*

Enter GARDINER *and a* Servant.

Gard. Sirrah, where be those men I caus'd to stay?
Serv. They do attend your pleasure, Sir, within.
Gard. Bid them come hither, and stay you without: [*Exit Servant.*
For by those men the fox of this same land,
That makes a goose of better than himself,
Must worried be even to his latest home;
Or Gardiner will fail in his intent.
As for the dukes of Suffolk and of Norfolk,
Whom I have sent for to come speak with me;
Howsoever outwardly they shadow it,
Yet in their hearts I know they love him not.
As for the earl of Bedford, he's but one,
And dares not gainsay what we do set down.

Enter the two Witnesses.

Now, my good friends, you know I sav'd your lives,
When, by the law, you had deserved death;
And then you promis'd me, upon your oaths,
To venture both your lives to do me good.
Both Wit. We swore no more than that we will perform.
Gard. I take your words; and that which you must do,
Is service for your God and for your king:
To root a rebel from this flourishing land,
One that's an enemy unto the church:
And therefore must you take your solemn oaths,

That you heard Cromwell, the lord chancellor,
Did wish a dagger at King Henry's heart.
Fear not to swear it, for I heard him speak it;
Therefore we'll shield you from ensuing harms.
  Both Wit. If you will warrant us the deed is good,
We'll undertake it.
  Gard. Kneel down, and I will here absolve you both:
This crucifix I lay upon your heads,
And sprinkle holy water on your brows:
The deed is meritorious that you do,
And by it shall you purchase grace from heaven.
  First Wit. Now, Sir, we'll undertake it, by our souls.
  Sec. Wit. For Cromwell never lov'd none of our sort.
  Gard. I know he doth not; and for both of you,
I will prefer you to some place of worth.
Now get you in, until I call for you,
For presently the dukes mean to be here. [*Exeunt Witnesses.*
Cromwell, sit fast; thy time's not long to reign.
The abbeys that were pull'd down by thy mean
Are now a mean for me to pull thee down.
Thy pride also thy own head lights upon,
For thou art he hath changed religion:—
But now no more, for here the dukes are come.

   Enter SUFFOLK, NORFOLK, *and* BEDFORD.

  Suf. Good even to my lord bishop.
  Nor. How fares my lord? what, are you all alone?
  Gard. No, not alone, my lords; my mind is troubled.
I know your honours muse wherefore I sent,
And in such haste. What, came you from the king?
  Nor. We did, and left none but Lord Cromwell with
   him.
  Gard. O, what a dangerous time is this we live in!
There's Thomas Wolsey, he's already gone,
And Thomas More, he follow'd after him:
Another Thomas yet there doth remain,
That is far worse than either of those twain;

And if with speed, my lords, we not pursue it,
I fear the king and all the land will rue it.
  Bed. Another Thomas? pray God, it be not Cromwell.
  Gard. My lord of Bedford, it is that traitor Cromwell.
  Bed. Is Cromwell false? my heart will never think it.
  Suf. My lord of Winchester, what likelihood
Or proof have you of this his treachery?
  Gard. My lord, too much.—Call in the men within.

Enter the Witnesses.

These men, my lord, upon their oaths, affirm
That they did hear Lord Cromwell in his garden
Wishing a dagger sticking at the heart
Of our King Henry: what is this but treason?
  Bed. If it be so, my heart doth bleed with sorrow.
  Suf. How say you, friends? What, did you hear these
    words?
  First Wit. We did, an't like your grace.
  Nor. In what place was Lord Cromwell when he spake
    them?
  Sec. Wit. In his garden; where we did attend a suit,
Which we had waited for two years and more.
  Suf. How long is 't since you heard him speak these
    words?
  Sec. Wit. Some half-year since.
  Bed. How chance that you conceal'd it all this time?
  First Wit. His greatness made us fear; that was the cause.
  Gard. Ay, ay, his greatness, that's the cause indeed,
And to make his treason here more manifest,
He calls his servants to him round about,
Tells them of Wolsey's life, and of his fall;
Says that himself hath many enemies,
And gives to some of them a park, or manor,
To others leases, lands to other some:
What need he do this in his prime of life,
And if he were not fearful of his death?
  Suf. My lord, these likelihoods are very great.

Bed. Pardon me, lords, for I must needs depart;
Their proofs are great, but greater is my heart.
                                        [*Exit Bedford.*
  Nor. My friends, take heed of that which you have said;
Your souls must answer what your tongues report:
Therefore take heed, be wary what you do.
  Sec. Wit. My lord, we speak no more but truth.
  Nor.   Let him
Depart, my lord of Winchester: and let
These men be close kept till the day of trial.
  Gard. They shall, my lord: ho, take in these two men.
                                    [*Exeunt Witnesses, &c.*
My lords, if Cromwell have a public trial,
That which we do is void, by his denial:
You know the king will credit none but him.
  Nor. 'Tis true; he rules the king even as he pleases.
  Suf. How shall we do for to attach him, then?
  Gard. Marry, thus, my lords; by an act he made himself,
With an intent to entrap some of our lives;
And this it is: *If any counsellor
Be convicted of high treason, he shall
Be executed without public trial:*
This act, my lords, he caus'd the king to make.
  Suf. He did, indeed, and I remember it;
And now 'tis like to fall upon himself.
  Nor. Let us not slack it; 'tis for England's good:
We must be wary, else he'll go beyond us.
  Gard. Well hath your grace said, my good lord of Norfolk:
Therefore let us go presently to Lambeth;
Thither comes Cromwell from the court to-night.
Let us arrest him; send him to the Tower;
And in the morning cut off the traitor's head.
  Nor. Come, then, about it; let us guard the town:
This is the day that Cromwell must go down.
  Gard. Along, my lords. Well, Cromwell is half dead;
He shaked my heart, but I will shake his head.   [*Exeunt.*

ACT V.

Scene I. *A street in London.*

Enter BEDFORD.

Bed. My soul is like a water greatly troubled;
And Gardiner is the man that makes it so.
O Cromwell, I do fear thy end is near;
Yet I'll prevent their malice if I can:
And, in good time, see where the man doth come,
Who little knows how near's his day of doom.

Enter CROMWELL, *with his train.* BEDFORD *makes as though he
would speak to him.* CROMWELL *goes on.*

Crom. You're well encounter'd, my good lord of Bedford.
I see your honour is address'd to talk.
Pray, pardon me; I am sent for to the king,
And do not know the business yet myself:
So fare you well, for I must needs be gone.
  Exit Cromwell, &c.

Bed. Be gone you must; well, what the remedy?
I fear too soon you must be gone indeed.
The king hath business; but little dost thou know,
Who's busy for thy life; thou think'st not so.

Re-enter CROMWELL, *attended.*

Crom. The second time well met, my lord of Bedford:
I am very sorry that my haste is such.
Lord marquis Dorset being sick to death,
I must receive of him the privy seal.
At Lambeth soon, my lord, we'll talk our fill. [*Exit.*

Bed. How smooth and easy is the way to death!

Enter a Messenger.

Mes. My lord, the dukes of Norfolk and of Suffolk,
Accompanied with the bishop of Winchester,

Entreat you to come presently to Lambeth,
On earnest matters that concern the state.
   Bed. To Lambeth! so: go fetch me pen and ink;
I and Lord Cromwell there shall talk enough:
Ay, and our last, I fear, an if he come.   [*Writes.*
Here, take this letter,—bear it to Lord Cromwell;
Bid him read it; say it concerns him near:
Away, be gone, make all the haste you can.
To Lambeth do I go a woful man.   [*Exeunt.*

     Scene II. *A street near the Thames.*
     Enter CROMWELL, *attended.*

   Crom. Is the barge ready? I will straight to Lambeth:
And, if this one day's business once were past,
I'd take my ease to-morrow after trouble.

     Enter Messenger.
How now, my friend, what, wouldst thou speak with me?
   Mes. Sir, here's a letter from my lord of Bedford.
     [*Gives him a letter. Cromwell puts it in his pocket.*
   Crom. O good, my friend, commend me to thy lord:
Hold, take these angels; drink them for thy pains.
   Mes. He doth desire your grace to read it straight,
Because he says it doth concern you near.
   Crom. Bid him assure himself of that. Farewell.
To-morrow, tell him, he shall hear from me.—
Set on before there, and away to Lambeth.   [*Exeunt.*

     Scene III. *Lambeth.*
Enter GARDINER, SUFFOLK, NORFOLK, BEDFORD, *Lieutenant of the Tower, a* Sergeant-at-Arms, *a* Herald, *and* Halberds.

   Gard. Halberds, stand close unto the water-side;
Sergeant-at-arms, be you bold in your office;
Herald, deliver now your proclamation.
   Her. This is to give notice to all the king's subjects, the late Lord Cromwell, lord chancellor of England, vicar-general over

the realm, him to hold and esteem as a traitor against the crown
and dignity of England. So God save the king.
 Gard. Amen.
 Bed.   Amen, and root thee from the land!
For whilst thou liv'st, the truth can never stand.
 Nor. Make a lane there, the traitor is at hand.
Keep back Cromwell's men; drown them, if they come on.
Sergeant, your office.

 Enter CROMWELL, *attended. The halberd-men make a lane.*

 Crom. What means my lord of Norfolk by these words?
Sirs, come along.
 Gard.   Kill them, if they come on.
 Ser. Lord Thomas Cromwell, in King Henry's name,
I do arrest your honour of high treason.
 Crom. Sergeant, me of treason?
        [*Cromwell's Attendants offer to draw.*
 Suf. Kill them; if they draw a sword.
 Crom. Hold; I charge you, as you love me, draw not a
    sword.
Who dares accuse Cromwell of treason now?
 Gard. This is no place to reckon up your crime;
Your dove-like looks were view'd with serpents' eyes.
 Crom. With serpents' eyes, indeed; by thine they were.
But, Gardiner, do thy worst: I fear thee not.
My faith compar'd with thine, as much shall pass
As doth the diamond excel the glass.
Attach'd of treason, no accusers by!
Indeed, what tongue dares speak so foul a lie?
 Nor. My lord, my lord, matters are too well known;
And it is time the king had note thereof.
 Crom. The king! let me go to him face to face;
No better trial I desire than that.
Let him but say, that Cromwell's faith was feign'd,
Then let my honour and my name be stain'd.
If e'er my heart against the king was set,
O, let my soul in judgment answer it!

Then if my faith's confirmèd with his reason,
'Gainst whom hath Cromwell then committed treason?

Suf. My lord, my lord, your matter shall be tried;
Meantime, with patience pray content yourself.

Crom. Perforce I must with patience be content:—
O, dear friend Bedford, dost thou stand so near?
Cromwell rejoiceth one friend sheds a tear.
And whither is't? Which way must Cromwell now?

Gard. My lord, you must unto the Tower. Lieutenant,
Take him unto your charge.

Crom. Well, where you please; but yet before I part,
Let me confer a little with my men.

Gard. Ay, as you go by water, so you shall.

Crom. I have some business present to impart.

Nor. You may not stay: Lieutenant, take your charge.

Crom. Well, well, my lord, you second Gardiner's text.
Norfolk, farewell! thy turn will be the next.

[*Exeunt Cromwell and Lieutenant.*

Gard. His guilty conscience makes him rave, my lord.

Nor. Ay, let him talk; his time is short enough.

Gard. My lord of Bedford, come; you weep for him
That would not shed a single tear for you.

Bed. It grieves me for to see his sudden fall.

Gard. Such success wish I unto traitors all. [*Exeunt.*

SCENE IV. *London. A street.*

Enter two Citizens.

First Cit. Why, can this news be true? Is't possible?
The great Lord Cromwell arrested upon treason?
I hardly will believe it can be so.

Sec. Cit. It is too true, Sir. Would 'twere otherwise,
Condition I spent half the wealth I have!
I was at Lambeth, saw him there arrested,
And afterward committed to the Tower.

First Cit. What, was't for treason that he was committed?

Sec. Cit. Kind, noble gentleman! I may rue the time:

All that I have, I did enjoy by him;
And if he die, then all my state is gone.
 First Cit. It may be hop'd that he shall not die,
Because the king did favour him so much.
 Sec. Cit. O, Sir, you are deceiv'd in thinking so.
The grace and favour he had with the king
Hath caus'd him have so many enemies.
He that in court secure will keep himself,
Must not be great, for then he's envied at.
The shrub is safe, when as the cedar shakes;
For where the king doth love above compare,
Of others they as much more envied are.
 First Cit. 'Tis pity that this nobleman should fall,
He did so many charitable deeds.
 Sec. Cit. 'Tis true; and yet you see in each estate
There's none so good, but some one doth him hate;
And they before would smile him in the face,
Will be the foremost to do him disgrace.
What, will you go along unto the court?
 First Cit. I care not if I do, and hear the news,
How men will judge what shall become of him.
 Sec. Cit. Some will speak hardly, some will speak in pity.
Go you to the court? I'll go into the city;
There I am sure to hear more news than you.
 First Cit. Why then we soon will meet again. Adieu.
[*Exeunt.*

SCENE V. *A room in the Tower.*

Enter CROMWELL.

Crom. Now, Cromwell, hast thou time to meditate,
And think upon thy state, and of the time.
Thy honours came unsought, ay, and unlook'd for;
Thy fall as sudden, and unlook'd for too.
What glory was in England that I had not?
Who in this land commanded more than Cromwell?
Except the king, who greater than myself?
But now I see what after-ages shall;

The greater men, more sudden is their fall.
And now I do remember, the earl of Bedford
Was very desirous for to speak to me;
And afterward sent unto me a letter,
The which I think I still have in my pocket;
Now may I read it, for I now have leisure,
And this I take it is: [*Reads.*

    My lord, come not this night to Lambeth,
    For, if you do, your state is overthrown;
    And much I doubt your life, an if you come:
    Then if you love yourself, stay where you are.

O God, O God! had I but read this letter,
Then had I been free from the lion's paw:
Deferring this to read until to-morrow.
I spurn'd at joy, and did embrace my sorrow.

    Enter Lieutenant *of the Tower*, Officers, &c.

Now, Master Lieutenant, when's this day of death?
  Lieu. Alas, my lord, would I might never see it!
Here are the dukes of Suffolk and of Norfolk,
Winchester, Bedford, and Sir Richard Radcliff,
With others still; but why they come I know not.
  Crom. No matter wherefore. Cromwell is prepar'd
For Gardiner has my life and state ensnar'd.
Bid them come in, or you shall do them wrong,
For here stands he who some think lives too long.
Learning kills learning, and, instead of ink
To dip his pen, Cromwell's heart-blood doth drink.

Enter the Dukes *of* SUFFOLK *and* NORFOLK; *the* Earl *of* BEDFORD,
  GARDINER *Bishop of* Winchester, Sir RICHARD RADCLIFF, *and*
  Sir RALPH SADLER.

  Nor. Good morrow, Cromwell. What, alone, so sad?
  Crom. One good among you, none of you are bad.
For my part, it best fits me be alone;
Sadness with me, not I with any one.
What, is the king acquainted with my cause?
  Nor. He is; and he hath answer'd us, my lord.

Crom. How shall I come to speak with him myself?
Gard. The king is so advertis'd of your guilt,
He'll by no means admit you to his presence.
Crom. No way admit me! am I so soon forgot?
Did he but yesterday embrace my neck,
And said that Cromwell was even half himself?
And are his princely ears so much bewitch'd
With scandalous ignomy, and slanderous speeches,
That now he doth deny to look on me?
Well, my lord of Winchester, no doubt but you
Are much in favour with his majesty:
Will you bear a letter from me to his grace?
Gard. Pardon me; I will bear no traitor's letters.
Crom. Ha!—Will you do this kindness then, to tell him
By word of mouth what I shall say to you?
Gard. That will I.
Crom. But, on your honour, will you?
Gard. Ay, on my honour.
Crom. Bear witness, lords.—Tell him, when he hath known
you,
And tried your faith but half so much as mine,
He'll find you to be the falsest-hearted man
Living in England: pray you, tell him this.
Bed. Be patient, good my lord, in these extremes.
Crom. My kind and honourable lord of Bedford,
I know your honour always lov'd me well:
But, pardon me, this still shall be my theme;
Gardiner's the cause makes Cromwell so extreme.
Sir Ralph Sadler, I pray a word with you;
You were my man, and all that you possess
Came by my means: Sir, to requite all this,
Say will you take this letter here of me,
And give it with your own hands to the king?
Sad. I kiss your hand, and never will I rest
Ere to the king this be deliverèd.   [*Exit Sadler.*
Crom. Why then yet Cromwell hath one friend in store.
Gard. But all the haste he makes shall be but vain.

Here 's a discharge, Sir, for your prisoner,
To see him executed presently: [*To the Lieutenant.*
My lord, you hear the tenure of your life.
    Crom. I do embrace it; welcome my last date,
And of this glistering world I take last leave:
And, noble lords, I take my leave of you.
As willingly I go to meet with death,
As Gardiner did pronounce it with his breath.
From treason is my heart as white as snow;
My death procurèd only by my foe.
I pray, commend me to my sovereign king,
And tell him in what sort his Cromwell died,
To lose his head before his cause was tried;
But let his grace, when he shall hear my name,
Say only this: Gardiner procur'd the same.

             Enter young CROMWELL.

    Lieu. Here is your son, Sir, come to take his leave.
    Crom. To take his leave? Come hither, Harry Cromwell;
Mark, boy, the last words that I speak to thee:
Flatter not Fortune, neither fawn upon her;
Gape not for state, yet lose no spark of honour;
Ambition, like the plague, see thou eschew it;
I die for treason, boy, and never knew it.
Yet let thy faith as spotless be as mine,
And Cromwell's virtues in thy face shall shine:
Come, go along, and see me leave my breath,
And I'll leave thee upon the floor of death.
    Son. O father, I shall die to see that wound,
Your blood being spilt will make my heart to swound.
    Crom. How, boy! not dare to look upon the axe?
How shall I do then to have my head struck off?
Come on, my child, and see the end of all;
And after say, that Gardiner was my fall.
    Gard. My lord, you speak it of an envious heart;
I have done no more than law and equity.
    Bed. O, my good lord of Winchester, forbear:

'Twould better have beseem'd you to be absent,
Than with your words disturb a dying man.
   Crom. Who, me, my lord? no: he disturbs not me.
My mind he stirs not, though his mighty shock
Hath brought more peers' heads down unto the block.—
Farewell, my boy! all Cromwell can bequeath,
My hearty blessing;—so I take my leave.
   Exec. I am your death's-man; pray, my lord, forgive me.
   Crom. Even with my soul. Why, man, thou art my doctor,
And bring'st me precious physic for my soul.—
My lord of Bedford, I desire of you
Before my death a corporal embrace.
                                              [*Cromwell embraces him.*
Farewell, great lord; my love I do commend,
My heart to you; my soul to heaven I send.
This is my joy, that ere my body fleet,
Your honour'd arms are my true winding-sheet.
Farewell, dear Bedford; my peace is made in heaven.
Thus falls great Cromwell, a poor ell in length,
To rise to unmeasur'd height, wing'd with new strength,
The land of worms, which dying men discover:
My soul is shrin'd with heaven's celestial cover.
                               Exeunt Cromwell, Officers, &c.
   Bed. Well, farewell Cromwell! sure the truest friend
That ever Bedford shall possess again.—
Well, lords, I fear that when this man is dead,
You'll wish in vain that Cromwell had a head.

      Enter an Officer, *with* Cromwell's *head.*

   Offi. Here is the head of the deceased Cromwell.
   Bed. Pray thee, go hence, and bear his head away
Unto his body; inter them both in clay.   [*Exit Officer.*

      Enter Sir Ralph Sadler.

   Sad. How now, my lords? What, is Lord Cromwell dead?
   Bed. Lord Cromwell's body now doth want a head.

Sad. O God, a little speed had sav'd his life.
Here is a kind reprieve come from the king,
To bring him straight unto his majesty.
  Suf. Ay, ay, Sir Ralph, reprieves come now too late.
  Gard. My conscience now tells me this deed was ill
Would Christ that Cromwell were alive again!
  Nor. Come, let us to the king, who, well I know,
Will grieve for Cromwell, that his death was so.
                                            [*Exeunt omnes.*

THE TRAGEDY OF LOCRINE.

DRAMATIS PERSONÆ.

BRUTUS, king of Britain.
LOCRINE,⎫
CAMBER,⎬ his sons.
ALBANACT,⎭
CORINEUS,⎫ brothers to Brutus.
ASSARACUS,⎭
THRASIMACHUS, son of Corineus.
DEBON, an old British officer.
HUMBER, king of the Scythians.
HUBBA, his son.
SEGAR,⎫ Scythian com-
THRASSIER,⎭ manders.
STRUMBO, a cobbler.
TROMPART, his servant.
OLIVER, a clown.
WILLIAM, his son.
MADAN, son of Locrine and Guendolen.
GUENDOLEN, daughter to Corineus, and wife of Locrine.
ESTRILD, wife to Humber.
SABREN, daughter of Locrine and Estrild.
DOROTHY, Strumbo's wife.
MARGERY, daughter to Oliver.

Ghosts of Albanact and Corineus; Ate, the Goddess of Revenge, as Chorus; Lords, a Captain, Soldiers, and Attendants.

SCENE.—*Britain.*

ACT I.

Thunder and Lightning.

Enter ATE *in black, with a burning torch in one hand, and a bloody sword in the other. Presently let there come forth a Lion running after a Bear; then come forth an Archer, who must kill the Lion in a dumb show, and then depart.* ATE *remains.*

Ate. In pœnam sectatur et umbra.*
A mighty lion, ruler of the woods,

* *l. s.* The shade or ghost pursues for punishment.

Of wondrous strength and great proportion,
With hideous noise scaring the trembling trees,
With yelling clamours shaking all the earth,
Travers'd the groves, and chas'd the wandering beasts:
Long did he range amid the shady trees,
And drave the silly beasts before his face;
When suddenly from out a thorny bush
A dreadful archer with his bow y-bent,
Wounded the lion with a dismal shaft:
So he him struck, that it drew forth the blood,
And fill'd his furious heart with fretting ire.
But all in vain he threat'neth teeth and paws
And sparkleth fire from forth his flaming eyes,
For the sharp shaft gave him a mortal wound:
So valiant Brute, the terror of the world,
Whose only looks did scare his enemies,
The archer Death brought to his latest end.
O, what may long abide above this ground,
In state of bliss and healthful happiness! [*Exit.*

SCENE I. *A chamber in the Royal Palace.*

Enter BRUTUS, *carried in a chair;* LOCRINE, CAMBER, ALBA-
NACT, CORINEUS, GUENDOLEN, ASSARACUS, DEBON, *and*
THRASIMACHUS.

Bru. Most loyal lords, and faithful followers,
That have with me, unworthy general,
Passèd the greedy gulf of ocean,
Leaving the confines of fair Italy,
Behold, your Brutus draweth nigh his end,
And I must leave you, though against my will.
My sinews shrink, my numbèd senses fail,
A chilling cold possesseth all my bones;
Black ugly Death, with visage pale and wan,
Presents himself before my dazzled eyes,
And with his dart prepared is to strike.
These arms, my lords, these never-daunted arms,

That oft have quell'd the courage of my foes,
And eke dismay'd my neighbours' arrogance,
Now yield to death, o'erlaid with crookèd age,
Devoid of strength and of their proper force.
Even as the lusty cedar worn with years,
That far abroad her dainty odour throws,
'Mongst all the daughters of proud Lebanon!
This heart, my lords, this ne'er-appallèd heart,
That was a terror to the bordering lands,
A doleful scourge unto my neighbour kings,
Now by the weapons of impartial death
Is clove asunder, and bereft of life:
As when the sacred oak with thunderbolts,
Sent from the fiery circuit of the heavens,
Sliding along the air's celestial vaults,
Is rent and cloven to the very roots.
In vain, therefore, I struggle with this foe;
Then welcome death, since God will have it so.

    Assar. Alas! my lord, we sorrow at your case,
And grieve to see your person vexèd thus.
But whatsoe'er the Fates determinèd have,
It lieth not in us to disannul;
And he that would annihilate their minds,
Soaring with Icarus too near the sun,
May catch a fall with young Bellerophon.
For when the fatal sisters have decreed
To separate us from this earthly mould,
No mortal force can countermand their minds.
Then, worthy lord, since there's no way but one,
Cease your laments, and leave your grievous moan.

    Cor. Your highness knows how many victories,
How many trophies I erected have
Triumphantly in every place we came.
The Grecian monarch, warlike Pandrasus,
And all the crew of the Molossians;
Goffarius, the arm-strong king of Gauls,
Have felt the force of our victorious arms,

And to their cost beheld our chivalry.
Where'er Aurora, handmaid of the sun,
Where'er the sun, bright guardian of the day,
Where'er the joyful day with cheerful light,
Where'er the light illuminates the world,
The Trojans' glory flies with golden wings,
Wings that do soar beyond fell envy's flight.
The fame of Brutus and his followers
Pierceth the skies, and, with the skies, the throne
Of mighty Jove, commander of the world.
Then, worthy Brutus, leave these sad laments;
Comfort yourself with this your great renown,
And fear not death, though he seem terrible.

Bru. Nay, Corineus, you mistake my mind,
In construing wrong the cause of my complaints,
I fear'd to yield myself to fatal death!
God knows it was the least of all my thought:
A greater care torments my very bones,
And makes me tremble at the thought of it;
And in you, lordings, doth the substance lie.

Thra. Most noble lord, if aught your loyal peers
Accomplish may, to ease your lingering grief,
I, in the name of all, protest to you,
That we will boldly enterprise the same,
Were it to enter to black Tartarus,
Where triple Cerberus, with his venomous throat,
Scareth the ghosts with high-resounding noise.
We'll either rent the bowels of the earth,
Searching the entrails of the brutish earth,
Or, with Ixion's over-daring son,
Be bound in chains of ever-during steel.

Bru. Then hearken to your sovereign's latest words,
In which I will unto you all unfold
Our royal mind and resolute intent.
When golden Hebe, daughter to great Jove,
Cover'd my manly cheeks with youthful down,
The unhappy slaughter of my luckless sire

Drove me and old Assaracus, mine eam,
As exiles from the bounds of Italy;
So that perforce we were constrain'd to fly
To Græcia's monarch, noble Pandrasus.
There I alone did undertake your cause,
There I restor'd your antique liberty,
Though Græcia frown'd, and all Molossia storm'd;
Though brave Antigonus, with martial band,
In pitchèd field encounter'd me and mine;
Though Pandrasus and his contributaries,
With all the rout of their confederates,
Sought to deface our glorious memory,
And wipe the name of Trojans from the earth:
Him did I captivate with this mine arm,
And by compulsion forc'd him to agree
To certain articles we did propound.
From Græcia through the boisterous Hellespont
We came unto the fields of Lestrigon,
Whereas our brother Corineus was,
Since when we passèd the Cilician gulf,
And so transfreighting the Illyrian sea,
Arrivèd on the coasts of Aquitain;
Where, with an army of his barbarous Gauls,
Goffarius and his brother Gathelus
Encountering with our host, sustain'd the foil;
And for your sakes my Turnus there I lost,
Turnus, that slew six hundred men-at-arms,
All in an hour, with his sharp battle-axe.
From thence upon the stronds of Albion
To Corus' haven happily we came,
And quell'd the giants, come of Albion's race
With Gogmagog, son to Samotheus,
The cursèd captain of that damnèd crew;
And in that isle at length I placèd you.
Now let me see, if my laborious toils,
If all my care, if all my grievous wounds,
If all my diligence, were well employ'd.

Cor. When first I follow'd thee and thine, brave king,
I hazarded my life and dearest blood
To purchase favour at your princely hands;
And for the same, in dangerous attempts,
In sundry conflicts, and in divers broils,
I show'd the courage of my manly mind.
For this I combated with Gathelus,
The brother to Goffarius of Gaul;
For this I fought with furious Gogmagog,
A savage captain of a savage crew;
And for these deeds brave Cornwall I receiv'd,
A grateful gift given by a gracious king;
And for this gift, his life and dearest blood
Will Corineus spend for Brutus' good.
  Deb. And what my friend, brave prince, hath vow'd to you,
The same will Debon do unto his end.
  Bru. Then, loyal peers, since you are all agreed,
And resolute to follow Brutus' 'hests,
Favour my sons, favour these orphans, lords,
And shield them from the dangers of their foes.
Locrine, the column of my family,
And only pillar of my weaken'd age,
Locrine, draw near, draw near unto thy sire,
And take thy latest blessings at his hands:
And, for thou art the eldest of my sons,
Be thou a captain to thy brethren,
And imitate thy agèd father's steps,
Which will conduct thee to true honour's gate:
For if thou follow sacred virtue's lore,
Thou shalt be crowned with a laurel branch,
And wear a wreath of sempiternal fame,
Sorted amongst the glorious happy ones.
  Loc. If Locrine do not follow your advice,
And bear himself in all things like a prince
That seeks to amplify the great renown
Left unto him for an inheritage
By those that were his glorious ancestors,

Let me be flung into the ocean,
Or swallow'd in the bowels of the earth:
Or let the ruddy lightning of great Jove
Descend upon this my devoted head.
  Bru. But for I see you all to be in doubt,
Who shall be matchèd with our royal son,
Locrine, receive this present at my hand;
              [Taking Guendolen by the hand.
A gift more rich than are the wealthy mines
Found in the bowels of America.
Thou shalt be spousèd to fair Guendolen:
Love her, and take her, for she is thine own,
If so thy uncle and herself do please.
  Cor. And herein how your highness honours me,
It cannot now be in my speech express'd;
For careful parents glory not so much
At their own honour and promotion,
As for to see the issue of their blood
Seated in honour and prosperity.
  Guen. And far be it from any maiden's thoughts
To contradict her agèd father's will.
Therefore, since he to whom I must obey,
Hath given me now unto your royal self,
I will not stand aloof from off the lure,
Like crafty dames that most of all deny
That which they most desire to possess.
  Bru. Then now, my son, thy part is on the stage,
            [Turning to Locrine, who kneels.
For thou must bear the person of a king.
              [Puts the crown on his head.
Locrine, stand up, and wear the regal crown,
And think upon the state of majesty,
That thou with honour well mayst wear the crown:
And, if thou tend'rest these my latest words,
As thou requir'st my soul to be at rest,
As thou desir'st thine own security,
Cherish and love thy new-betrothèd wife.

Loc. No longer let me well enjoy the crown,
Than I do honour Guendolen.
  Bru. Camber!
  Cam.   My lord.
  Bru.   The glory of mine age,
And darling of thy mother Imogen,
Take thou the South for thy dominion.
From thee there shall proceed a royal race,
That shall maintain the honour of this land,
And sway the regal sceptre with their hands.
                              [*Turning to Albanact.*
And Albanact, thy father's other joy,
Youngest in years, but not the young'st in mind,
A perfect pattern of all chivalry,
Take thou the North for thy dominion;
A country full of hills and ragged rocks,
Replenished with fierce, untamed beasts,
As correspondent to thy martial thoughts.
Live long, my sons, with endless happiness,
And bear concordance firm among yourselves.
Obey the counsels of these fathers grave,
That you may better bear out violence.—
But suddenly, through weakness of my age,
And the defect of youthful puissance,
My malady increaseth more and more,
And cruel Death hasteneth his quicken'd pace,
To dispossess me of my earthly shape.
Mine eyes wax dim, o'ercast with clouds of age,
The pangs of death compass my crazèd bones;
Thus to you all my blessings I bequeath,
And, with my blessings, this my fleeting soul.
My glass is run, and all my miseries
Do end with life; death closeth up mine eyes,
My soul in haste flies to the Elysian fields.   [*Dies.*
  Loc. Accursèd stars, damn'd and accursèd stars,
T'abbreviate my noble father's life!
Hard-hearted gods, and ye too envious fates,

Thus to cut off my father's fatal thread!
Brutus, that was a glory to us all,
Brutus, that was a terror to his foes,
Alas! too soon by Demogorgon's knife
The martial Brutus is bereft of life.
   Cor. No sad complaints may move just Æacus,
No dreadful threats can fear just Rhadamanth.
Wert thou as strong as mighty Hercules,
That tam'd the hugest monsters of the world,
Play'dst thou as sweet on the sweet-sounding lute
As did the spouse of fair Eurydice,
That did enchant the waters with his noise,
And made stones, birds, and beasts, to lead a dance,
Constrain'd the hilly trees to follow him,
Thou couldst not move the judge of Erebus,
Nor move compassion in grim Pluto's heart;
For fatal Mors expecteth all the world,
And every man must tread the way of death.
Brave Tantalus, the valiant Pelops' sire,
Guest to the gods, suffer'd untimely death;
And old Tithonus, husband to the Morn,
And eke grim Minos, whom just Jupiter
Deign'd to admit unto his sacrifice.
The thundering trumpets of blood-thirsty Mars,
The fearful rage of fell Tisiphone,
The boisterous waves of humid ocean,
Are instruments and tools of dismal death.
Then, noble cousin, cease to mourn his chance,
Whose age and years were signs that he should die.
It resteth now that we inter his bones,
That was a terror to his enemies.
Take up the corse, and princes, hold him dead,
Who while he liv'd uphold the Trojan state.
Sound drums and trumpets; march to Troynovant,
There to provide our chieftain's funeral.   [*Exeunt.*

140   THE TRAGEDY OF   [ACT I.

SCENE II. *The house of* STRUMBO.

Enter STRUMBO *above, in a gown, with ink and paper in his hand.*

Strum. Either the four elements, the seven planets, and all the particular stars of the pole antarctic, are adversative against me, or else I was begotten and born in the wane of the moon, when everything, as Lactantius in his fourth book of Constultations doth say, goeth arseward. Ay, masters, ay, you may laugh, but I must weep; you may joy, but I must sorrow; shedding salt tears from the watery fountains of my moist, dainty, fair eyes along my comely and smooth cheeks, in as great plenty as the water runneth from the bucking-tubs, or red wine out of the hogsheads. For trust me, gentlemen and my very good friends, and so forth, the little god, nay the desperate god, with one of his vengible bird-bolts, hath shot me into the heel: so not only, but also, (oh fine phrase!) *I burn, I burn, and I burn-a; in love, in love, and in love-a.* Ah! Strumbo, what hast thou seen? not Dina with the ass Tom? Yea, with these eyes, thou hast seen her; and therefore pull them out, for they will work thy bale. Ah! Strumbo, what hast thou heard? not the voice of the nightingale, but a voice sweeter than hers; yea, with these ears hast thou heard it, and therefore cut them off, for they have caused thy sorrow. Nay, Strumbo, kill thyself, drown thyself, hang thyself, starve thyself. Oh, but then I shall leave my sweetheart. Oh my heart! Now, pate, [*scratching his head*] for thy master! I will 'dite an aliquant love-pistle to her, and then she hearing the grand verbosity of my scripture, will love me presently. [*Writes.*] My pen is naught; gentlemen, lend me a knife; I think the more haste the worse speed. [*Writes again, and then reads.*]

So it is, Mistress Dorothy, and the sole essence of my soul, that the little sparkles of affection kindled in me towards your sweet self, hath now increased to a great flame, and will, ere it be long, consume my poor heart, except you with the pleasant water of your secret fountain quench the furious heat of the same. Alas, I am a gentleman of good fame and name, majestical, in apparel comely, in gait portly. Let not therefore your gentle heart be so hard as to despise a proper tall young man of a handsome life; and by despising him, not only but also to kill him. Thus expecting time and tide, I bid you farewell.

Your servant,
SIGNIOR STRUMBO.

O wit! O pate! O memory! O hand! O ink! O paper! Well, now I will send it away. Trompart, Trompart! What a villain is this? Why, sirrah, come when your master calls you. Trompart!

Enter TROMPART.

Trom. Anon, Sir.

Strum. Thou knowest, my pretty boy, what a good master I have been to thee ever since I took thee into my service.

Trom. Ay, Sir.

Strum. And how I have cherished thee always, as if thou hadst been the fruit of my loins, flesh of my flesh, and bone of my bone.

Trom. Ay, Sir.

Strum. Then show thyself herein a trusty servant; and carry this letter to Mistress Dorothy, and tell her—[*Whispers him. Exit Trompart.*] Nay, masters, you shall see a marriage by-and-by. But here she comes. Now must I frame my amorous passions.

Enter DOROTHY *and* TROMPART.

Dor. Signior Strumbo, well met. I received your letters by your man here, who told me a pitiful story of your anguish; and so understanding your passions were so great, I came hither speedily.

Strum. O, my sweet and pigsney, the fecundity of my ingeny is not so great that may declare unto you the sorrowful sobs and broken sleeps that I suffered for your sake; and therefore I desire you to receive me into your familiarity:

For your love doth lie
As near and as nigh

> Unto my heart within,
> As mine eye to my nose,
> My leg unto my hose,
> And my flesh unto my skin.

Dor. Truly, master Strumbo, you speak too learnedly for me to understand the drift of your mind; and therefore tell your tale in plain terms, and leave off your dark riddles.

Strum. Alas, mistress Dorothy, this is my luck, that when I most would, I cannot be understood; so that my great learning is an inconvenience unto me. But to speak in plain terms, I love you, mistress Dorothy, if you like to accept me into your familiarity.

Dor. If this be all, I am content.

Strum. Sayest thou so, sweet wench, let me lick thy toes. Farewell, mistress. If any of you be in love [*turning to the audience*], provide ye a cap-case full of new-coined words, and then shall you soon have the *succado de labres*, and something else. [*Exeunt.*

Scene III. *An apartment in the palace.*

Enter Locrine, Guendolen, Camber, Albanact, Corineus, Assaracus, Debon, *and* Thrasimachus.

Loc. Uncle, and princes of brave Brittany,
Since that our noble father is entomb'd,
As best beseem'd so brave a prince as he,
If so you please, this day my love and I,
Within the temple of Concordia,
Will solemnize our royal marriage.

Thra. Right noble lord, your subjects every one
Must needs obey your highness at command;
Especially in such a case as this,
That much concerns your highness' great content.

Loc. Then frolic, lordings, to fair Concord's walls,
Where we will pass the day in knightly sports,
The night in dancing and in figur'd masks,
And offer to god Risus all our tasks. [*Exeunt.*

ACT II.

A room with two doors.

Enter ATE, *as before. After a little lightning and thundering, let there come forth this Show:—Enter at one door* PERSEUS *and* ANDROMEDA, *hand in hand, and* CEPHEUS *also, with swords and targets. Then let there come out of another door* PHINEUS, *in black armour, with Æthiopians after him, driving in* PERSEUS; *and having taken away* ANDROMEDA, *let them depart.* ATE *remains.*

Ate. *Regit omnia numen.*[*]
When Perseus married fair Andromeda,
The only daughter of King Cepheus,
He thought he had establish'd well his crown,
And that his kingdom should for aye endure.
But lo! proud Phineus with a band of men,
Compos'd of sun-burnt Æthiopians,
By force of arms the bride he took from him,
And turn'd their joy into a flood of tears.
So fares it with young Locrine and his love;—
He thinks this marriage tendeth to his weal,
But this foul day, this foul accursèd day,
Is the beginning of his miseries.
Behold where Humber and his Scythians
Approacheth nigh with all his warlike train.—
It needs not, I, the sequel should declare,
What tragic chances fall out in this war.   [*Exit.*

SCENE I. *The seacoast of Britain.*

Enter HUMBER, HUBBA, ESTRILD, SEGAR, *and their* Soldiers.

Hum. At length the snail doth climb the highest tops,
Ascending up the stately castle walls;
At length the water with continual drops

---
[*] *I. e.* The Divinity or Fate rules all things.

Doth penetrate the hardest marble stone;
At length we are arriv'd in Albion.
Nor could the barbarous Dacian sovereign,
Nor yet the ruler of brave Belgia,
Stay us from cutting over to this isle,
Where as I hear a troop of Phrygians,
Under the conduct of Posthumius' son,
Have pitched up lordly pavilions,
And hope to prosper in this lovely isle.
But I will frustrate all their foolish hopes,
And teach them that the Scythian emperor
Leads Fortune tied in a chain of gold.
Constraining her to yield unto his will,
And grace him with their regal diadem;
Which I will have, maugre their treble hosts,
And all the power their petty kings can make.

Hub. If she that rules fair Rhamnus' golden gate*
Grant us the honour of the victory,
As hitherto she always favour'd us,
Right noble father, we will rule the land
Enthronized in seats of topaz stones;
That Locrine and his brethren all may know,
None must be king but Humber and his son.

Hum. Courage, my son; Fortune shall favour us,
And yield to us the coronet of bay,
That decketh none but noble conquerors.
But what saith Estrild to these regions?
How liketh she the temperature thereof?
Are they not pleasant in her gracious eyes?

Est. The plains, my lord, garnish'd with Flora's wealth,
And overspread with party-colour'd flowers,
Do yield sweet contentation to my mind.
The airy hills enclos'd with shady groves,
The groves replenish'd with sweet chirping birds,
The birds resounding heavenly melody,
Are equal to the groves of Thessaly;

* *I. e.* Fortune, one of whose principal seats was Rhamnus, in Attica.

Where Phœbus with the learnèd ladies nine,
Delight themselves with music's harmony,
And from the moisture of the mountain tops
The silent springs dance down with murmuring streams,
And water all the ground with crystal waves.
The gentle blasts of Eurus' modest wind,
Moving the pattering leaves of Sylvan's woods,
Do equal it with Tempe's paradise;
And thus consorted all to one effect,
Do make me think these are the happy isles,
Most fortunate, if Humber may them win.

Hub. Madam, where resolution leads the way,
And courage follows with embolden'd pace,
Fortune can never use her tyranny:
For valiantness is like unto a rock,
That standeth in the waves of ocean;
Which though the billows beat on every side,
And Boreas fell, with his tempestuous storms,
Bloweth upon it with a hideous clamour,
Yet it remaineth still unmoveable.

Hum. Kingly resolvèd, thou glory of thy sire.—
But, worthy Segar, what uncouth novelties
Bring'st thou unto our royal majesty?

Seg. My lord, the youngest of all Brutus' sons,
Stout Albanact, with millions of men,
Approacheth nigh, and meaneth ere the morn
To try your force by dint of fatal sword.

Hum. Tut, let him come with millions of hosts,
He shall find entertainment good enough,
Yea, fit for those that are our enemies;
For we'll receive them at the lances' points,
And massacre their bodies with our blades:
Yea, though they were in number infinite,
More than the mighty Babylonian queen,
Semiramis, the ruler of the West,
Brought 'gainst the emperor of the Scythians,

Yet would we not start back one foot from them,
That they might know we are invincible.
  Hub. Now, by great Jove, the supreme king of heaven,
And the immortal gods that live therein,
When as the morning shows his cheerful face,
And Lucifer, mounted upon his steed,
Brings in the chariot of the golden sun,
I'll meet young Albanact in open field,
And crack my lance upon his burgonet,
To try the valour of his boyish strength.
There will I show such ruthful spectacles,
And cause so great effusion of blood,
That all his boys shall wonder at my strength:
As when the warlike queen of Amazons,
Penthesiléa, armèd with her lance,
Girt with a corslet of bright-shining steel,
Coop'd up the faint-heart Grecians in the camp.
  Hum. Spoke like a warlike knight, my noble son;
Nay, like a prince that seeks his father's joy.
Therefore to-morrow, ere fair Titan shine,
And bashful Eos, messenger of light,
Expels the liquid sleep from out men's eyes,
Thou shalt conduct the right wing of the host;
The left wing shall be under Segar's charge;
The rearward shall be under me myself.
And lovely Estrild, fair and gracious,
If Fortune favour me in mine attempts,
Thou shalt be queen of lovely Albion.
Fortune *shall* favour me in mine attempts,
And make thee queen of lovely Albion!
Come, let us in, and muster up our train,
And furnish up our lusty soldiers;
That they may be a bulwark to our state,
And bring our wishèd joys to perfect end.   [*Exeunt.*

Scene II. *The cobbler's stall of Strumbo.*

Enter Strumbo, Dorothy, *and* Trompart, *cobbling shoes, and singing.*

Trom. *We cobblers lead a merry life:*
All. *Dan, dan, dan, dan.*
Strum. *Void of all envy and of strife:*
All. *Dan diddle dan.*
Dor. *Our ease is great, our labour small:*
All. *Dan, dan, dan, dan.*
Strum. *And yet our gains be much withal:*
All. *Dan diddle dan.*
Dor. *With this art so fine and fair:*
All. *Dan, dan, dan, dan.*
Trom. *No occupation may compare:*
All. *Dan diddle dan.*
Dor. *For merry pastime and joyful glee:*
    Dan, dan, dan, dan.
Strum. *Most happy men we cobblers be:*
    Dan diddle dan.
Trom. *The can stands full of nappy ale:*
    Dan, dan, dan, dan.
Strum. *In our shop still withouten fail:*
    Dan diddle dan.
Dor. *This is our meat, this is our food:*
    Dan, dan, dan, dan.
Trom. *This brings us to a merry mood:*
    Dan diddle dan.
Strum. *This makes us work for company:*
    Dan, dan, dan, dan.
Dor. *To pull the tankards cheerfully:*
    Dan diddle dan.
Trom. *Drink to thy husband, Dorothy:*
    Dan, dan, dan, dan.
Dor. *Why, then, my Strumbo, here's to thee:*
    Dan diddle dan.

Strum. *Drink thou the rest, Trompart, amain:*
Dan, dan, dan, dun.
Dor. *When that is gone, we'll fill't again:*
Dan diddle dan.

Enter a Captain.

Capt. The poorest state is furthest from annoy:
How merrily he sitteth on his stool!
But when he sees that needs he must be press'd,
He'll turn his note, and sing another tune.
Ho, by your leave, master cobbler.

Strum. You are welcome, gentleman. What, will you any old shoes or buskins, or will you have your shoes clouted? I will do them as well as any cobbler in Caithness whatsoever.

Capt. O master cobbler, you are far deceived in me; for don't you see this? [*Showing him press-money.*] I come not to buy any shoes, but to buy yourself. Come, Sir, you must be a soldier in the king's cause.

Strum. Why, but hear you, Sir. Has your king any commission to take any man against his will? I promise you, I can scant believe it: or did he give you commission?

Capt. O, Sir, you need not care for that: I need no commission. Hold here: I command you, in the name of our king Albanact, to appear to-morrow in the town-house of Caithness.

Strum. King Nactaball!* I cry God mercy; what have we to do with him, or he with us? But you, Sir, master Capontail, draw your pasteboard, or else, I promise you, I'll give you a canvasado with a bastinado over your shoulders, and teach you to come hither with your implements.

Capt. I pray thee, good fellow, be content; I do the king's command.

Strum. Put me out of your book then.

Capt. I may not.

Strum. No! Well, come, Sir, will your stomach serve you? By gogs blue-hood and halidom, I will have a bout with you.

[*Strumbo snatches up a staff. They fight.*

* A contemptuous perversion of the king's name.

Enter THRASIMACHUS.

Thra. How now, what noise, what sudden clamour 's
 this?
My captain and the cobbler hard at fight!
Sirs, what 's your quarrel?
 Capt. Nothing, Sir, but that he will not take press-money.
 Thra. Here, good fellow, take it at my command, unless
you mean to be stretched.
 Strum. Truly, master gentleman, I lack no money: if
you please I will resign it to one of these poor fellows.
 Thra. No such matter:
Look you be at the common-house to-morrow.
 [*Exeunt Thrasimachus and Captain.*
 Strum. O wife, I have spun a fair thread! If I had been
quiet, I had not been pressed, and therefore well may I
wail ment. But come, sirrah, shut up, for we must to the
wars. [*Exeunt.*

Scene III. *The camp of Albanact.*

Enter ALBANACT, DEBON, THRASIMACHUS, *and Lords.*

Alba. Brave cavaliers, princes of Albany,
Whose trenchant blades, with our deceasèd sire,
Passing the frontiers of brave Græcia,
Were bathed in our enemies' lukewarm blood,
Now is the time to manifest your wills,
Your haughty minds and resolutions.
Now opportunity is offerèd
To try your courage and your earnest zeal,
Which you always protest to Albanact;
For at this time, yea, at this present time,
Stout fugitives, come from the Scythians' bounds,
Have pester'd every place with mutinies.
But trust me, lordings, I will never cease
To persecute the rascal runagates,
Till all the rivers, stainèd with their blood,
Shall fully show their fatal overthrow.

Deb. So shall your highness merit great renown,
And imitate your agèd father's steps.
  Alba. But tell me, cousin, cam'st thou through the plains?
And saw'st thou there the faint-heart fugitives,
Mustering their weather-beaten soldiers?
What order keep they in their marshalling?
  Thra. After we pass'd the groves of Caledon,
Where murmuring rivers slide with silent streams,
We did behold the straggling Scythians' camp,
Replete with men, and storèd with munition.
There might we see the valiant-minded knights,
Fetching careers along the spacious plains.
Humber and Hubba arm'd in azure blue,
Mounted upon their coursers white as snow,
Went to behold the pleasant flowering fields:
Hector and Troilus, Priamus' lovely sons,
Chasing the Grecians over Simois,
Were not to be compar'd to these two knights.
  Alba. Well hast thou painted out in eloquence
The portraiture of Humber and his son,
As fortunate as was Polycrates.
Yet shall they not escape our conquering swords,
Or boast of aught but of our clemency.

        Enter STRUMBO *and* TROMPART, *crying often,*
Wildfire and pitch, wildfire and pitch.
  Thra. What, Sirs, what mean you by these clamours made,
These outcries raisèd in our stately court?
  Strum. Wildfire and pitch, wildfire and pitch.
  Thra. Villains, I say, tell us the cause hereof.
  Strum. Wildfire and pitch, wildfire and pitch.
  Thra. Tell me, you villains, why you make this noise,
Or, with my lance I'll prick your bowels out.
  Alba. Where are your houses? where's your dwelling-place?
  Strum. Place! Ha! ha! ha! laugh a month and a day at him. Place! I cry God mercy: Why, do you think that

such poor honest men as we be, hold our habitacles in kings'
palaces? Ha! ha! ha! But because you seem to be an
abominable chieftain, I will tell you our state:
     From the top to the toe,
     From the head to the shoe,
     From the beginning to the ending,
     From the building to the brending.
 This honest fellow and I had our mansion-cottage in the
suburbs of this city, hard by the temple of Mercury; and by
the common soldiers of the Shitens, the Scythians, (what do
you call them?) with all the suburbs, were burnt to the
ground; and the ashes are left there for the country wives to
wash bucks withal:
     And that which grieves me most,
      My loving wife,
      (O cruel strife!)
     The wicked flames did roast.
     And therefore, Captain Crust,
      We will continually cry,
      Except you seek a remedy,
      Our houses to re-edify,
     Which now are burnt to dust.

    [*Both cry Wildfire and pitch, wildfire and pitch.*

 Alba. Well, we must remedy these outrages,
And throw revenge upon their hateful heads.
And you, good fellows, for your houses burnt,
We will remunerate you store of gold,
And build your houses by our palace-gate.
 Strum. Gate! O petty treason to my person, nowhere else
but by your backside? Gate! O, how I am vexed in my
choler! Gate! I cry God mercy. Do you hear, master king?
If you mean to gratify such poor men as we be, you must
build our houses by the tavern.
 Alba. It shall be done, Sir.
 Strum. Near the tavern; ay, by our lady. Sir, it was
spoken like a good fellow. Do you hear, Sir? When our

152 THE TRAGEDY OF [ACT II.

house is builded, if you do chance to pass or repass that way,
we will bestow a quart of the best wine upon you.
                                     [*Exeunt Strumbo and Trompart.*
    Alba. It grieves me, lordings, that my subjects' goods
Should thus be spoiled by the Scythians,
Who, as you see, with lightfoot foragers,
Depopulate the places where they come:
But, cursèd Humber, thou shalt rue the day,
That e'er thou cam'st unto Cathnesia.   [*Exeunt.*

SCENE IV. *The camp of Humber.*

Enter HUMBER, HUBBA, SEGAR, THRASSIER, *and their forces.*

    Hum. Hubba, go take a coronet of our horse,
As many lanciers, and light-armèd knights,
As may suffice for such an enterprise,
And place them in the grove of Caledon:
With these, when as the skirmish doth increase,
Retire thou from the shelter of the wood,
And set upon the weaken'd Trojans' backs;
For policy, being join'd with chivalry,
Can never be put back from victory.   [*Exit Hubba.*

Enter ALBANACT; STRUMBO *and* Clowns *with him.*

    Alba. Thou base-born Hun, how durst thou be so bold,
As once to menace warlike Albanact,
The great commander of these regions?
But thou shalt buy thy rashness with thy death,
And rue too late thy over-bold attempts;
For with this sword, this instrument of death,
That hath been drenchèd in my foemen's blood,
I'll separate thy body from thy head,
And set that coward blood of thine abroach.
    Strum. Nay, with this staff, great Strumbo's instrument,
I'll crack thy cockscomb, paltry Scythian.
    Hum. Naught reck I of thy threats, thou princox boy,
Nor do I fear thy foolish insolence:

And, but thou better use thy bragging blade,
Than thou dost rule thy overflowing tongue,
Superbious Briton, thou shalt know too soon
The force of Humber and his Scythians.
  [*They fight. Humber and his soldiers fly. Albanact and
  his forces follow.*
  Strum. O horrible, terrible!

SCENE V. *Another part of the field of battle.*

Alarum. Enter HUMBER *and his Soldiers.*

Hum. How bravely this young Briton, Albanact,
Darteth abroad the thunderbolts of war,
Beating down millions with his furious mood,
And in his glory triumphs over all,
Moving the massy squadrons off the ground!
Heaps hills on hills, to scale the starry sky:
As when Briareus, arm'd with an hundred hands,
Flung forth an hundred mountains at great Jove:
As when the monstrous giant Monychus
Hurl'd mount Olympus at great Mars's targe,
And shot huge cedars at Minerva's shield.
How doth he overlook with haughty front
My fleeting hosts, and lifts his lofty face
Against us all that now do fear his force!
Like as we see the wrathful sea from far,
In a great mountain heap'd, with hideous noise,
With thousand billows beat against the ships,
And toss them in the waves like tennis-balls.
  [*An alarm sounded.*
Ah me! I fear my Hubba is surpris'd. [*Exit.*

Alarum again. Enter ALBANACT, CAMBER, THRASIMACHUS,
  DEBON, *and their Forces.*

Alba. Follow me, soldiers, follow Albanact;
Pursue the Scythians flying through the field;
Let none of them escape with victory!

That they may know the Britons' force is more
Than all the power of the trembling Huns.

   Thra. Forward, brave soldiers, forward; keep the chase.
He that takes captive Humber or his son,
Shall be rewarded with a crown of gold.

An alarum sounded; then they fight. HUMBER *and his Army
retreat. The Britons pursue.* HUMBA *enters at their rear, and
kills* DEBON: STRUMBO *falls down;* ALBANACT *runs out, and
afterwards enters wounded.*

   Alba. Injurious Fortune, hast thou cross'd me thus?
Thus in the morning of my victories,
Thus in the prime of my felicity,
To cut me off by such hard overthrow!
Hadst thou no time thy rancour to declare,
But in the spring of all my dignities?
Hadst thou no place to spit thy venom out,
But on the person of young Albanact?
I that erewhile did scare mine enemies,
And drove them almost to a shameful flight;
I that erewhile full lion-like did fare
Amongst the dangers of the thick throng'd pikes,
Must now depart, most lamentably slain
By Humber's treacheries and Fortune's spites.
Curs'd be her charms, damn'd be her cursed charms,
That do delude the wayward hearts of men,
Of men that trust unto her fickle wheel,
Which never leaveth turning upside-down!
O gods, O heavens, allot me but the place
Where I may find her hateful mansion.
I'll pass the Alps to wat'ry Meroe,
Where fiery Phœbus in his chariot,
The wheels whereof are deck'd with emeralds,
Casts such a heat, yea such a scorching heat,
As spoileth Flora of her chequer'd grass;
I'll overturn the mountain Caucasus,
Where fell Chimæra in her triple shape,

Rolleth hot flames from out her monstrous paunch,
Scaring the beasts with issue of her gorge;
I'll pass the frozen zone, where icy flakes
Stopping the passage of the fleeting ships,
Do lie, like mountains, in the congeal'd sea:
Where if I find that hateful house of hers,
I'll pull the fickle wheel from out her hands,
And tie herself in everlasting bands.
But all in vain I breathe these threatenings:
The day is lost, the Huns are conquerors,
Debon is slain, my men are done to death,
The currents swift swim violently with blood,
And last, (O that this last might so long last!)
Myself with wounds past all recovery,
Must leave my crown for Humber to possess.

Strum. Lord have mercy upon us, masters! I think this is a holy-day; every man lies sleeping in the fields: but God knows full sore against their wills.   [*Falls.*

Thra. Fly, noble Albanact, and save thyself,
The Scythians follow with great celerity,
And there's no way but flight or speedy death;
Fly, noble Albanact, and save thyself,
              [*Exit Thrasimachus. Alarum.*

Alba. Nay, let them fly that fear to die the death,
That tremble at the name of fatal Mors.
Ne'er shall proud Humber boast or brag himself,
That he hath put young Albanact to flight:
And lest he should triumph at my decay,
This sword shall reave his master of his life,
That oft hath sav'd his master's doubtful life:
But oh, my brethren, if you care for me,
Revenge my death upon his traitorous head.

    Et vos queis domus est nigrantis regia Ditis,
    Qui regitis rigido Stygios moderamine lucos,
    Nox cæci regina poli, furialis Erinnys,
    Diique deæque omnes, Albanum tollite regem,

Tollite flumineis undis rigidaque palude!
Nunc me fata vocant, hoc condam pectore ferrum.*)

                                          [Stabs himself.

           Enter TROMPART, *who sees* STRUMBO.

Trom. O, what hath he done? his nose bleeds; but I smell a fox: look where my master lies. Master, master!

Strum. Let me alone, I tell thee, for I am dead.

Trom. Yet one word, good master.

Strum. I will not speak, for I am dead, I tell thee.

    Trom. And is my master dead?   [*Singing.*
O sticks and stones, brickbats and bones,
   And is my master dead?
O you cockatrices, and you bablatrices,
   That in the woods dwell:
You briers and brambles, you cook-shops and shambles,
   Come, howl and yell!
With howling and shrieking, with wailing and weeping,
   Come you to lament,
Of colliers of Croydon, and rustics of Roydon,
   And fishers of Kent;—
For Strumbo the cobbler, the fine merry cobbler
   Of Caithness town,
At this same stour, at this very hour,
   Lies dead on the ground.

O master, thieves, thieves, thieves!

Strum. Where be they? cox me tunny, bobekin! let me be rising: be gone; we shall be robbed by-and-by.

                              [*Exeunt Strumbo and Trompart.*

---

* *I. e.* And you who sway in Pluto's royal house,
And govern with stern power the Stygian realms,
Night, queen of cloudy heavens—thou fearful fury,
And you, ye gods and goddesses, receive
The Alban sovereign to your gloomy lake
And over-flowing streams!—The summoning fates
Decree, and through this bosom goes the sword.

Scene VI. *The camp of the Huns.*

Enter HUMBER, HUBBA, SEGAR, THRASSIER, ESTRILD *and*
Soldiers.

Hum. Thus from the dreadful shocks of furious Mars,
Thund'ring alarums, and Rhamnusia's drum,
We are retir'd with joyful victory.
The slaughter'd Trojans, sweltering in their blood,
Infect the air with their dead carcasses,
And are a prey for every ravenous bird.
 Est. So perish they that are our enemies!
So perish they that love not Humber's weal!
And, mighty Jove, commander of the world,
Protect my love from all false treacheries!
 Hum. Thanks, lovely Estrild, solace to my soul!
But, valiant Hubba, for thy chivalry
Declar'd against the men of Albany,
Lo! here a flow'ring garland wreath'd of bay,
As a reward for this thy forward mind.
 [*Sets it on Hubba's head.*
 Hub. This unexpected honour, noble sire,
Will prick my courage unto braver deeds,
And cause me to attempt such hard exploits,
That all the world shall sound of Hubba's name.
 Hum. And now, brave soldiers, for this good success,
Carouse whole cups of Amazonian wine,
Sweeter than Nectar, or Ambrosia;
And cast away the clouds of cursèd care,
With goblets crown'd with Semeleius' gifts.
Now let us march to Abus' silver streams,
That clearly glide along the champain fields,
And moist the grassy meads with humid drops.
Sound drums and trumpets, sound up cheerfully,
Sith we return with joy and victory. [*Exeunt.*

ACT III.

Enter ATE *as before. Then this dumb show. A crocodile sitting on a river's bank, and a little snake stinging it. Both of them fall into the water.*

Até. *Scelera in authorem cadunt.**)
High on a bank, by Nilus' boisterous streams,
Fearfully sat the Egyptian crocodile,
Dreadfully grinding in her sharp long teeth
The broken bowels of a silly fish:
His back was arm'd against the dint of spear,
With shields of brass that shone like burnish'd gold:
And as he stretchèd forth his cruel paws,
A subtle adder creeping closely near,
Thrusting his forkèd sting into his claws,
Privily shed his poison through his bones,
Which made him swell, that there his bowels burst,
That did so much in his own greatness trust.
So Humber having conquer'd Albanact,
Doth yield his glory unto Locrine's sword.
Mark what ensues, and you may easily see
That all our life is but a tragedy. [*Exit.*

SCENE I. *Troynovant. An apartment in the Royal Palace.*

Enter LOCRINE, GUENDOLEN, CORINEUS, ASSARACUS, THRASI-
MACHUS, *and* CAMBER.

Loc. And is this true? Is Albanactus slain?
Hath cursèd Humber, with his straggling host,
With that his army made of mongrel curs,
Brought our redoubted brother to his end?
O that I had the Thracian Orpheus' harp,
For to awake out of the infernal shade
Those ugly devils of black Erebus,—
That might torment the damnèd traitor's soul!

* *I. e.* The criminal must answer for his crime.

O that I had Amphion's instrument,
To quicken with his vital notes and tunes
'The flinty joints of every stony rock,'
By which the Scythians might be punishèd!
For, by the lightning of almighty Jove,
The Hun shall die, had he ten thousand lives:
And would to God he had ten thousand lives,
That I might with the arm-strong Hercules
Crop off so vile an hydra's hissing heads!
But say, my cousin (for I long to hear),
How Albanact came by untimely death?

   Thra. After the traitorous host of Scythians
Enter'd the field with martial equipage,
Young Albanact, impatient of delay,
Led forth his army 'gainst the straggling mates;
Whose multitude did daunt our soldiers' minds.
Yet nothing could dismay the forward prince:
Who with a courage most heroical,
Like to a lion 'mongst a flock of lambs,
Made havoc of the faint-heart fugitives,
Hewing a passage through them with his sword.
Yea, we had almost given them the repulse,
When, suddenly from out the silent wood,
Hubba, with twenty thousand soldiers,
Cowardly came upon our weaken'd backs,
And murder'd all with fatal massacre:
Amongst the which old Debon, martial knight,
With many wounds was brought unto the death;
And Albanact, oppress'd with multitude,
Whilst valiantly he fell'd his enemies,
Yielded his life and honour to the dust.
He being dead, the soldiers fled amain;
And I alone escapèd them by flight,
To bring you tidings of these accidents.

   Loc. Not agèd Priam, king of stately Troy,
Grand emperor of barbarous Asia,
When he beheld his noble-minded sons

Slain traitorously by all the Myrmidons,
Lamented more than I for Albanact.
 Guen. Not Hecuba the queen of Ilion,
When she beheld the town of Pergamus,
Her palace, burnt with all-devouring flames,
Her fifty sons and daughters, fresh of hue,
Murder'd by wicked Pyrrhus' bloody sword,
Shed such sad tears as I for Albanact.
 Cam. The grief of Niobe, fair Amphion's queen,
For her seven sons magnanimous in field,
For her seven daughters, fairer than the fairest,
Is not to be compar'd with my laments.
 Cor. In vain you sorrow for the slaughter'd prince,
In vain you sorrow for his overthrow;
He loves not most that doth lament the most,
But he that seeks to 'venge the injury.
Think you to quell the enemies' warlike train
With childish sobs and womanish laments?
Unsheathe your swords, unsheathe your conquering swords,
And seek revenge, the comfort for this sore!
In Cornwall, where I hold my regiment,
Even just ten thousand valiant men-at-arms
Hath Corineus ready at command,
All these and more, if need shall more require,
Hath Corineus ready at command.
 Cam. And in the fields of martial Cambria,
Close by the boisterous Isca's silver streams,
Where light-foot fairies skip from bank to bank,
Full twenty thousand brave courageous knights
Well exercis'd in feats of chivalry,
In manly manner most invincible,
Young Camber hath, with gold and victual;
All these and more, if need shall more require,
I offer up to 'venge my brother's death.
 Loc. Thanks, loving uncle, and good brother too;
For this revenge, for this sweet word, revenge,
Must ease and cease my wrongful injuries:

And by the sword of bloody Mars I swear,
Ne'er shall sweet quiet enter this my front;
                    [*Touching his forehead.*
Till I be 'vengèd on his traitorous head,
That slew my noble brother Albanact.
Sound drums and trumpets; muster up the camp;
For we will straight march to Albania.   [*Exeunt.*

SCENE II. *The banks of the river, afterward the Humber.*

Enter HUMBER, ESTRILD, HUBBA, THRASSIMB, *and*
Soldiers.

Hum. Thus are we come, victorious conquerors
Unto the flowing current's silver streams,
Which, in memorial of our victory,
Shall be agnominated by our name,
And talkèd of by our posterity:
For sure I hope before the golden sun
Posteth his horses to fair Thetis' plains,
To see the water turned into blood,
And change his bluish hue to rueful red,
By reason of the fatal massacre
Which shall be made upon the virent plains.

Enter the Ghost of ALBANACT.

Ghost. See how the traitor doth presage his harm;
See how he glories at his own decay;
See how he triumphs at his proper loss;
O Fortune vile, unstable, fickle, frail!
    Hum. Methinks I see both armies in the field.
The broken lances climb the crystal skies;
Some headless lie, some breathless, on the ground,
And every place is strew'd with carcasses:
Behold the grass hath lost its pleasant green,
The sweetest sight that ever might be seen.
    Ghost. Ay, traitorous Humber, thou shalt find it so;
Yea to thy cost thou shalt the same behold,

With anguish, sorrow, and with sad laments.
The grassy plains, that now do please thine eyes,
Shall ere the night be colour'd all with blood.
The shady groves which now enclose thy camp,
And yield sweet savour to thy damnèd corps,
Shall ere the night be figur'd all with blood.
The profound stream that passeth by thy tents,
And with his moisture serveth all thy camp,
Shall ere the night converted be to blood.—
Yea with the blood of those thy straggling boys:
For now revenge shall ease my lingering grief,
And now revenge shall glut my longing soul. [*Exit.*

Hub. Let come what will, I mean to bear it out:
And either live with glorious victory,
Or die with fame renown'd for chivalry.
He is not worthy of the honeycomb,
That shuns the hives because the bees have stings.
That likes me best that is not got with ease,
Which thousand dangers do accompany;
For nothing can dismay our regal mind,
Which aims at nothing but a golden crown,
The only upshot of mine enterprises.
Were they enchainèd in grim Pluto's court,
And kept for treasure 'mongst his hellish crew,
I'd either quell the triple Cerberus,
And all the army of his hateful hags,
Or roll the stone with wretched Sisyphus.

Hum. Right martial be thy thoughts, my noble son,
And all thy words savour of chivalry.

Enter SEGAR, *hastily.*

But, warlike Segar, what strange accidents
Make you to leave the warding of the camp?

Segar. To arms, my lord, to honourable arms:
Take helm and targe in hand: The Britons come
With greater multitude than erst the Greeks
Brought to the ports of Phrygian Tenedos.

Hum. But what saith Segar to these accidents?
What counsel gives he in extremities?
  Segar. Why this, my lord, experience teacheth us,
That resolution is sole help at need;
And this, my lord, our honour teacheth us,
That we be bold in every enterprise.
Then, since there is no way but fight or die,
Be resolute, my lord, for victory.
  Hum. And resolute, Segar, I mean to be.
Perhaps some blissful star will favour us,
And comfort bring to our perplexèd state.
Come, let us in, and fortify our camp,
So to withstand their strong invasion. [*Exeunt.*

SCENE III. *Before the hood of a peasant.*

Enter STRUMBO, TROMPART, OLIVER, *and his son* WILLIAM.

  Strum. Nay, neighbour Oliver, if you be so hot, come, prepare yourself, you shall find two as stout fellows of us, as any in all the North.
  Oliv. No, by my dorth, neighbour Strumbo; Ich zee dat you are a man of small 'zideration, dat will zeek to injure your old vreends, one of your vamiliar guests; and derefore zeeing your 'pinion is to deal withouten reazon, Ich and my zon William will take dat course dat shall be fardest vrom reason. How zay you? will you have my daughter or no?
  Strum. A very hard question, neighbour, but I will solve it as I may. What reason have you to demand it of me?
  Will. Marry, Sir, what reason had you, when my sister was in the barn, to tumble her upon the hay, and to fish her belly?
  Strum. Mass, thou say'st true. Well, but would you have me marry her therefore? No, I scorn her, and you, and you: ay, I scorn you all.
  Oliv. You will not have her then?
  Strum. No, as I am a true gentleman.

Will. Then will we school you, ere you and we part hence. [*They fight.*

Enter MARGERY. *She snatches the staff out of her brother's hand, as he is fighting.*

Strum. Ay, you come in pudding-time, or else I had dress'd them.

Mar. You, master saucebox, lobcock, cockscomb; you, slopsauce, lickfingers, will you not hear?

Strum. Who speak you to? me?

Mar. Ay, Sir, to you, John Lackhonesty, Littlewit. Is it you that will have none of me?

Strum. No, by my troth, mistress Nicebice. How fine you can nick-name me! I think you were brought up in the university of Bridewell, you have your rhetoric so ready at your tongue's end, as if you were never well warned when you were young.

Mar. Why then, goodman Codshead, if you will have none of me, farewell.

Strum. If you be so plain, mistress Driggle-draggle, fare you well.

Mar. Nay, master Strumbo, ere you go from hence, we must have more words. You will have none of me? [*They fight.*

Strum. O, my head, my head! Leave, leave, leave; I will, I will, I will.

Mar. Upon that condition I let thee alone.

Oliv. How now, master Strumbo? Hath my daughter taught you a new lesson?

Strum. Ay, but hear you, goodman Oliver; it will not be for my ease to have my head broken every day; therefore remedy this, and we shall agree.

Oliv. Well, zon, well (for you are my zon now), all shall be remedied. Daughter, be friends with him. [*They shake hands.*

[*Exeunt Oliver, William, and Margery.*

Strum. You are a sweet nut; the devil crack you! Masters, I think it be my luck. My first wife was a loving quiet wench; but this, I think, would weary the devil. I would she might be burnt as my other wife was; if not, I must run to the halter for help. O Codpiece, thou hast undone thy master; this it is to be meddling with warm plackets. [*Exeunt.*

SCENE IV. *The camp of Locrine.*

Enter LOCRINE, CAMBER, CORINEUS, THRASIMACHUS, *and* ASSARACUS.

Loc. Now am I guarded with an host of men,
Whose haughty courage is invincible.
Now am I hemm'd with troops of soldiers,
Such as might force Bellona to retire,
And make her tremble at their puissance.
Now sit I like the mighty god of war,
When, armèd with his coat of adamant,
Mounted in's chariot drawn with mighty bulls,
He drove the Argives over Xanthus' streams.
Now, cursèd Humber, doth thy end draw nigh,
Down goes the glory of thy victories,
And all thy fame, and all thy high renown,
Shall in a moment yield to Locrine's sword.
Thy bragging banners cross'd with argent streams,
The ornaments of thy pavilions,
Shall all be captivated with this hand;
And thou thyself at Albanactus' tomb
Shalt offer'd be, in satisfaction
Of all the wrongs thou didst him when he liv'd.—
But canst thou tell me, brave Thrasimachus,
How far we distant are from Humber's camp?

Thra. My lord, within yon foul accursèd grove,
That bears the tokens of our overthrow,
This Humber hath intrench'd his damnèd camp.
March on, my lord, because I long to see
The treacherous Scythians swelt'ring in their gore.

Loc. Sweet Fortune, favour Locrine with a smile,
That I may 'venge my noble brother's death!
And in the midst of stately Troynovant

I'll build a temple to thy deity,
Of perfect marble, and of jacinth stones,
That it shall pass the high pyramidés,
Which with their top surmount the firmament.

 Cam. The arm-strong offspring of the 'doubted night,
Stout Hercules, Alcmena's mighty son,
That tam'd the monsters of the threefold world,
And rid the oppressèd from the tyrants' yokes,
Did never show such valiantness in fight,
As I will now for noble Albanact.

 Cor. Full fourscore years hath Corineus liv'd,
Sometimes in war, sometimes in quiet peace,
And I yet feel myself to be as strong
As erst I was in summer of mine age;
Able to toss this great unwieldy club,
Which hath been painted with my foemen's brains:
And with this club I'll break the strong array
Of Humber and his straggling soldiers,
Or lose my life amongst the thickest press,
And die with honour in my latest days:
Yet, ere I die, they all shall understand,
What force lies in stout Corineus' hand.

 Thra. And if Thrasimachus detract the fight,
Either for weakness, or for cowardice,
Let him not boast that Brutus was his eam,
Or that brave Corineus was his sire.

 Loc. Then courage, soldiers, first for your safety,
Next for your peace, last for your victory. [*Exeunt.*

  Scene V. *The field of battle.*

 Alarum. Enter Humber *and* Segar *at one side of the stage,
and* Corineus *at the other.*

 Cor. Art thou that Humber, prince of fugitives,
That by thy treason slew'st young Albanact?

 Hub. I am his son that slew young Albanact;
And if thou take not heed, proud Phrygian,

I'll send thy soul unto the Stygian lake,
There to complain of Humber's injuries.
   Cor. You triumph, Sir, before the victory,
For not so soon is Corineus slain.
But, cursèd Scythians, you shall rue the day,
That e'er you came into Albania.
So perish they that envy Britain's wealth,
So let them die with endless infamy:
And he that seeks his sovereign's overthrow,
Would this my club might aggravate his woe.
                 [*Strikes them with his club. Exeunt fighting.*

SCENE VI. *Another part of the field.*

Enter HUMBER.

   Hum. Where may I find some desert wilderness,
Where I may breathe out curses as I would,
And scare the earth with my condemning voice;
Where every echo's repercussion
May help me to bewail mine overthrow,
And aid me in my sorrowful laments?
Where may I find some hollow uncouth rock,
Where I may damn, condemn, and ban my fill,
The heavens, the hell, the earth, the air, the fire;
And utter curses to the concave sky
Which may infect the airy regions,
And light upon the Briton Locrine's head?
You ugly spirits that in Cocytus mourn,
And gnash your teeth with dolorous laments;
You fearful dogs, that in black Lethe howl,
And scare the ghosts with your wide open throats;
You ugly ghosts, that flying from these dogs
Do plunge yourselves in Pyriphlegethon;
Come all of you, and with your shrieking notes
Accompany the Britons' conquering host.
Come, fierce Erinnys, horrible with snakes;
Come, ugly furies, armèd with your whips;

You threefold judges of black Tartarus,
And all the army of your hellish fiends,
With new-found torments rack proud Locrine's bones!
O gods and stars! damn'd be the gods and stars,
That did not drown me in fair Thetis' plains!
Curst be the sea, that with outrageous waves,
With surging billows, did not rive my ships
Against the rocks of high Ceraunia,
Or swallow me into her wat'ry gulf!
Would God we had arriv'd upon the shore
Where Polyphemus and the Cyclops dwell;
Or where the bloody Anthropophagi
With greedy jaws devour the wandering wights!

Enter the Ghost of ALBANACT.

But why comes Albanactus' bloody ghost,
To bring a cor'sive to our miseries?
Is't not enough to suffer shameful flight,
But we must be tormented now with ghosts,
With apparitions fearful to behold?
 Ghost. Revenge, revenge for blood.
 Hum. So, naught will satisfy you, wandering ghost,
But dire revenge; nothing but Humber's fall;
Because he conquer'd you in Albany.
Now, by my soul, Humber would be condemn'd
To Tantal's hunger, or Ixion's wheel,
Or to the vulture of Prometheus,
Rather than that this murder were undone.
When as I die, I'll drag thy cursèd ghost
Through all the rivers of foul Erebus,
Through burning sulphur of the limbo-lake,
To allay the burning fury of that heat,
That rageth in mine everlasting soul.
 Ghost. Vindicta! vindicta! [*Exeunt.*

ACT IV.

Enter ATE *as before. Then* OMPHALE, *having a club in her hand, and a lion's skin on her back;* HERCULES *following with a distaff.* OMPHALE *turns about, and taking off her pantofle, strikes* HERCULES *on the head; then they depart.* ATE *remains.*

Atè. *Quem non Argolici mandata severa tyranni,*
Non potuit Juno vincere, vicit amor.*
Stout Hercules, the mirror of the world,
Son to Alcmena and great Jupiter,
After so many conquests won in field,
After so many monsters quell'd by force,
Yielded his valiant heart to Omphale,
A fearful woman, void of manly strength.
She took the club, and wore the lion's skin;
He took the wheel, and maidenly 'gan spin.
So martial Locrine, cheer'd with victory,
Falleth in love with Humber's concubine,
And so forgetteth peerless Guendolen:
His uncle Corineus storms at this,
And forceth Locrine for his grace to sue.
Lo here the sum; the process doth ensue. [*Exit.*

SCENE I. *The camp of* LOCRINE.

Enter LOCRINE, CAMBER, CORINEUS, ASSARACUS, THRASI-
MACHUS, *and* Soldiers.

Loc. Thus from the fury of Bellona's broils,
With sound of drum, and trumpets' melody,
The Britain king returns triumphantly.
The Scythians slain with great occision,
Do equalize the grass in multitude;
And with their blood have stain'd the streaming brooks,

* *I. e.* He whom the tyrant's mandate could not move,
Nor Juno's self subdue, submits to love.

Offering their bodies, and their dearest blood,
As sacrifice to Albanactus' ghost.
Now, cursèd Humber, hast thou paid thy due,
For thy deceits and crafty treacheries,
For all thy guiles, and damnèd stratagems,
With loss of life and ever-during shame.
Where are thy horses trapp'd with burnish'd gold?
Thy trampling coursers rul'd with foaming bits?
Where are thy soldiers, strong and numberless?
Thy valiant captains, and thy noble peers?
Even as the country clowns with sharpest scythes
Do mow the wither'd grass from off the earth,
Or as the ploughman with his piercing share
Renteth the bowels of the fertile fields,
And rippeth up the roots with razors keen,
So Locrine, with his mighty curtle-axe,
Hath cropped off the heads of all thy Huns:
So Locrine's peers have daunted all thy peers,
And drove thine host unto confusion,
That thou mayst suffer penance for thy fault,
And die for murdering valiant Albanact.

Cor. And thus, yea thus, shall all the rest be serv'd
That seek to enter Albion, 'gainst our wills.
If the brave nation of the Troglodytes,
If all the coal-black Æthiopians,
If all the forces of the Amazons,
If all the hosts of the barbarian lands,
Should dare to enter this our little world,
Soon should they rue their overbold attempts;
That after us our progeny may say,
There lie the beasts that sought to usurp our land.

Loc. Ay, they are beasts that seek to usurp our land,
And like to brutish beasts they shall be serv'd.
For, mighty Jove, the supreme king of heaven,
That guides the concourse of the meteors,
And rules the motion of the azure sky,
Fights always for the Britons' safety.

But stay; methinks I hear some shrieking noise,
That draweth near to our pavilion.

Enter Soldiers, *leading in* ESTRILD.

Est. What prince soe'er, adorn'd with golden crown,
Doth sway the regal sceptre in his hand,
And thinks no chance can ever throw him down,
Or that his state shall everlasting stand,
Let him behold poor Estrild in this plight,
The perfect platform of a troubled wight.
Once was I guarded with Mavortial bands,
Compass'd with princes of the noblest blood;
Now am I fallen into my foemen's hands,
And with my death must pacify their mood.
O life, the harbour of calamities!
O death, the haven of all miseries!
I could compare my sorrows to thy woe,
Thou wretched queen of wretched Pergamus,
But that thou view'dst thy enemy's overthrow.
Nigh to the rock of high Caphareus,
Thou saw'st their death and then departedst thence:
I must abide the victors' insolence.
The gods that pitied thy continual grief,
Transform'd thy corps, and with thy corps thy care:
Poor Estrild lives, despairing of relief,
For friends in trouble are but few and rare.
What, said I, few? ay, few or none at all,
For cruel Death made havoc of them all.
Thrice happy they, whose fortune was so good
To end their lives, and with their lives their woes!
Thrice hapless I, whom Fortune so withstood,
That cruelly she gave me to my foes!
O soldiers, is there any misery
To be compar'd to Fortune's treachery?

Loc. Camber, this same should be the Scythian queen.

Cam. So may we judge by her lamenting words.

Loc. So fair a dame mine eyes did never see;
With floods of woes o'erwhelm'd she seems to be.
　　Cam. O, hath she not a cause for to be sad?
　　Loc. [*aside*]. If she have cause to weep for Humber's death,
And shed salt tears for her own overthrow,
Locrine may well bewail his proper grief,
Locrine may move his own peculiar woe.—
Humber, being conquer'd, died a speedy death,
And felt not long his lamentable smart:
I, being the conqueror, live a lingering life,
And feel the force of Cupid's sudden dart.
I gave him cause to die a speedy death;
He left me cause to wish a speedy death.
O, that sweet face, painted with nature's dye,
Those roseal cheeks mix'd with a snowy white,
That decent neck surpassing ivory,
Those comely breasts which Venus well might spite,
Are like to snares, which wily fowlers wrought,
Wherein my yielding heart is prisoner caught!
The golden tresses of her dainty hair,
Which shine like rubies glittering with the sun,
Have so entrapp'd poor Locrine's love-sick heart,
That from the same no way it can be won.
How true is that which oft I heard declare,
One dram of joy must have a pound of care.
　　Est. Hard is their fall, who from a golden crown
Are cast into a sea of wretchedness.
　　Loc. Hard is their thrall, who still by Cupid's frown
Are wrapp'd in waves of endless carefulness. [*Aside.*
　　Est. O kingdom, subject to all miseries!
　　Loc. O love, the extrem'st of all extremities! [*Aside.*
　　　　　　　　　　　　　　　　　　　　[*Goes into his chair.*
　　First Sold. My lord, in ransacking the Scythian tents,
I found this lady, and to manifest
That earnest zeal I bear unto your grace,
I here present her to your majesty.

SCENE I.] LOCRINE. 173

Second Sold. He lies, my lord; I found the lady first,
And here present her to your majesty.
 First Sold. Presumptuous villain, wilt thou take my prize?
 Second Sold. Nay, rather thou depriv'st me of my right.
 First Sold. Resign thy title, caitiff, unto me,
Or with my sword I'll pierce thy coward's loins.
 Second Sold. Soft words, good sir; 'tis not enough to
   speak:
A barking dog doth seldom strangers bite.
 Loc. Unreverent villains, strive you in our sight?
Take them hence, jailer, to the dungeon;
There let them lie, and try their quarrel out.
But thou, fair princess, be no whit dismay'd,
But rather joy that Locrine favours thee.
 Est. How can he favour me that slew my spouse?
 Loc. The chance of war, my love, took him from thee.
 Est. But Locrine was the causer of his death.
 Loc. He was an enemy to Locrine's state,
And slew my noble brother Albanact.
 Est. But he was link'd to me in marriage-bond,
And would you have me love his slaughterer?
 Loc. Better to love, than not to live at all.
 Est. Better to die renown'd for chastity,
Than live with shame and endless infamy.
What would the common sort report of me,
If I forget my love, and cleave to thee?
 Loc. Kings need not fear the vulgar sentences.
 Est. But ladies must regard their honest name.
 Loc. Is it a shame to live in marriage-bonds?
 Est. No, but to be a strumpet to a king.
 Loc. If thou wilt yield to Locrine's burning love,
Thou shalt be queen of fair Albania.
 Est. But Guendolen will undermine my state.
 Loc. Upon mine honour, thou shalt have no harm.
 Est. Then lo! brave Locrine, Estrild yields to thee;
And, by the gods, whom thou dost invocate,
By the dread ghost of thy deceased sire,

By thy right hand, and by thy burning love,
Take pity on poor Estrild's wretched thrall.

    Cori. Hath Locrine then forgot his Guendolen,
That thus he courts the Scythian's paramour?
What, are the words of Brute so soon forgot?
Are my deserts so quickly out of mind?
Have I been faithful to thy sire, now dead?
Have I protected thee from Humber's hand,
And dost thou quit me with ingratitude?
Is this the guerdon for my grievous wounds?
Is this the honour for my labours past?
Now, by my sword, Locrine, I swear to thee,
This injury of thine shall be repaid.

    Loc. Uncle, scorn you your royal sovereign,
As if we stood for ciphers in the court?
Upbraid you me with those your benefits?
Why, 'twas a subject's duty so to do.
What you have done for our deceasèd sire,
We know; and all know, you have your reward.

    Cori. Avaunt, proud princox! brav'st thou me withal?
Assure thyself, though thou be emperor,
Thou ne'er shalt carry this unpunishèd.

    Camb. Pardon, my brother, noble Corineus,
Pardon this once, and it shall be amended.

    Assa. Cousin, remember Brutus' latest words,
How he desirèd you to cherish them:
Let not this fault so much incense your mind,
Which is not yet passèd all remedy.

    Cori. Then, Locrine, lo! I reconcile myself;
But as thou lov'st thy life, so love thy wife.
But if thou violate those promises,
Blood and revenge shall light upon thy head.
Come, let us back to stately Troynovant,
Where all these matters shall be settled.

    Loc. [*aside*]. Millions of devils wait upon thy soul!
Legions of spirits vex thy impious ghost!
Ten thousand torments rack thy cursèd bones!

Let everything that hath the use of breath,
Be instruments and workers of thy death! [*Exeunt.*

Scene II. *A forest.*

Enter Humber, *his hair hanging over his shoulders, his arms all
bloody, and a dart in his hand.*

Hum. What basilisk was hatch'd in this place,
Where everything consumed is to naught?
What fearful fury haunts these cursèd groves,
Where not a root is left for Humber's meat?
Hath fell Alecto, with envenom'd blasts,
Breathed forth poison on these tender plains?
Hath triple Cerberus, with contagious foam,
Sow'd aconit among these wither'd herbs?
Hath dreadful Fames, with her charming rods,
Brought barrenness on every fruitful tree?
What, not a root, nor fruit, nor beast, nor bird,
To nourish Humber in this wilderness!
What would you more, you fiends of Erebus?
My very entrails burn for want of drink;
My bowels cry, Humber, give us some meat;
But wretched Humber can give you no meat,
These foul accursèd groves afford no meat,
This fruitless soil, this ground, brings forth no meat,
The gods, hard-hearted gods, yield me no meat:
Then how can Humber give you any meat? [*Retires back.*

Enter Strumbo, *wearing a Scotch cap, with a pitchfork in his
hand.*

Strum. How do you, masters, how do you? how have you
'scaped hanging this long time? I' faith I have 'scaped many
a scouring this year; but I thank God I have pass'd them all
with a good coraggio, and my wife and I are in great love
and charity now, I thank my manhood and my strength. For
I will tell you, masters: Upon a certain day at night I came
home, to say the very truth, with my stomach full of wine,
and ran up into the chamber, where my wife soberly sat

rocking my little baby, leaning her back against the bed, singing lullaby. Now when she saw me come with my nose foremost, thinking that I had been drunk (as I was indeed), she snatched up a fagot-stick in her hand, and came furiously marching towards me, with a big face, as though she would have eaten me at a bit; thundering out these words unto me: *Thou drunken knave, where hast thou been so long? I shall teach thee how to benight me another time:* and so she began to play knaves trumps. Now, although I trembled, fearing she would set her ten commandments in my face, I ran within her, and delighted her so with the sport I made, that ever after she would call me *sweet husband;* and so banished brawling for ever. And to see the good-will of the wench!—She bought with her portion a yard of land, and by that I am now become one of the richest men in our parish. Well, masters, what's o'clock? It is now breakfast time; you shall see what meat I have here for my breakfast.

[*Sits down, and takes out his victuals.*

Hum. Was ever land so fruitless as this land?
Was ever grove so graceless as this grove?
Was ever soil so barren as this soil?
Oh no: the land where hungry Fames dwelt,
May no ways equalize this cursèd land;
No, even the climate of the torrid zone
Brings forth more fruit than this accursèd grove.
Ne'er came sweet Ceres, ne'er came Venus here;
Triptolemus, the god of husbandmen,
Ne'er sow'd his seed in this foul wilderness.
The hunger-bitten dogs of Acheron,
Chas'd from the nine-fold Pyriphlegethon,
Have set their footsteps in this damnèd ground.
The iron-hearted Furies, arm'd with snakes,
Scatter'd huge Hydras over all the plains;
Which have consum'd the grass, the herbs, the trees,
Which have drunk up the flowing water-springs.

[*Strumbo, hearing his voice, starts up, and puts his meat in his pocket, endeavouring to hide himself.*

Thou great commander of the starry sky,
That guid'st the life of every mortal wight,
From the inclosures of the fleeting clouds
Rain down some food, or else I faint and die:
Pour down some drink, or else I faint and die.
O Jupiter, hast thou sent Mercury [*Seeing Strumbo.*
In clownish shape to minister some food?
Some meat, some meat, some meat!
    Strum. O alas, Sir, you are deceived. I am not Mercury;
I am Strumbo.
    Hum. Give me some meat, villain, give me some meat,
Or 'gainst this rock I'll dash thy cursèd brains,
And rent thy bowels with my bloody hands.
Give me some meat, villain; give me some meat!
    Strum. By the faith of my body, good fellow, I had rather
give a whole ox, than that thou shouldst serve me in that
sort. Dash out my brains! O horrible! terrible! I think I
have a quarry of stones in my pocket. [*Aside.*
    [*He makes as though he would give him some, and as he
    puts out his hand, the Ghost of Albanact enters, and
    strikes him on the hand. Strumbo runs out, Humber
    following him.*
    Ghost. Lo, here the gift of fell ambition,
Of usurpation and of treachery!
Lo, here the harms that wait upon all those
That do intrude themselves in others' lands,
Which are not under their dominion. [*Exit.*

    SCENE III. *A chamber in the Royal Palace.*

    Enter LOCRINE.

    Loc. Seven years hath agèd Corineus liv'd
To Locrine's grief, and fair Estrilda's woe,
And seven years more he hopeth yet to live.
O supreme Jove, annihilate this thought!
Should he enjoy the air's fruition,
Should he enjoy the benefit of life,
Should he contemplate the radiant sun,

That makes my life equal to dreadful death?
Venus, convey this monster from the earth,
That disobeyeth thus thy sacred 'hests!
Cupid, convey this monster to dark hell,
That disannuls thy mother's sugar'd laws!
Mars, with thy target all beset with flames,
With murdering blade bereave him of his life,
That hind'reth Locrine in his sweetest joys!
And yet, for all his diligent aspéct,
His wrathful eyes, piercing like lynxes' eyes,
Well have I overmatch'd his subtilty.
Nigh Durolitum, by the pleasant Ley,
Where brackish Thamis slides with silver streams,
Making a breach into the grassy downs,
A curious arch, of costly marble wrought,
Hath Locrine framèd underneath the ground;
The walls whereof, garnish'd with diamonds,
With opals, rubies, glistering emeralds,
And interlacèd with sun-bright carbuncles,
Lighten the room with artificial day:
And from the Ley with water-flowing pipes
The moisture is deriv'd into this arch,
Where I have plac'd fair Estrild secretly.
Thither eftsoons, accompanied with my page,
I visit covertly my heart's desire,
Without suspicion of the meanest eye,
For love aboundeth still with policy.
And thither still means Locrine to repair,
Till Atropos cut off mine uncle's life. [*Exit.*

Scene IV. *The entrance of a cave, near which runs the river, afterward the Humber.*

Enter Humber.

Hum. *O vita, misero longa, felici brevis!
Eheu malorum fames extremum malum!**

* *I. e.* O life, long to the wretched—to the happy, short!
Alas! of all evils, hunger is the worst.

Long have I livèd in this desert cave,
With eating haws and miserable roots,
Devouring leaves and beastly excrements.
Caves were my beds, and stones my pillow-biers,
Fear was my sleep, and horror was my dream;
For still, methought, at every boisterous blast,
Now Locrine comes, now, Humber, thou must die;
So that for fear and hunger Humber's mind
Can never rest, but always trembling stands.
O, what Danubius now may quench my thirst?
What Euphrates, what light-foot Euripus
May now allay the fury of that heat,
Which raging in my entrails eats me up?
You ghastly devils of the nine-fold Styx,
You damnèd ghosts of joyless Acheron,
You mournful souls, vex'd in Abyssus' vaults,
You coal-black devils of Avernus' pond,
Come, with your flesh-hooks rent my famish'd arms,
These arms that have sustain'd their master's life.
Come, with your razors rip my bowels up,
With your sharp fire-forks crack my starvèd bones:
Use me as you will, so Humber may not live.
Accursèd gods, that rule the starry poles,
Accursèd Jove, king of the cursèd gods,
Cast down your lightning on poor Humber's head,
That I may leave this death-like life of mine!
What! hear you not? and shall not Humber die?
Nay, I will die, though all the gods say nay.
And, gentle Abus, take my troubled corse,
Take it, and keep it from all mortal eyes,
That none may say, when I have lost my breath,
The very floods conspirèd Humber's death.
[*Flings himself into the river.*

Enter the Ghost *of* ALBANACT.

Ghost. En cædem sequitur cædes, in cæde quiesco.*

* *I. e.* Lo! death to death succeeds—In death I rest.

Humber is dead. Joy heavens, leap earth, dance trees—
Now mayst thou reach thy apples, Tantalus,
And with them feed thy hunger-bitten limbs.
Now Sisyphus, leave the tumbling of thy rock,
And rest thy restless bones upon the same.
Unbind Ixion, cruel Rhadamanth,
And lay proud Humber on the whirling wheel.
Back will I post to hell-mouth Tænarus,
And pass Cocytus, to the Elysian fields,
And tell my father Brutus of these news. [Exit.

ACT V.

Enter ATE, *as before. Then enter* JASON, *leading* CREON'S *daughter;* MEDEA *following, with a garland in her hand. She puts the garland on the head of* CREON'S *daughter; sets it on fire; and then, killing her and* JASON, *departs.*

  Até. *Non tam Trinacriis exæstuat Ætna cavernis,*
  Lœsæ furtivo quam cor mulieris amore.*
Medea seeing Jason leave her love,
And choose the daughter of the Theban king,
Went to her devilish charms to work revenge;—
And raising up the triple Hecaté,
With all the rout of the condemnèd fiends,
Framèd a garland by her magic skill,
With which she wrought Jason and Creon's ill.
So Guendolen, seeing herself misused,
And Humber's paramour possess her place,
Flies to the dukedom of Cornubia,
And with her brother, stout Thrasimachus,
Gathering a power of Cornish soldiers,
Gives battle to her husband and his host,
Nigh to the river of great Mercia.

 * *I. e.* Not with such tumult, in Sicilia's caves,
  Does Ætna rage, as doth the woman's heart,
  When rous'd to madness by clandestine fires!

The chances of this dismal massacre
That which ensueth shortly will unfold. [*Exit.*

Scene I. *A chamber in the Royal Palace.*

Enter Locrine, Camber, Assabacus, *and* Thrasimachus.

Assa. But tell me, cousin, died my brother so?
Now who is left to helpless Albion,
That as a pillar might uphold our state,
That might strike terror to our daring foes?
Now who is left to hapless Brittany,
That might defend her from the barbarous hands
Of those that still desire her ruinous fall,
And seek to work her downfall and decay?
  Cam. Ay, uncle, death's our common enemy,
And none but death can match our matchless power.
Witness the fall of Albioneus' crew,
Witness the fall of Humber and his Huns;
And this foul death hath now increas'd our woe,
By taking Corineus from this life,
And in his room leaving us worlds of care.
  Thra. But none may more bewail his mournful hearse,
Than I that am the issue of his loins.
Now foul befall that cursèd Humber's throat,
That was the causer of his ling'ring wound!
  Loc. Tears cannot raise him from the dead again.—
But where's my lady mistress, Guendolen?
  Thra. In Cornwall, Locrine, is my sister now,
Providing for my father's funeral.
  Loc. And let her there provide her mourning weeds,
And mourn for ever her own widowhood.
Ne'er shall she come within our palace gate,
To countercheck brave Locrine in his love.
Go, boy, to Durolitum, down the Ley,
Unto the arch where lovely Estrild lies;
Bring her and Sabren straight unto the court:
She shall be queen in Guendolena's room.

Let others wail for Corineus' death;
I mean not so to macerate my mind,
For him that barr'd me from my heart's desire.
    Thra. Hath Locrine then forsook his Guendolen?
Is Corineus' death so soon forgot?
If there be gods in heaven, as sure there be,
If there be fiends in hell, as needs there must,
They will revenge this thy notorious wrong,
And pour their plagues upon thy cursèd head.
    Loc. What, prat'st thou, peasant, to thy sovereign?
Or art thou strucken in some ecstasy?
Dost thou not tremble at our royal looks?
Dost thou not quake, when mighty Locrine frowns?
Thou beardless boy, were't not that Locrine scorns
To vex his mind with such a heartless child,
With the sharp point of this my battle-axe
I'd send thy soul to Pyriphlegethon.
    Thra. Though I be young and of a tender age,
Yet will I cope with Locrine when he dares.
My noble father with his conquering sword
Slew the two giant kings of Aquitain.
Thrasimachus is not so degenerate,
That he should fear and tremble at the looks
Or taunting words of a Venerean squire.
    Loc. Menacest thou thy royal sovereign?
Uncivil, not beseeming such as thou.
Injurious traitor (for he is no less
That at defiance standeth with his king),
Leave these thy taunts, leave these thy bragging words,
Unless thou mean'st to leave thy wretched life.
    Thra. If princes stain their glorious dignity
With ugly spots of monstrous infamy,
They lose their former estimation,
And throw themselves into a hell of hate.
    Loc. Wilt thou abuse my gentle patience,
As though thou didst our high displeasure scorn?
Proud boy, that thou mayst know thy prince is mov'd,

Yea, greatly mov'd at this thy swelling pride:
We banish thee for ever from our court.
  Thra. Then, losel Locrine, look unto thyself;
Thrasimachus will 'venge this injury.   [*Exit.*
  Loc. Farewell, proud boy, and learn to use thy tongue.
  Assa. Alas, my lord, you should have call'd to mind
The latest words that Brutus spake to you;
How he desirèd you, by the obedience
That children ought to bear unto their sire,
To love and favour Lady Guendolen.
Consider this, that if the injury
Do move her mind, as certainly it will,
War and dissension follows speedily.
What though her power be not so great as yours?
Have you not seen a mighty elephant
Slain by the biting of a silly mouse?
Even so the chance of war inconstant is.
  Loc. Peace, uncle, peace, and cease to talk hereof;
For he that seeks, by whispering this or that,
To trouble Locrine in his sweetest life,
Let him persuade himself to die the death.
    Enter ESTRILD, SABREN, *and a Page.*
  Est. O say me, page, tell me, where is the king.
Wherefore doth he send for me to the court?
Is it to die? is it to end my life?
Say me, sweet boy; tell me and do not feign.
  Page. No, trust me, madam: if you will credit the little
honesty that is yet left me, there is no such danger as you
fear. But prepare yourself; yonder's the king.
  Est. Then, Estrild, lift thy dazzled spirits up,
And bless that blessèd time, that day, that hour,
That warlike Locrine first did favour thee.
Peace to the king of Brittany, my love!   [*Kneeling.*
Peace to all those that love and favour him!
  Loc. Doth Estrild fall with such submission   [*Raising her.*
Before her servant, king of Albion?

184 THE TRAGEDY OF [ACT V.

Arise, fair lady, leave this lowly cheer;   [*Taking her up.*
Lift up those looks that cherish Locrine's heart,
That I may freely view that roseal face,
Which so entangled hath my love-sick breast.
Now to the court, where we will court it out,
And pass the night and day in Venus' sports.
Frolic, brave peers; be joyful with your king.   [*Exeunt.*

SCENE II. *The camp of Guendolen.*

Enter GUENDOLEN, THRASIMACHUS, MADAN, *and* Soldiers.

Guen. You gentle winds, that with your modest blasts
Pass through the circuit of the heavenly vault,
Enter the clouds, unto the throne of Jove,
And bear my prayers to his all-hearing ears,
For Locrine hath forsaken Guendolen,
And learn'd to love proud Humber's concubine.
You happy sprites, that in the concave sky
With pleasant joy enjoy your sweetest love,
Shed forth those tears with me, which then you shed
When first you woo'd your ladies to your wills:
Those tears are fittest for my woful case,
Since Locrine shuns my nothing-pleasant face.
Blush heavens, blush sun, and hide thy shining beams;
Shadow thy radiant locks in gloomy clouds;
Deny thy cheerful light unto the world,
Where nothing reigns but falsehood and deceit.
What said I? falsehood? ay, that filthy crime,
For Locrine hath forsaken Guendolen.
Behold the heavens do wail for Guendolen;
The shining sun doth blush for Guendolen;
The liquid air doth weep for Guendolen;
The very ground doth groan for Guendolen!
Ay, they are milder than the Britain king,
For he rejecteth luckless Guendolen.

Thra. Sister, complaints are bootless in this cause;
This open wrong must have an open plague,

This plague must be repaid with grievous war;
This war must finish soon with Locrine's death:
His death must soon extinguish our complaints.
　Guen. O no; his death will more augment my woes:
He was my husband, brave Thrasimachus,
More dear to me than th' apple of mine eye;
Nor can I find in heart to work his scathe.
　Thra. Madam, if not your proper injuries,
Nor my exile, can move you to revenge,
Think on our father Corineus' words;
His words to us stand always for a law.
Should Locrine live, that caus'd my father's death?
Should Locrine live, that now divorceth you?
The heavens, the earth, the air, the fire reclaim;
And then why should all we deny the same?
　Guen. Then henceforth farewell womanish complaints!
All childish pity henceforth then farewell!
But cursèd Locrine, look unto thyself;
For Nemesis, the mistress of revenge,
Sits arm'd at all points on our dismal blades:
And cursèd Estrild, that inflam'd his heart,
Shall, if I live, die a reproachful death.
　Mad. Mother, though nature makes me to lament
My luckless father's froward lechery,
Yet, for he wrongs my lady mother thus,
I, if I could, myself would work his death.
　Thra. See, madam, see! the desire of revenge
Is in the children of a tender age.—
Forward, brave soldiers, into Mercia,
Where we shall brave the coward to his face. 　　[*Exeunt.*

Scene III. *The camp of Locrine.*

Enter Locrine, Estrild, Sabren, Assaracus, *and* Soldiers.

　Loc. Tell me, Assaracus, are the Cornish choughs
In such great number come to Mercia?
And have they pitchèd there their petty host,
So close unto our royal mansion?

Assa. They are, my lord, and mean incontinent
To bid defiance to your majesty.
   Loc. It makes me laugh, to think that Guendolen
Should have the heart to come in arms against me.
   Est. Alas, my lord, the horse will run amain,
When as the spur doth gall him to the bone:
Jealousy, Locrine, hath a wicked sting.
   Loc. Say'st thou so, Estrild, beauty's paragon?
Well, we will try her choler to the proof,
And make her know, Locrine can brook no braves.
March on, Assaracus; thou must lead the way,
And bring us to their proud pavilion. [*Exeunt.*

SCENE IV. *The field of battle.*

Thunder and lightning.   Enter the Ghost *of* CORINEUS.

   Ghost. Behold, the circuit of the azure sky
Throws forth sad throbs, and grievously suspires,
Prejudicating Locrine's overthrow.
The fire casteth forth sharp darts of flames;
The great foundation of the triple world
Trembleth and quaketh with a mighty noise,
Presaging bloody massacres at hand.
The wandering birds that flutter in the dark
(When hellish Night in cloudy chariot seated,
Casteth her mists on shady Tellus' face,
With sable mantles covering all the earth),
Now fly abroad amid the cheerful day,
Foretelling some unwonted misery.
The snarling curs of darken'd Tartarus,
Sent from Avernus' ponds by Rhadamanth,
With howling ditties pester every wood.
The wat'ry Naiads, and the light-foot Fauns,
And all the rabble of the woody nymphs,
All trembling hide themselves in shady groves,
And shroud themselves in hideous hollow pits.
The boisterous Boreas thund'reth forth revenge;

The stony rocks cry out on sharp revenge:
The thorny bush pronounceth dire revenge.   [*Alarum.*
Now, Corineus, stay and see revenge,
And feed thy soul with Locrine's overthrow.
Behold they come; the trumpets call them forth:
The roaring drums summon the soldiers.
Lo where their army glistereth on the plains.
Throw forth thy lightning, mighty Jupiter,
And pour thy plagues on cursèd Locrine's head!

Enter LOCRINE, ESTRILD, ASSARACUS, SABREN *and their* Soldiers *at one side;* THRASIMACHUS, GUENDOLEN, MADAN, *and their* Followers *at another.*

Loc. What, is the tiger started from his cave?
Is Guendolen come from Cornubia,
That thus she braveth Locrine to the teeth?
And hast thou found thine armour, pretty boy,
Accompanied with these thy straggling mates?
Believe me, but this enterprise was bold,
And well deserveth commendation.

Guen. Ay, Locrine, traitorous Locrine, we are come,
With full pretence to seek thine overthrow.
What have I done, that thou shouldst scorn me thus?
What have I said, that thou shouldst me reject?
Have I been disobedient to thy words?
Have I bewray'd thy arcane secrecy?
Have I dishonourèd thy marriage bed
With filthy crimes, or with lascivious lusts?
Nay, it is thou that hast dishonour'd it;
Thy filthy mind, o'ercome with filthy lusts,
Yieldeth unto affection's filthy darts.
Unkind, thou wrong'st thy first and truest feere;
Unkind, thou wrong'st thy best and dearest friend;
Unkind, thou scorn'st all skilful Brutus' laws;
Forgetting father, uncle, and thyself.

Est. Believe me, Locrine, but the girl is wise,

And well would seem to make a vestal nun:
How finely frames she her oration!
 Thra. Locrine, we came not here to fight with words,
Words that can never win the victory;
But, for you are so merry in your frumps,
Unsheathe your swords, and try it out by force,
That we may see who hath the better hand.
 Loc. Think'st thou to dare me, bold Thrasimachus?
Think'st thou to fear me with thy taunting braves?
Or do we seem too weak to cope with thee?
Soon shall I show thee my fine cutting blade,
And with my sword, the messenger of death,
Seal thee a quittance for thy bold attempts. [*Exeunt.*

  Scene V. *The entrance of a cave.*

  Enter Locrine *and* Estrild, *in flight.*

 Loc. O fair Estrilda, we have lost the field;
Thrasimachus hath won the victory,
And we are left to be a laughing-stock,
Scoff'd at by those that are our enemies.
Ten thousand soldiers, arm'd with sword and shield,
Prevail against an hundred thousand men.
Thrasimachus, incens'd with fuming ire,
Rageth amongst the faint-heart soldiers,
Like to grim Mars, when, cover'd with his targe,
He fought with Diomedes in the field,
Close by the banks of silver Simois. [*Alarum.*
O lovely Estrild, now the chase begins:
Ne'er shall we see the stately Troynovant,
Mounted on coursers garnish'd all with pearls;
Ne'er shall we view the fair Concordia,
Unless as captives we be thither brought.
Shall Locrine then be taken prisoner
By such a youngling as Thrasimachus?
Shall Guendolena captivate my love?
Ne'er shall mine eyes behold that dismal hour,

Ne'er will I view that ruthful spectacle;
For with my sword, this my sharp curtle-axe,
I'll cut in-sunder my accursèd heart.
But, O you judges of the nine-fold Styx,
Which with incessant torments rack the ghosts
Within the bottomless Abyssus' pits;
You gods, commanders of the heavenly spheres,
Whose will and laws irrevocable stand,
Forgive, forgive, this foul accursèd sin!
Forget, O gods, this foul condemnèd fault!
And now, my sword, that in so many fights [*Kisses his sword.*
Hast sav'd the life of Brutus and his son,
End now his life that wisheth still for death,
Work now his death that wisheth still for death,
Work now his death that hateth still his life!
Farewell, fair Estrild, beauty's paragon,
Fram'd in the front of forlorn miseries!
Ne'er shall mine eyes behold thy sunshine eyes,
But when we meet in the Elysian fields:
Thither I go before with hasten'd pace.
Farewell, vain world, and thy enticing snares!
Farewell, foul sin, and thy enticing pleasures;
And welcome, death, the end of mortal smart,
Welcome to Locrine's over-burden'd heart!
                                         [*Stabs himself, and dies.*

    Est. Break heart, with sobs and grievous suspires!
Stream forth, you tears, from out my wat'ry eyes;
Help me to mourn for warlike Locrine's death!
Pour down your tears, you wat'ry regions,
For mighty Locrine is bereft of life!
O fickle Fortune! O unstable world!
What else are all things that this globe contains,
But a confusèd chaos of mishaps?
Wherein, as in a glass, we plainly see
That all our life is but a tragedy;
Since mighty kings are subject to mishap,
Since martial Locrine is bereft of life.

Shall Estrild live then after Locrine's death?
Shall love of life bar her from Locrine's sword?
O no; this sword that hath bereft his life,
Shall now deprive me of my fleeting soul.
Strengthen these hands, O mighty Jupiter,
That I may end my woful misery!
Locrine, I come; Locrine, I follow thee! [*Kills herself.*

Alarum. Enter SABREN.

Sab. What doleful sight, what ruthful spectacle
Hath Fortune offer'd to my hapless heart?
My father slain with such a fatal sword,
My mother murder'd by a mortal wound!
What Thracian dog, what barbarous Myrmidon,
Would not relent at such a ruthful case?
What fierce Achilles, what hard stony Hint,
Would not bemoan this mournful tragedy?
Locrine, the map of magnanimity,
Lies slaughter'd in this foul accursed cave.
Estrild, the perfect pattern of renown,
Nature's sole wonder, in whose beauteous breasts
All heavenly grace and virtue was enshrin'd,
Both massacred, are dead within this cave;
And with them dies fair Pallas and sweet Love.
Here lies a sword, and Sabren hath a heart;
This blessed sword shall cut my cursed heart,
And bring my soul unto my parents' ghosts,
That they that live and view our tragedy,
May mourn our case with mournful plaudite.
[*Attempts to kill herself.*
Ah me, my virgin hands are too, too weak!
To penetrate the bulwark of my breast.
My fingers, us'd to tune the amorous lute,
Are not of force to hold this steely glaive:
So I am left to wail my parents' death,
Not able for to work my proper death.
Ah, Locrine, honour'd for thy nobleness,

SCENE V.] LOCRINE. 191

Ah, Estrild, famous for thy constancy,
Ill may they fare that wrought your mortal ends!
                                    [*Retires back.*

Enter GUENDOLEN, THRASIMACHUS, MADAN, *and* Soldiers.

Guen. Search, soldiers, search; find Locrine and his love,
Find the proud strumpet, Humber's concubine,
That I may change those her so pleasing looks
To pale and ignominious aspéct.
Find me the issue of their cursèd love,
Find me young Sabren, Locrine's only joy,
That I may glut my mind with lukewarm blood,
Swiftly distilling from the bastard's breast.
My father's ghost still haunts me for revenge,
Crying, *Revenge my over-hasten'd death.*
My brother's exile and mine own divorce
Banish remorse clean from my brazen heart,
All mercy from mine adamantine breasts.

Thra. Nor doth thy husband, lovely Guendolen,
That wonted was to guide our stayless steps,
Enjoy this light: see where he murder'd lies
By luckless lot and froward frowning fate;
And by him lies his lovely paramour,
Fair Estrild, gorèd with a dismal sword,
And, as it seems, both murder'd by themselves;
Clasping each other in their feebled arms,
With loving zeal, as if for company
Their uncontented corse were yet content
To pass foul Styx in Charon's ferry-boat.

Guen. And hath proud Estrild then prevented me?
Hath she escapèd Guendolena's wrath,
By violently cutting off her life?
Would God she had the monstrous Hydra's lives,
That every hour she might have died a death
Worse than the swing of old Ixion's wheel,
And every hour revive to die again!
As Tityus, bound to houseless Caucasus,

Doth feed the substance of his own mishap,
And every day for want of food doth die,
And every night doth live, again to die.
But stay; methinks I hear some fainting voice,
Mournfully weeping for their luckless death.

[Sabren comes forward.

   Sab. You mountain nymphs which in these deserts reign,
Cease off your hasty chase of savage beasts!
Prepare to see a heart oppress'd with care;
Address your ears to hear a mournful style!
No human strength, no words can work my weal,
Care in my heart so tyrant-like doth deal.
You Dryades, and light-foot Satyri,
You gracious fairies, which at even-tide
Your closets leave, with heavenly beauty stor'd,
And on your shoulders spread your golden locks;
You savage bears, in caves and darken'd dens,
Come wail with me the martial Locrine's death;
Come mourn with me for beauteous Estrild's death!
Ah! loving parents, little do you know
What sorrow Sabren suffers for your thrall.

   Guen. But may this be, and is it possible?
Lives Sabren yet to expiate my wrath?
Fortune, I thank thee for this courtesy;
And let me never see one prosperous hour,
If Sabren die not a reproachful death.

   Sab. Hard-hearted Death, that, when the wretched call,
Art farthest off, and seldom hear'st at all;
But in the midst of fortune's good success
Uncallèd com'st, and sheer'st our life in twain;
When will that hour, that blessèd hour draw nigh,
When poor distressèd Sabren may be gone?
Sweet Atropos, cut off my fatal thread!
Where art thou, Death? shall not poor Sabren die?

   Guen. Yes, damsel, yes, Sabren shall surely die,
Though all the world should seek to save her life,
And not a common death shall Sabren die,

SCENE V.]   LOCRINE.   193

But, after strange and grievous punishments,
Shortly inflicted on thy bastard's head,
Thou shalt be cast into the cursèd streams,
And feed the fishes with thy tender flesh.
  Sab. And think'st thou then, thou cruel homicide,
That these thy deeds shall be unpunished?
No, traitor, no; the gods will 'venge these wrongs,
The fiends of hell will mark these injuries.
Never shall these blood-sucking mastiff curs
Bring wretched Sabren to her latest home.
For I myself, in spite of thee and thine,
Mean to abridge my former destinies;
And that which Locrine's sword could not perform,
This present stream shall present bring to pass.
                                    [*She drowns herself.*
  Guen. One mischief follows on another's neck.
Who would have thought so young a maid as she
With such a courage would have sought her death?
And, for because this river was the place
Where little Sabren resolutely died,
Sabren for ever shall this stream be call'd.
And as for Locrine, our deceasèd spouse,
Because he was the son of mighty Brute,
To whom we owe our country, lives, and goods,
He shall be buried in a stately tomb,
Close by his agèd father Brutus' bones,
With such great pomp and great solemnity,
As well beseems so brave a prince as he.
Let Estrild lie without the shallow vaults,
Without the honour due unto the dead,
Because she was the author of this war.
Retire, brave followers, unto Troynovant,
Where we will celebrate these exequies,
And place king Locrine in his father's tomb.
                                           [*Exeunt.*

                    Enter ATE.

  Ate. Lo! here the end of lawless treachery,

Shakespeare, Doubtful Plays.   13

Of usurpation and ambitious pride.
And they that for their private amours dare
Turmoil our land, and set their broils abroach,
Let them be warnèd by these premises.
And as a woman was the only cause
That civil discord was then stirrèd up,
So let us pray for that renownèd maid
That eight and thirty years the sceptre sway'd
In quiet peace and sweet felicity;
And every wight that seeks her grace's smart,
Would that this sword were piercèd in his heart! [*Exit.*

A YORKSHIRE TRAGEDY.

DRAMATIS PERSONÆ

HUSBAND.
MASTER OF A COLLEGE.
A KNIGHT, a Magistrate.
SEVERAL GENTLEMEN.
OLIVER, }
RALPH, } servants.
SAMUEL, }
Other SERVANTS and OFFICERS.
THREE LITTLE BOYS.

WIFE.
MAID SERVANT.

SCENE.—*Calverly, in Yorkshire.*

ACT I.

SCENE I. *A servant's room in Calverly Hall.*

Enter OLIVER *and* RALPH.

Oliv. Sirrah Ralph, my young mistress is in such a pitiful passionate humour for the long absence of her love—

Ralph. Why, can you blame her? Why, apples hanging longer on the tree than when they are ripe, make so many fallings; so mad wenches, because they are not gathered in time, are fain to drop off themselves, and then 'tis common you know for every man to take them up.

Oliv. Mass, thou say'st true, 'tis common indeed. But sirrah, is neither our young master returned, nor our fellow Sam come from London?

Ralph. Neither of either, as the puritan bawd says. 'Slid

I hear Sam. Sam's come; here he is; tarry;—come i' faith: now my nose itches for news.

Oliv. And so does mine elbow.

Sam. [*within*]. Where are you there? Boy, look you walk my horse with discretion. I have rid him sinfully: I warrant his skin sticks to his back with very heat. If he should catch cold and get the cough of the lungs, I were well served, were I not?

Enter SAMUEL.

What, Ralph and Oliver!

Both. Honest fellow Sam, welcome i' faith. What tricks hast thou brought from London?

Sam. You see I am hanged after the truest fashion; three hats, and two glasses bobbing upon them; two rebato wires upon my breast, a cap-case by my side, a brush at my back, an almanack in my pocket, and three ballads in my codpiece. Now am I the true picture of a common serving-man.

Oliv. I'll swear thou art; thou mayst set up when thou wilt: there's many a one begins with less, I can tell thee, that proves a rich man ere he dies. But what's the news from London, Sam?

Ralph. Ay, that's well said; what's the news from London, sirrah? My young mistress keeps such a puling for her love.

Sam. Why, the more fool she; ay, the more ninnyhammer she.

Oliv. Why, Sam, why?

Sam. Why, he is married to another long ago.

Both. I' faith? You jest.

Sam. Why, did you not know that till now? Why, he's married, beats his wife, and has two or three children by her. For you must note, that any woman bears the more when she is beaten.

Ralph. Ay, that's true, for she bears the blows.

Oliv. Sirrah Sam, I would not for two years' wages my

young mistress knew so much; she'd run upon the left hand of her wit, and ne'er be her own woman again.

Sam. And I think she were blest in her cradle, had he never come in her bed. Why, he has consumed all, pawned his lands, and made his university brother stand in wax for him: there's a fine phrase for a scrivener. Puh! he owes more than his skin is worth.

Oliv. Is't possible?

Sam. Nay, I'll tell you moreover, he calls his wife whore, as familiarly as one would call Moll and Doll; and his children bastards, as naturally as can be.—But what have we here? I thought 'twas something pulled down my breeches; I quite forgot my two poking-sticks: these came from London. Now, anything is good here that comes from London.

Oliv. Ay, far fetched, you know, Sam,—But speak in your conscience i' faith; have not we as good poking-sticks i' the country as need to be put in the fire?

Sam. The mind of a thing is all; the mind of a thing is all; and as thou saidst even now, far-fetched are the best things for ladies.

Oliv. Ay, and for waiting-gentlewomen too.

Sam. But Ralph, what, is our beer sour this thunder?

Ralph. No, no, it holds countenance yet.

Sam. Why, then follow me; I'll teach you the finest humour to be drunk in: I learned it at London last week.

Both. I' faith? Let's hear it, let's hear it.

Sam. The bravest humour! 'twould do a man good to be drunk in it: they call it knighting in London, when they drink upon their knees.

Both. 'Faith, that's excellent.

Sam. Come, follow me; I'll give you all the degrees of it in order. [*Exeunt.*

SCENE II. *Another apartment in Calverly Hall.*

Enter WIFE.

Wife. What will become of us? All will away:
My husband never ceases in expense,
Both to consume his credit and his house;
And 'tis set down by heaven's just decree,
That Riot's child must needs be beggary.
Are these the virtues that his youth did promise?
Dice and voluptuous meetings, midnight revels,
Taking his bed with surfeits; ill beseeming
The ancient honour of his house and name?
His fortunes cannot answer his expense.
And this not all, but that which kills me most,
When he recounts his losses and false fortunes,
The weakness of his state so much dejected,
Not as a man repentant, but half mad,
He sits, and sullenly locks up his arms,
Forgetting heaven, looks downward; which makes him
Appear so dreadful that he frights my heart:
Walks heavily, as if his soul were earth;
Not penitent for those his sins are past,
But vex'd his money cannot make them last:
A fearful melancholy, ungodly sorrow.
O, yonder he comes; now in despite of ills
I'll speak to him, and I will hear him speak,
And do my best to drive it from his heart.

Enter HUSBAND.

Hus. Pox o' the last throw! It made five hundred angels
Vanish from my sight. I'm damn'd, I'm damn'd;
The angels have forsook me. Nay, it is
Certainly true; for he that has no coin
Is damn'd in this world; he is gone, he's gone.
Wife. Dear husband.
Hus. O! most punishment of all, I have a wife.

Wife. I do entreat you, as you love your soul,
Tell me the cause of this your discontent.

Hus. A vengeance strip thee naked! thou art the cause,
The effect, the quality, property; thou, thou, thou. [*Exit.*

Wife. Bad turn'd to worse; both beggary of the soul
And of the body;—and so much unlike
Himself at first, as if some vexèd spirit
Had got his form upon him. He comes again.

Re-enter HUSBAND.

He says I am the cause: I never yet
Spoke less than words of duty and of love.

Hus. If marriage be honourable, then cuckolds are honourable, for they cannot be made without marriage. Fool! what meant I to marry to get beggars? Now must my eldest son be a knave or nothing; he cannot live upon the fool, for he will have no land to maintain him. That mortgage sits like a snaffle upon mine inheritance, and makes me chew upon iron. My second son must be a promoter; and my third a thief, or an under-putter; a slave pander. O beggary, beggary, to what base uses dost thou put a man! I think the devil scorns to be a bawd; he bears himself more proudly, has more care of his credit. Base, slavish, abject, filthy poverty!

Wife. Good Sir, by all our vows I do beseech you,
Show me the true cause of your discontent.

Hus. Money, money, money; and thou must supply me.

Wife. Alas, I am the least cause of your discontent;
Yet what is mine, either in rings or jewels,
Use to your own desire; but I beseech you,
As you are a gentleman by many bloods,'
Though I myself be out of your respect,
Think on the state of the three lovely boys
You have been father to.

Hus. Puh! bastards, bastards, bastards; begot in tricks, begot in tricks.

Wife. Heaven knows how those words wrong me: but I may
Endure these griefs among a thousand more.
O, call to mind your lands already mortgag'd,
Yourself wound into debts, your hopeful brother
At the university in bonds for you,
Like to be seiz'd upon; and——
    Hus.   Have done, thou harlot,
Whom, though for fashion-sake I married,
I never could abide. Think'st thou, thy words
Shall kill my pleasures? Fall off to thy friends;
Thou and thy bastards beg; I will not bate
A whit in humour. Midnight, still I love you,
And revel in your company! Curb'd in!
Shall it be said in all societies,
That I broke custom? that I flagg'd in money?
No, those thy jewels I will play as freely
As when my state was fullest.
    Wife.   Be it so.
    Hus. Nay, I protest (and take that for an earnest)
                                              [*Spurns her.*
I will for ever hold thee in contempt,
And never touch the sheets that cover thee,
But be divorc'd in bed, till thou consent
Thy dowry shall be sold, to give new life
Unto those pleasures which I most affect.
    Wife. Sir, do but turn a gentle eye on me,
And what the law shall give me leave to do,
You shall command.
    Hus. Look it be done. Shall I want dust,
And like a slave wear nothing in my pockets
                                [*Holds his hands in his pockets.*
But my bare hands, to fill them up with nails?
O much against my blood! Let it be done;
I was never made to be a looker-on,
A bawd to dice; I'll shake the drabs myself,
And make them yield: I say, look it be done.

Wife. I take my leave: It shall. [*Exit.*
Hus.   Speedily, speedily
I hate the very hour I chose a wife:
A trouble, trouble! Three children, like three evils,
Hang on me. Fie, fie, fie! Strumpet and bastards!

Enter three GENTLEMEN.

Strumpet and bastards!
  First Gent. Still do these loathsome thoughts jar on your
      tongue?
Yourself to stain the honour of your wife,
Nobly descended? Those whom men call mad,
Endanger others; but he's more than mad
That wounds himself; whose own words do proclaim
Scandals unjust, to soil his better name:
It is not fit; I pray, forsake it.
  Second Gent. Good Sir, let modesty reprove you.
  Third Gent. Let honest kindness sway so much with you.
  Hus. Good den; I thank you, Sir; how do you? Adieu!
I am glad to see you. Farewell instructions, admonitions!
                                                          [*Exeunt Gentlemen.*

Enter a SERVANT.

How now, sirrah? What would you?
  Ser. Only to certify you, Sir, that my mistress was met
by the way, by them who were sent for her up to London by
her honourable uncle, your worship's late guardian.
  Hus. So, Sir, then she is gone; and so may you be;
But let her look the thing be done she wots of,
Or hell will stand more pleasant than her house
At home. [*Exit Servant.*

Enter a GENTLEMAN.

  Gent. Well or ill met, I care not.
  Hus.   No, nor I.
  Gent. I am come with confidence to chide you.
  Hus.   Who? me?

Chide me? Do't finely, then; let it not move me:
For if thou chid'st me angry, I shall strike.
    Gent. Strike thine own follies, for 'tis they deserve
To be well beaten. We are now in private;
There's none but thou and I. Thou art fond and peevish;
An unclean rioter; thy lands and credit
Lie now both sick of a consumption:
I am sorry for thee. That man spends with shame
That with his riches doth consume his name;
And such art thou.
    Hus. Peace!
    Gent. No, thou shalt hear me further.
Thy father's and forefathers' worthy honours,
Which were our county's monuments, our grace,
Follies in thee begin now to deface.
The spring-time of thy youth did fairly promise
Such a most fruitful summer to thy friends,
It scarce can enter into men's beliefs,
Such dearth should hang upon thee. We that see it,
Are sorry to believe it. In thy change,
This voice into all places will be hurl'd—
Thou and the devil have deceiv'd the world.
    Hus. I'll not endure thee.
    Gent.   But of all the worst,
Thy virtuous wife, right honourably allied,
Thou hast proclaim'd a strumpet.
    Hus. Nay, then, I know thee;
Thou art her champion, thou; her private friend;
The party you wot on.
    Gent.   O ignoble thought!
I am past my patient blood. Shall I stand idle,
And see my reputation touch'd to death?
    Hus. It has gall'd you, this; has it?
    Gent. No, monster; I will prove
My thoughts did only tend to virtuous love.
    Hus. Love of her virtues? there it goes.
    Gent.   Base spirit,

To lay thy hate upon the fruitful honour
Of thine own bed!   [*They fight, and the Husband is hurt.*
Hus.   O!
Gent.   Wilt thou yield it yet?
Hus. Sir, Sir, I have not done with you.
Gent. I hope, nor ne'er shall do.   [*They fight again.*
Hus. Have you got tricks? Are you in cunning with me?
Gent. No, plain and right:
He needs no cunning that for truth doth fight.
                              [*Husband falls down.*
Hus. Hard fortune! am I levell'd with the ground?
Gent. Now, Sir, you lie at mercy.
Hus.   Ay, you slave.
Gent. Alas, that hate should bring us to our grave!
You see, my sword's not thirsty for your life:
I am sorrier for your wound than you yourself.
You're of a virtuous house; show virtuous deeds;
'Tis not your honour, 'tis your folly bleeds.
Much good has been expected in your life;
Cancel not all men's hopes: you have a wife,
Kind and obedient; heap not wrongful shame
On her and your posterity; let only sin be sore,
And by this fall, rise never to fall more.
And so I leave you.   [*Exit.*
Hus.   Has the dog left me, then,
After his tooth has left me? O, my heart
Would fain leap after him. Revenge, I say;
I'm mad to be reveng'd. My strumpet wife,
It is thy quarrel that rips thus my flesh,
And makes my breast spit blood;—but thou shalt bleed.
Vanquish'd? got down? unable even to speak?
Surely 'tis want of money makes men weak:
Ay, 'twas that o'erthrew me: I'd ne'er been down else. [*Exit.*

SCENE III. *Another room in the same.*

Enter WIFE, *in a riding-suit, and a* SERVANT.

Ser. 'Faith, mistress, if it might not be presumption
In me to tell you so, for his excuse
You had small reason, knowing his abuse.

Wife. I grant I had; but alas,
Why should our faults at home be spread abroad?
'Tis grief enough within doors. At first sight
Mine uncle could run o'er his prodigal life
As perfectly as if his serious eye
Had number'd all his follies:
Knew of his mortgag'd lands, his friends in bonds,
Himself wither'd with debts; and in that minute
Had I added his usage and unkindness,
'Twould have confounded every thought of good:
Where now, fathering his riots on his youth,
Which time and tame experience will shake off,—
Guessing his kindness to me (as I smooth'd him
With all the skill I had, though his deserts
Are in form uglier than an unshap'd bear),
He's ready to prefer him to some office
And place at court; a good and sure relief
To all his stooping fortunes. 'Twill be a means, I hope,
To make new league between us, and redeem
His virtues with his lands.

Ser. I should think so, mistress. If he should not now
be kind to you, and love you, and cherish you up, I should
think the devil himself kept open house in him.

Wife. I doubt not but he will. Now prithee leave me; I
think I hear him coming.

Ser. I am gone. [*Exit.*

Wife. By this good means I shall preserve my lands,
And free my husband out of usurers' hands.
Now there's no need of sale; my uncle 's kind:

I hope, if aught, this will content his mind.
Here comes my husband.

Enter HUSBAND.

Hus. Now, are you come? Where's the money? Let's see the money. Is the rubbish sold? those wise-acres, your lands? Why when? The money? Where is it? Pour it down; down with it, down with it: I say, pour't on the ground; let's see it, let's see it.

Wife. Good Sir, keep but in patience, and I hope my words shall like you well. I bring you better comfort than the sale of my dowry.

Hus. Ha! What's that?

Wife. Pray, do not fright me, Sir, but vouchsafe me hearing. My uncle, glad of your kindness to me and mild usage (for so I made it to him), hath, in pity of your declining fortunes, provided a place for you at court, of worth and credit; which so much overjoyed me—

Hus. Out on thee, filth! over and overjoyed, when I'm in torment? [*Spurns her.*] Thou politic whore, subtiler than nine devils, was this thy journey to nunck? to set down the history of me, of my state and fortunes? Shall I that dedicated myself to pleasure, be now confined in service? to crouch and stand, like an old man, i' the hams; my hat off? I that could never abide to uncover my head i' the church? Base slut! this fruit bear thy complaints.

Wife. O, heaven knows
That my complaints were praises, and best words,
Of you and your estate. Only, my friends
Knew of your mortgag'd lands, and were possess'd
Of every accident before I came.
If you suspect it but a plot in me,
To keep my dowry, or for mine own good,
Or my poor children's (though it suits a mother
To show a natural care in their reliefs),
Yet I'll forget myself to calm your blood:
Consume it, as your pleasure counsels you.

And all I wish even clemency affords;
Give me but pleasant looks and modest words.
   Hus. Money, whore, money, or I'll—   [*Draws a dagger.*

        Enter a SERVANT, *hastily.*

What the devil! How now! thy hasty news?
   Ser. May it please you, Sir—
   Hus. What! may I not look upon my dagger? Speak, villain, or I will execute the point on thee: Quick, short.
   Ser. Why, Sir, a gentleman from the university stays below to speak with you.   [*Exit.*
   Hus. From the university? so; university:—that long word runs through me.   [*Exit.*
   Wife. Was ever wife so wretchedly besot?
Had not this news stepp'd in between, the point
Had offer'd violence unto my breast.
That which some women call great misery,
Would show but little here; would scarce be seen
Among my miseries. I may compare,
For wretched fortunes, with all wives that are.
Nothing will please him, until all be nothing.
He calls it slavery to be preferr'd;
A place of credit, a base servitude.
What shall become of me, and my poor children,
Two here, and one at nurse? my pretty beggars!
I see how ruin with a palsied hand
Begins to shake this ancient seat to dust:
The heavy weight of sorrow draws my lids
Over my dankish eyes: I can scarce see;
This grief will last;—it wakes and sleeps with me.   [*Exit.*

   SCENE IV.   *Another apartment in the same.*

    Enter HUSBAND *and the* MASTER *of a College.*

   Hus. Please you draw near, Sir; you're exceeding welcome.

Mast. That's my doubt; I fear I come not to be welcome.

Hus. Yes, howsoever.

Mast. 'Tis not my fashion, Sir, to dwell in long circumstance, but to be plain and effectual; therefore to the purpose. The cause of my setting forth was piteous and lamentable. That hopeful young gentleman, your brother, whose virtues we all love dearly, through your default and unnatural negligence lies in bond executed for your debt,—a prisoner; all his studies amazed, his hope struck dead, and the pride of his youth muffled in these dark clouds of oppression.

Hus. Umph, umph, umph!

Mast. O, you have killed the towardest hope of all our university: wherefore, without repentance and amends, expect ponderous and sudden judgments to fall grievously upon you. Your brother, a man who profited in his divine employments, and might have made ten thousand souls fit for heaven, is now by your careless courses cast into prison, which you must answer for; and assure your spirit it will come home at length.

Hus. O God! O!

Mast. Wise men think ill of you; others speak ill of you; no man loves you: nay, even those whom honesty condemns, condemn you: And take this from the virtuous affection I bear your brother; never look for prosperous hour, good thoughts, quiet sleep, contented walks, nor anything that makes man perfect, till you redeem him. What is your answer? How will you bestow him? Upon desperate misery, or better hopes?—I suffer till I hear your answer.

Hus. Sir, you have much wrought with me; I feel you in my soul: you are your art's master. I never had sense till now; your syllables have cleft me. Both for your words and pains I thank you. I cannot but acknowledge grievous wrongs done to my brother; mighty, mighty, mighty, mighty wrongs. Within, there!

Enter a SERVANT.

Hus. Fill me a bowl of wine. [*Exit Servant.*] Alas, poor brother, bruised with an execution for my sake!

Mast. A bruise indeed makes many a mortal sore, Till the grave cure them.

Re-enter SERVANT *with wine.*

Hus. Sir, I begin to you; you've chid your welcome.

Mast. I could have wished it better for your sake. I pledge you, Sir:—To the kind man in prison.

Hus. Let it be so. Now, Sir, if you please to spend but a few minutes in a walk about my grounds below, my man here shall attend you. I doubt not but by that time to be furnished of a sufficient answer, and therein my brother fully satisfied.

Mast. Good Sir, in that the angels would be pleas'd, And the world's murmurs calm'd; and I should say, I set forth then upon a lucky day.

[*Exeunt Master and Servant.*

Hus. O thou confused man! Thy pleasant sins have undone thee; thy damnation has beggared thee. That heaven should say we must not sin, and yet made women! give our senses way to find pleasure, which being found, confounds us! Why should we know those things so much misuse us? O, would virtue had been forbidden! We should then have proved all virtuous; for 'tis our blood to love what we are forbidden. Had not drunkenness been forbidden, what man would have been fool to a beast, and zany to a swine,—to show tricks in the mire? What is there in three dice, to make a man draw thrice three thousand acres into the compass of a little round table, and with the gentleman's palsy in the hand shake out his posterity, thieves or beggars? 'Tis done; I have don't i' faith: terrible, horrible misery!—How well was I left! Very well, very well. My lands showed like a full moon about me; but now the moon's in the last quarter,—waning, waning; and I am mad to think that moon was mine; mine and my father's, and my forefathers'; generations, generations.—Down goes the house of us; down, down it sinks. Now is the name a beggar; begs in me. That name which hundreds of years has made this shire famous, in me and my posterity runs out. In my seed five are made miserable besides myself: my riot is now my brother's gaoler, my wife's sighing, my three boys' penury, and mine own confusion.

Why sit my hairs upon my cursèd head? [*Tears his hair.*
Will not this poison scatter them? O, my brother 's
In execution among devils that
Stretch him and make him give; and I in want,
Not able to relieve, nor to redeem him!
Divines and dying men may talk of hell,
But in my heart its several torments dwell;
Slavery and misery. Who, in this case,
Would not take up money upon his soul?
Pawn his salvation, live at interest?
I that did ever in abundance dwell,
For me to want, exceeds the throes of hell.

Enter a little Boy with a top and scourge.

Son. What ail you, father? Are you not well? I cannot scourge my top as long as you stand so. You take up all the room with your wide legs. Puh! you cannot make me afraid with this; I fear no vizards, nor bugbears.

[*He takes up the child by the skirts of his long coat with one hand, and draws his dagger with the other.*

Hus. Up, Sir, for here thou hast no inheritance left.
Son. O, what will you do, father? I am your white boy.
Hus. Thou shalt be my red boy; take that. [*Strikes him.*
Son. O, you hurt me, father.
Hus. My eldest beggar,
Thou shalt not live to ask an usurer bread;
To cry at a great man's gate; or follow,
Good your honour, by a coach; no, nor your brother:
'Tis charity to brain you.

Son. How shall I learn, now my head 's broke?

Hus. Bleed, bleed,   [*Stabs him.*
Rather than beg. Be not thy name's disgrace:
Spurn thou thy fortunes first; if they be base,
Come view thy second brother's. Fates! My children's blood
Shall spin into your faces; you shall see,
How confidently we scorn beggary!   [*Exit with his Son.*

Scene V. *A bed-room in the same.*

A Maid discovered with a Child in her arms; the Mother on a couch by her, asleep.

Maid. Sleep, sweet babe; sorrow makes thy mother sleep:
It bodes small good when heaviness falls so deep.
Hush, pretty boy; thy hopes might have been better.
'Tis lost at dice, what ancient honour won:
Hard, when the father plays away the son!
Nothing but misery survives in this house;
Ruin and desolation. O!

Enter HUSBAND, *with his Son bleeding.*

Hus. Whore, give me that boy. [*Strives with her for the child.*
Maid. O help, help! Out alas! murder, murder!
Hus. Are you gossiping, you prating, sturdy quean?
I'll break your clamour with your neck. Down stairs;
Tumble, tumble headlong. So:—
                  [*He throws her down and stabs the child.*
The surest way to charm a woman's tongue,
Is—break her neck: a politician did it.*
Son. Mother, mother; I am kill'd, mother. [*Wife awakes.*
Wife. Ha, who's that cried? O me! my children!
Both, both, bloody, bloody! [*Catches up the youngest child.*
Hus. Strumpet, let go the boy, let go the beggar.

---

* The reference here is to the Earl of Leicester, the death of whose first wife is said, in the celebrated libel called *Leicester's Commonwealth*, to have been occasioned by her being thrown down stairs at Cunmor, by her husband's order.

Wife. O my sweet husband!
Hus. Filth, harlot.
Wife. O, what will you do, dear husband?
Hus. Give me the bastard.
Wife. Your own sweet boy—
Hus. There are too many beggars.
Wife. Good my husband—
Hus. Dost thou prevent me still?
Wife. O God!
Hus. Have at his heart.   [*Stabs at the child in her arms.*
Wife. O, my dear boy!
Hus. Brat, thou shalt not live to shame thy house—
Wife. O heaven!   [*She is hurt, and sinks down.*
Hus. And perish!—Now be gone:
There's whores enough, and want would make thee one.

Enter a SERVANT.

Ser. O Sir, what deeds are these?
Hus.   Base slave, my vassal!
Com'st thou between my fury to question me?
Ser. Were you the devil, I would hold you, Sir.
Hus. Hold me? Presumption! I'll undo thee for it.
Ser. 'Sblood, you have undone us all, Sir.
Hus. Tug at thy master?
Ser. Tug at a monster.
Hus. Have I no power? shall my slave fetter me?
Ser. Nay then the devil wrestles; I am thrown.
Hus. O villain! now I'll tug thee, now I'll tear thee;
Set quick spurs to my vassal; bruise him, trample him.
So; I think thou wilt not follow me in haste.
My horse stands ready saddled. Away, away;
Now to my brat at nurse, my sucking beggar:
Fates, I'll not leave you one to trample on!   [*Exit.*

14*

SCENE VI. *Court before the house.*

Enter HUSBAND; *to him the* MASTER *of the College.*

Mast. How is it with you, Sir?
Methinks you look of a distracted colour.
  Hus. Who, I, Sir? 'Tis but your fancy.
Please you walk in, Sir, and I'll soon resolve you,
I want one small part to make up the sum,
And then my brother shall rest satisfied.
  Mast. I shall be glad to see it: Sir, I'll attend you.
[*Exeunt.*

SCENE VII. *A room in the house.*

The WIFE, SERVANT, *and* CHILDREN, *discovered.*

Ser. O, I am scarce able to heave up myself,
He has so bruis'd me with his devilish weight,
And torn my flesh with his blood-hasty spur:
A man before of easy constitution,
Till now Hell-power supplied, to his soul's wrong:
O, how damnation can make weak men strong!

Enter the MASTER *of the College and two* SERVANTS.

Ser. O, the most piteous deed, Sir, since you came!
  Mast. A deadly greeting! Hath he summ'd up these
To satisfy his brother? Here's another;
And by the bleeding infants, the dead mother.
  Wife. O! O!
  Mast. Surgeons! surgeons! she recovers life:—
One of his men all faint and bloodied!
  First Ser. Follow; our murderous master has took horse
To kill his child at nurse. O, follow quickly.
  Mast. I am the readiest; it shall be my charge
To raise the town upon him.
  First Ser. Good Sir, do follow him.
[*Exeunt Master and two Servants.*

Wife. O my children!

First Ser. How is it with my most afflicted mistress?

Wife. Why do I now recover? Why half live,
To see my children bleed before mine eyes?
A sight able to kill a mother's breast, without
An executioner.—What, art thou mangled too?

First Ser. I, thinking to prevent what his quick mischiefs
Had so soon acted, came and rush'd upon him.
We struggled; but a fouler strength than his
O'erthrew me with his arms; then did he bruise me,
And rent my flesh, and robb'd me of my hair;
Like a man mad in execution,
Made me unfit to rise and follow him.

Wife. What is it has beguil'd him of all grace,
And stole away humanity from his breast?
To slay his children, purpose to kill his wife,
And spoil his servants—

Enter a SERVANT.

Ser. Please you to leave this most accursèd place:
A surgeon waits within.

Wife. Willing to leave it?
'Tis guilty of sweet blood, innocent blood:
Murder has took this chamber with full hands,
And will ne'er out as long as the house stands. [*Exeunt.*

SCENE VIII. *A high road.*

Enter HUSBAND. *He falls.*

Hus. O stumbling jade, the spavin overtake thee!
The fifty diseases stop thee!
O, I am sorely bruis'd! Plague founder thee!
Thou run'st at ease and pleasure. Heart of chance!
To throw me now, within a flight o' the town,
In such plain even ground too! 'Sfoot, a man

May dice upon it, and throw away the meadows.
Filthy beast!
    [*Cry within.*] Follow, follow, follow!
    Hus. Ha! I hear sounds of men, like hue and cry.
Up, up, and struggle to thy horse; make on;
Dispatch that little beggar, and all's done.
    [*Cry within.*] Here, here; this way, this way!
    Hus. At my back! O,
What fate have I! my limbs deny me go.
My will is barr'd; beggary claims a part.
O, could I here reach to the infant's heart!

        Enter the MASTER *of the College,* three GENTLEMEN, *and*
                Attendants *with halberds.*

    All. Here, here; yonder, yonder.
    Mast. Unnatural, flinty, more than barbarous!
The Scythians, or the marble-hearted Fates,
Could not have acted more remorseless deeds,
In their relentless natures, than these of thine.
Was this the answer I long waited on?
The satisfaction for thy prison'd brother?
    Hus. Why, he can have no more of us than our skins,
And some of them want but fleaing.
    First Gent. Great sins have made him impudent.
    Mast. He has shed so much blood, that he cannot blush.
    Sec. Gent. Away with him, bear him to the justice's.
A gentleman of worship dwells at hand:
There shall his deeds be blaz'd.
    Hus.   Why, all the better.
My glory 'tis to have my action known;
I grieve for nothing, but I miss'd of one.
    Mast. There's little of a father in that grief:
Bear him away.   [*Exeunt.*

Scene IX. *A room in the house of a Magistrate.*

Enter a Knight *and three* Gentlemen.

Knight. Endanger'd so his wife? murder'd his children?
First Gent. So the cry goes.
Knight. I am sorry I e'er knew him;
That ever he took life and natural being
From such an honour'd stock, and fair descent,
Till this black minute without stain or blemish.
First Gent. Here come the men.

Enter Master *of the College, &c. with the* Prisoner.

Knight. The serpent of his house! I am sorry
For this time, that I am in place of justice.
Mast. Please you, Sir—
Knight. Do not repeat it twice; I know too much:
Would it had ne'er been thought on! Sir, I bleed for you.
First Gent. Your father's sorrows are alive in me.
What made you show such monstrous cruelty?
Hus. In a word, Sir, I have consumed all, played away
long-acre; and I thought it the charitablest deed I could do,
to cozen beggary, and knock my house o' the head.
Knight. O, in a cooler blood you will repent it.
Hus. I repent now that one is left unkill'd;
My brat at nurse. I would full fain have wean'd him.
Knight. Well, I do not think, but in to-morrow's judgment,
The terror will sit closer to your soul',
When the dread thought of death remembers you:
To further which, take this sad voice from me,
Never was act play'd more unnaturally.
Hus. I thank you, Sir.
Knight. Go, lead him to the gaol:
Where justice claims all, there must pity fail.
Hus. Come, come; away with me. [*Exeunt Husband, &c.*

Mast. Sir, you deserve the worship of your place:
Would all did so! In you the law is grace.
   Knight. It is my wish it should be so.—Ruinous man!
The desolation of his house, the blot
Upon his predecessors' honour'd name!
That man is nearest shame, that is past shame.   [*Exeunt.*

Scene X. *Before Calverly Hall.*

Enter Husband *guarded*, Master *of the College*, Gentlemen, *and Attendants.*

   Hus. I am right against my house,—seat of my ancestors:
I hear my wife's alive, but much endanger'd.
Let me entreat to speak with her, before
The prison gripe me.

           His Wife *is brought in.*

   Gent. See, here she comes of herself.
   Wife. O my sweet husband, my dear distressèd husband,
Now in the hands of unrelenting laws,
My greatest sorrow, my extremest bleeding;
Now my soul bleeds.
   Hus. How now? Kind to me? Did I not wound thee?
Left thee for dead?
   Wife. Tut, far, far greater wounds did my breast feel;
Unkindness strikes a deeper wound than steel.
You have been still unkind to me.
   Hus. 'Faith, and so I think I have;
I did my murders roughly out of hand,
Desperate and sudden; but thou hast devis'd
A fine way now to kill me: thou hast given mine eyes
Seven wounds apiece. Now glides the devil from me,
Departs at every joint; heaves up my nails.
O, catch him torments that were ne'er invented!
Bind him one thousand more, you blessèd angels
In that pit bottomless! Let him not rise

To make men act unnatural tragedies;
To spread into a father, and in fury
Make him his children's executioner;
Murder his wife, his servants, and who not!—
For that man's dark, where heaven is quite forgot.
    Wife. O my repentant husband!
    Hus. O my dear soul, whom I too much have wrong'd:
For death I die, and for this have I long'd.
    Wife. Thou shouldst not, be assur'd, for these faults die,
If the law could forgive as soon as I.
                               [*The two children laid out.*
    Hus. What sight is yonder?
    Wife.   O, our two bleeding boys,
Laid forth upon the threshold.
    Hus. Here's weight enough to make a heart-string crack.
O, were it lawful that your pretty souls
Might look from heaven into your father's eyes,
Then should you see the penitent glasses melt,
And both your murders shoot upon my cheeks!
But you are playing in the angels' laps,
And will not look on me, who, void of grace,
Kill'd you in beggary.
O, that I might my wishes now attain,
I should then wish you living were again,
Though I did beg with you, which thing I fear'd:
O, 'twas the enemy my eyes so blear'd!
O, would you could pray heaven me to forgive,
That will unto my end repentant live!
    Wife. It makes me e'en forget all other sorrows,
And live apart with this.
    Offi.   Come, will you go?
    Hus. I'll kiss the blood I spilt, and then I'll go:
My soul is bloodied, well may my lips be so.
Farewell, dear wife; now thou and I must part;
I of thy wrongs repent me with my heart.
    Wife. O, stay; thou shalt not go.
    Hus. That's but in vain; you see it must be so.

Farewell ye bloody ashes of my boys!
My punishments are their eternal joys.
Let every father look into my deeds,
And then their heirs may prosper, while mine bleeds.
                    [*Exeunt Husband and Officers.*
    Wife. More wretched am I now in this distress,
Than former sorrows made me.
        Mast.   O kind wife,
Be comforted; one joy is yet unmurder'd;
You have a boy at nurse; your joy 's in him.
    Wife. Dearer than all is my poor husband's life.
Heaven give my body strength, which is yet faint
With much expense of blood, and I will kneel,
Sue for his life, number up all my friends
To plead for pardon for my dear husband's life.
    Mast. Was it in man to wound so kind a creature?
I'll ever praise a woman for thy sake.
I must return with grief; my answer 's set;
I shall bring news weighs heavier than the debt.
Two brothers, one in bond lies overthrown,
This on a deadlier execution.   [*Exeunt omnes.*

THE LONDON PRODIGAL.

DRAMATIS PERSONÆ.

FLOWERDALE SENIOR, a merchant.
MATTHEW FLOWERDALE, his son.
FLOWERDALE JUNIOR, brother to the merchant.
SIR LANCELOT SPURCOCK.
SIR ARTHUR GREENSHIELD, a military officer, } in love with Luce.
OLIVER, a Devonshire clothier,
WEATHERCOCK, a parasite to Sir Lancelot Spurcock.
CIVET, in love with Frances.
A Citizen.
DAFFODILL, } servants to Sir
ARTICHOKE, } Lancelot Spurcock.
DICK and RALPH, two cheating gamesters.
RUFFIAN, a pander.
DELIA, }
FRANCES, } daughters to Sir Lancelot Spurcock.
LUCE, }
Citizen's wife.

Sheriff and Officers, Lieutenant and Soldiers, Drawers, and other Attendants.

SCENE.—*London, and the parts adjacent.*

ACT I.

SCENE I. *London. A room in* FLOWERDALE JUNIOR'*. house.*

Enter FLOWERDALE SENIOR *and* FLOWERDALE JUNIOR.

Flow. Sen. Brother, from Venice, being thus disguis'd,
I come, to prove the humours of my son.
How hath he borne himself since my departure,
I leaving you his patron and his guide?

Flow. Jun. I' faith, brother, so, as you will grieve to hear, And I almost ashamèd to report it.

Flow. Sen. Why, how is't, brother? What, doth he spend beyond the allowance I left him?

Flow. Jun. How! beyond that? and far more. Why, your exhibition is nothing. He hath spent that, and since hath borrowed: protested with oaths, alleged kindred, to wring money from me,—*by the love I bore his father,—by the fortunes might fall upon himself,*—to furnish his wants: that done, I have had since, his bond, his friend and friend's bond. Although I know that he spends is yours, yet it grieves me to see the unbridled wildness that reigns over him.

Flow. Sen. Brother, what is the manner of his life? how is the name of his offences? If they do not relish altogether of damnation, his youth may privilege his wantonness. I myself ran an unbridled course till thirty, nay, almost till forty: —well, you see how I am. For vice once looked into with the eyes of discretion, and well balanced with the weights of reason, the course passed seem so abominable, that the landlord of himself, which is the heart of his body, will rather entomb himself in the earth, or seek a new tenant to remain in him; which once settled, how much better are they that in their youth have known all these vices, and left them, than those that knew little, and in their age run into them? Believe me, brother, they that die most virtuous, have in their youth lived most vicious; and none knows the danger of the fire more than he that falls into it.—But say, how is the course of his life? let's hear his particulars.

Flow. Jun. Why, I'll tell you, brother; he is a continual swearer, and a breaker of his oaths; which is bad.

Flow. Sen. I grant indeed to swear is bad, but the not keeping those oaths is better; for who will set by a bad thing? Nay, by my faith, I hold this rather a virtue than a vice. Well, I pray proceed.

Flow. Jun. He is a mighty brawler, and comes commonly by the worst.

Flow. Sen. By my faith, this is none of the worst neither;

for if he brawl, and be beaten for it, it will in time make him shun it; for what brings man or child more to virtue than correction?—What reigns over him else?

Flow. Jun. He is a great drinker, and one that will forget himself.

Flow. Sen. O best of all! vice should be forgotten: let him drink on, so he drink not churches. Nay, an this be the worst, I hold it rather a happiness in him, than any iniquity. Hath he any more attendants?

Flow. Jun. Brother, he is one that will borrow of any man.

Flow. Sen. Why, you see, so doth the sea; it borrows of all the small currents in the world to increase himself.

Flow. Jun. Ay, but the sea pays it again, and so will never your son.

Flow. Sen. No more would the sea neither, if it were as dry as my son.

Flow. Jun. Then, brother, I see you rather like these vices in your son, than any way condemn them.

Flow. Sen. Nay, mistake me not, brother; for though I slur them over now, as things slight and nothing, his crimes being in the bud, it would gall my heart, they should ever reign in him.

M. Flow. [*within*]. Ho! who's within, ho?

[*M. Flowerdale knocks within.*

Flow. Jun. That's your son; he is come to borrow more money.

Flow. Sen. For God's sake give it out I am dead; see how he'll take it. Say I have brought you news from his father. I have here drawn a formal will, as it were from myself, which I'll deliver him.

Flow. Jun. Go to, brother, no more: I will.

M. Flow. Uncle, where are you, uncle? [*Within.*

Flow. Jun. Let my cousin in there.

Flow. Sen. [*hastily, and in undertones*]. I am a sailor come from Venice, and my name is Christopher.

Enter M. FLOWERDALE.

M. Flow. By the Lord, in truth, uncle——

Flow. Jun. In truth would have served, cousin, without the lord.

M. Flow. By your leave, uncle, the Lord is the Lord of truth. A couple of rascals at the gate set upon me for my purse.

Flow. Jun. You never come, but you bring a brawl in your mouth.

M. Flow. By my truth, uncle, you must needs lend me ten pound.

Flow. Jun. Give my cousin some small beer here.

M. Flow. Nay look you, you turn it to a jest now. By this light, I should ride to Croydon fair, to meet Sir Lancelot Spurcock; I should have his daughter Luce: and for scurvy ten pound, a man shall lose nine hundred three score and odd pounds, and a daily friend beside! By this hand, uncle, 'tis true.

Flow. Jun. Why, anything is true, for aught I know.

M. Flow. To see now!—why, you shall have my bond, uncle, or Tom White's, James Brock's, or Nick Hall's; as good rapier-and-dagger-men as any be in England; let's be damned, if we do not pay you: the worst of us all will not damn ourselves for ten pound. A pox of ten pound.

Flow. Jun. Cousin, this is not the first time I have believed you.

M. Flow. Why, trust me now, you know not what may fall. If one thing were but true, I would not greatly care; I should not need ten pound;—but when a man cannot be believed, there's it.

Flow. Jun. Why, what is it, cousin?

M. Flow. Marry, this, uncle. Can you tell me if the *Kate and Hugh* be come home or no?

Flow. Jun. Ay, marry, is't.

M. Flow. By God, I thank you for that news. What, is't in the Pool, can you tell?

Flow. Jun. It is; what of that?

M. Flow. What? why then I have six pieces of velvet sent me, I'll give you a piece, uncle: for thus said the letter;—A piece of ash-colour, a three-piled black, a colour de roy, a crimson, a sad green, and a purple: yes i' faith.

Flow. Jun. From whom should you receive this?

M. Flow. From whom? why from my father; with commendations to you, uncle; and thus he writes:—"I know (saith he) thou hast much troubled thy kind uncle, whom, God willing, at my return I will see amply satisfied;" amply, I remember was the very word: so God help me.

Flow. Jun. Have you the letter here?

M. Flow. Yes, I have the letter here, here is the letter: no,—yes—no;—let me see; what breeches wore I o' Saturday? Let me see: o' Tuesday, my calamanco; o' Wednesday, my peachcolour satin; o' Thursday, my velure; o' Friday, my calamanco again; o' Saturday,—let me see,—o' Saturday,—for in those breeches I wore o' Saturday is the letter—O, my riding-breeches, uncle, those that you thought had been velvet; in those very breeches is the letter.

Flow. Jun. When should it be dated?

M. Flow. Marry, *decimo tertio Septembris*—no, no; *decimo tertio Octobris;* ay, *Octobris*, so it is.

Flow. Jun. Decimo tertio Octobris! and here I receive a letter that your father died in June. [*To Flow. Sen., as Christopher*] How say you, Kester?

Flow. Sen. Yes, truly, Sir, your father is dead; these hands of mine holp to wind him.

M. Flow. Dead?

Flow. Sen. Ay, Sir, dead.

M. Flow. 'Sblood, how should my father come dead?

Flow. Sen. I' faith, Sir, according to the old proverb:
The child was born, and cried,
Became a man, after fell sick, and died.

Flow. Jun. Nay, cousin, do not take it so heavily.

M. Flow. Nay, I cannot weep you extempore: marry, some two or three days hence I shall weep without any stintance. But I hope he died in good memory.

Flow. Sen. Very well, Sir, and set down everything in good order; and the *Catharine and Hugh*, you talked of, I came over in; and I saw all the bills of lading; and the velvet that you talked of, there is no such aboard.

M. Flow. By God, I assure you, then there is knavery abroad.

Flow. Sen. I'll be sworn of that: there's knavery abroad, although there were never a piece of velvet in Venice.

M. Flow. I hope he died in good estate.

Flow. Sen. To the report of the world he did; and made his will, of which I am an unworthy bearer.

M. Flow. His will! have you his will?

Flow. Sen. Yes, Sir, and in the presence of your uncle I was willed to deliver it. [*Delivers the will.*

Flow. Jun. I hope, cousin, now God hath blessed you with wealth, you will not be unmindful of me.

M. Flow. I'll do reason, uncle: yet, i' faith, I take the denial of this ten pound very hardly.

Flow. Jun. Nay, I denied you not.

M. Flow. By God, you denied me directly.

Flow. Jun. I'll be judged by this good fellow.

Flow. Sen. Not directly, Sir.

M. Flow. Why, he said he would lend me none, and that had wont to be a direct denial, if the old phrase hold. Well, uncle, come, we'll fall to the legacies. [*Reads.*] "In the name of God, Amen.—Item, I bequeath to my brother Flowerdale, three hundred pounds, to pay such trivial debts as I owe in London.

"Item, to my son Matthew Flowerdale, I bequeath two bale of false dice, videlicet, high men and low men, fulloms, stop-cater-traies, and other bones of function."

'Sblood what doth he mean by this?

Flow. Jun. Proceed, cousin!

M. Flow. [*reads*] "These precepts I leave him: Let him borrow of his oath; for of his word nobody will trust him. Let him by no means marry an honest woman; for the other will keep herself. Let him steal as much as he can, that a guilty conscience may bring him to his destinate repentance:"—I think he means hanging! An this were his last will and testament, the devil stood laughing at his bed's feet while he made it. 'Sblood, what doth he think to fob off his posterity with paradoxes?

Flow. Sen. This he made, Sir, with his own hands.

M. Flow. Ay, well; nay, come, good uncle, let me have this ten pound: imagine you have lost it, or were robb'd of it, or misreckon'd yourself so much; any way to make it come easily off, good uncle.

Flow. Jun. Not a penny.

Flow. Sen. I' faith, lend it him, Sir. I myself have an estate in the city worth twenty pound; all that I'll engage for him: he saith it concerns him in a marriage.

M. Flow. Ay, marry doth it. This is a fellow of some sense, this: come, good uncle.

Flow. Jun. Will you give your word for it, Kester?

Flow. Sen. I will, Sir, willingly.

Flow. Jun. Well, cousin, come to me an hour hence, you shall have it ready.

M. Flow. Shall I not fail?

Flow. Jun. You shall not; come or send.

M. Flow. Nay, I'll come myself.

Flow. Sen. By my troth, would I were your worship's man.

M. Flow. What? wouldst thou serve?

Flow. Sen. Very willingly, Sir.

M. Flow. Well, I'll tell thee what thou shalt do. Thou say'st thou hast twenty pound: go into Birchin-lane, put thyself into clothes: thou shalt ride with me to Croydon fair.

Flow. Sen. I thank you, Sir; I will attend you.

M. Flow. Well, uncle, you will not fail me an hour hence.

Flow. Jun. I will not, cousin.

M. Flow. What's thy name? Kester?

Flow. Sen. Ay, Sir.

M. Flow. Well, provide thyself! uncle, farewell till anon!
[*Exit M. Flowerdale.*

Flow. Jun. Brother, how do you like your son?
Flow. Sen. I' faith, brother, like a mad, unbridled colt,
Or as a hawk, that never stoop'd to lure:
The one must be tam'd with an iron bit,
The other must be watch'd, or still she's wild.
Such is my son; a while let him be so;
For counsel still is folly's deadly foe.
I'll serve his youth, for youth must have his course;
For being restrain'd, it makes him ten times worse:
His pride, his riot, all that may be nam'd,
Time may recall, and all his madness tam'd. [*Exeunt.*

SCENE II. *The high-street in Croydon. An inn appearing with an open drinking-booth before it.*

Enter Sir LANCELOT SPURCOCK, WEATHERCOCK, DAFFODIL, ARTICHOKE, LUCE, *and* FRANCES.

Sir Lanc. Sirrah, Artichoke, get you home before;
And as you prov'd yourself a calf in buying,
Drive home your fellow calves that you have bought.
    Art. Yes, forsooth: Shall not my fellow Daffodil go along with me?
    Sir Lanc. No, Sir, no; I must have one to wait on me.
    Art. Daffodil, farewell, good fellow Daffodil.
You may see, mistress, I am set up by the halves;
Instead of waiting on you, I 'm sent to drive home calves.
                                                    [*Exit.*
    Sir Lanc. I' faith, Franke, I must turn away this Daffodil;
He's grown a very foolish saucy fellow.
    Fran. Indeed la, father, he was so since I had him:
Before, he was wise enough for a foolish serving-man.
    Weath. But what say you to me, Sir Lancelot?
    Sir Lanc. O, about my daughters? Well, I will go forward.
Here's two of them, God save them; but the third,
O, she's a stranger in her course of life:
She hath refus'd you, Master Weathercock.

Weath. Ay, by the rood, Sir Lancelot, that she hath;
But had she tried me,
She should have found a man of me indeed.

Sir Lanc. Nay, be not angry, Sir, at her denial;
She hath refus'd seven of the worshipfull'st
And worthiest housekeepers this day in Kent:
Indeed, she will not marry, I suppose.

Weath. The more fool she.

Sir Lanc. What, is it folly to love chastity?

Weath. No, no, mistake me not, Sir Lancelot;
But 'tis an old proverb, and you know it well,
That women dying maids, lead apes in hell.

Sir Lanc. That is a foolish proverb and a false.

Weath. By the mass, I think it be, and therefore let it go: but who shall marry with Mistress Frances?

Fran. By my troth, they are talking of marrying me, sister.

Luce. Peace, let them talk:
Fools may have leave to prattle as they walk.

Daf. Sentences still, sweet mistress:
You have a wit, an 'twere your alabaster.

Luce. I' faith, and thy tongue trips trenchmore.

Sir Lanc. No, of my knighthood, not a suitor yet:
Alas, God help her, silly girl, a fool, a very fool;
But there's the other, black-brows, a shrewd girl,
She hath wit at will, and suitors two or three;
Sir Arthur Greenshield one, a gallant knight,
A valiant soldier, but his power but poor;
Then there's young Oliver, the De'nshire lad,
A wary fellow, marry full of wit,
And rich, by the rood; But there's a third, all air,
Light as a feather, changing as the wind;
Young Flowerdale.

Weath. O, he, Sir, he's a desperate Dick indeed;
Bar him your house.

Sir Lanc. Fie, Sir, not so: he's of good parentage.

Weath. By my fay and so he is, and a proper man.

Sir Lanc. Ay, proper enough, had he good qualities.

Weath. Ay, marry, there's the point, Sir Lancelot; for there's an old saying:—
> Be he rich, or be he poor,
> Be he high, or be he low:
> Be he born in barn or hall,
> 'Tis manners makes the man and all.

Sir Lanc. You are in the right, Master Weathercock.

Enter CIVET.

Civ. 'Soul, I think I am sure crossed, or witched, with an owl. I have haunted them, inn after inn, booth after booth, yet cannot find them. Ha, yonder they are; that's she. I hope to God 'tis she: nay, I know 'tis she now, for she treads her shoe a little awry.

Sir Lanc. Where is this inn? We are past it, Daffodil.

Daf. The good sign is here, Sir, but the back gate is before.

Civ. Save you, Sir. I pray, may I borrow a piece of a word with you?

Daf. No pieces, Sir.

Civ. Why then the whole. I pray, Sir, what may yonder gentlewomen be?

Daf. They may be ladies, Sir, if the destinies and mortality work.

Civ. What's her name, Sir?

Daf. Mistress Frances Spurcock, Sir Lancelot Spurcock's daughter.

Civ. Is she a maid, Sir?

Daf. You may ask Pluto and Dame Proserpine that: I would be loath to be riddled, Sir?

Civ. Is she married, I mean, Sir?

Daf. The Fates know not yet what shoemaker shall make her wedding-shoes.

Civ. I pray, where inn you, Sir? I would be very glad to bestow the wine of that gentlewoman.

Daf. At the *George*, Sir.

Civ. God save you, Sir.

Daf. I pray your name, Sir?

Civ. My name is Master Civet, Sir.

Daf. A sweet name! God be with you, good Master Civet.
[*Exit Civet.*

Sir Lanc. Ha, have we spied you, stout St. George? For all
Your dragon, you had best sell us good wine
That needs no ivy-bush. Well, we'll not sit by it,
As you do on your horse: This room shall serve:—
Drawer!

Enter Drawer.

Let me have sack for us old men:
For these young girls and knaves small wines are best.
A pint of sack,—no more.

Draw. A quart of sack in the Three Tuns. [*Exit.*

Sir Lanc. A pint, draw but a pint. Daffodil, call for wine to make yourselves drink.

Fran. And a cup of small beer, and a cake, good Daffodil.
[*Daffodil goes into the house, and returns with wine, &c.*

Enter M. FLOWERDALE, *and* FLOWERDALE SENIOR *as his Servant.*

M. Flow. How now? fie, sit in the open room? Now, good Sir Lancelot, and my kind friend, worshipful Master Weathercock! What, at your pint? A quart for shame.

Sir Lanc. Nay, royster, by your leave, we will away.

M. Flow. Come, give us some music, we'll go dance. Be gone, Sir Lancelot! what, and fair-day too?

Luce. 'Twere foully done, to dance within the fair.

M. Flow. Nay, if you say so, fairest of all fairs, then I'll not dance. A pox upon my tailor, he hath spoiled me a peach-colour satin suit, cut upon cloth of silver; but, if ever the rascal serve me such another trick, I'll give him leave, i' faith, to put me in the calendar of fools, and you, and you, Sir Lancelot, and Master Weathercock. My goldsmith, too, on t'other side—I bespoke thee, Luce, a carcanet of gold, and thought thou shouldst have had it for a fairing; and the rogue puts me in 'rearages for orient pearl: but thou shalt have it by Sunday night, wench.

Re-enter Drawer.

Draw. Sir, here is one hath sent you a pottle of Rhenish wine, brewed with rose-water.

M. Flow. To me?

Draw. No, Sir; to the knight; and desires his more acquaintance.

Sir Lanc. To me? what's he that proves so kind?

Daf. I have a trick to know his name, Sir. He hath a month's mind here to Mistress Frances; his name is Master Civet.

Sir Lanc. Call him in, Daffodil. [*Exit Daffodil.*

M. Flow. O, I know him, Sir; he is a fool, but reasonable rich: his father was one of these lease-mongers, these corn-mongers, these money-mongers; but he never had the wit to be a whore-monger.

Enter Civet.

Sir Lanc. I promise you, Sir, you are at too much charge.

Civ. The charge is small charge, Sir; I thank God, my father left me wherewithal. If it please you, Sir, I have a great mind to this gentlewoman here, in the way of marriage.

Sir Lanc. I thank you, Sir. Please you to come to Lewsham,
To my poor house, you shall be kindly welcome.
I knew your father; he was a wary husband. —
To pay here, Drawer.

Draw. All is paid, Sir; this gentleman hath paid all.

Sir Lanc. I' faith, you do us wrong;
But we shall live to make amends ere long.
Master Flowerdale, is that your man?

M. Flow. Yes, 'faith, a good old knave.

Sir Lanc. Nay then I think
You will turn wise, now you take such a servant:
Come, you'll ride with us to Lewsham; let's away;
'Tis scarce two hours to the end of day. [*Exeunt.*

ACT II.

SCENE I. *A road near* Sir LANCELOT SPURCOCK's *house, in Kent.*

Enter Sir ARTHUR GREENSHIELD, OLIVER, Lieutenant, *and* Soldiers.

Sir Arth. Lieutenant, lead your soldiers to the ships, There let them have their coats; at their arrival They shall have pay. Farewell; look to your charge.
Sol. Ay, we are now sent away, and cannot so much as speak with our friends.
Oli. No man, what e'er you used a zutch a fashion, thick you cannot take your leave of your vreens?
Sir Arth. Fellow, no more; Lieutenant, lead them off.
Sol. Well, if I have not my pay and my clothes, I'll venture a running away, though I hang for't.
Sir Arth. Away, sirrah: charm your tongue.

[*Exeunt Lieutenant and Soldiers.*

Oli. Bin you a presser, Sir?
Sir Arth. I am a commander, Sir, under the king.
Oli. 'Sfoot, man, an you be ne'er zutch a commander, shud a spoke with my vreens before I chid a gone; so chid.
Sir Arth. Content yourself, man; my authority will stretch to press so good a man as you.
Oli. Press me? I devy; press scoundrels, and thy measels. Press me! che scorns thee, i' faith; for secst thee, here's a worshipful knight knows, cham not to be pressed by thee.

Enter Sir LANCELOT, WEATHERCOCK, M. FLOWERDALE, FLOWERDALE SENIOR, LUCE, *and* FRANCES.

Sir Lanc. Sir Arthur, welcome to Lewsham; welcome, by my troth.—What's the matter, man? why are you vexed?
Oli. Why, man, he would press me.
Sir Lanc. O fie, Sir Arthur, press him? he is a man of reckoning.

Weath. Ay, that he is, Sir Arthur; he hath the nobles, the golden ruddocks he.

Sir Arth. The fitter for the wars: and were he not
In favour with your worships, he should see
That I have power to press so good as he.

Oli. Chill stand to the trial, so chill.

M. Flow. Ay, marry shall he. Press cloth and kersey, whitepot and drowsen broth! tut, tut, he cannot.

Oli. Well, Sir, though you vlouten cloth and karsey, che 'a zeen zutch a karsey-coat wear out the town sick a silken jacket as thick a one you wear.

M. Flow. Well said, vlittan vlattan.

Oli. Ay, and well said, cocknell, and Bow-bell too. What dost think cham aveard of thy zilken coat? no vear vor thee.

Sir Lanc. Nay come, no more: be all lovers and friends.

Weath. Ay, 'tis best so, good Master Oliver.

M. Flow. Is your name Master Oliver, I pray you?

Oli. What tit and be tit, and grieve you.

M. Flow. No, but I'd gladly know if a man might not have a foolish plot out of Master Oliver to work upon.

Oli. Work thy plots upon me! Stand aside: work thy foolish plots upon me, chill so use thee, thou wert never so used since thy dame bound thy head. Work upon me!

M. Flow. Let him come, let him come.

Oli. Zyrrha, zyrrha, if it were not vor shame, che would 'a given thee zutch a whister-poop under the ear, che would have made thee a vanged another at my feet: Stand aside, let me loose; cham all of a vlaming firebrand; stand aside.

M. Flow. Well, I forbear you for your friends' sake.

Oli. A vig for all my vreens; dost thou tell me of my vreens?

Sir Lanc. No more, good Master Oliver; no more,
Sir Arthur. And, maiden, here in the sight
Of all your suitors, every man of worth,
I'll tell you whom I fainest would prefer
To the hard bargain of your marriage-bed.
Shall I be plain among you, gentlemen?

Sir Arth. Ay, Sir, it is best.
Sir Lanc.   Then, Sir, first to you.
I do confess you a most gallant knight,
A worthy soldier, and an honest man:
But honesty maintains not a French hood;
Goes very seldom in a chain of gold;
Keeps a small train of servants; hath few friends.
And for this wild oats here, young Flowerdale,
I will not judge. God can work miracles;
But he were better make a hundred new,
Than thee a thrifty and an honest one.
 Weath. Believe me, he hath hit you there; he hath touched you to the quick; that he hath.
 M. Flow. Woodcock o' my side! Why, Master Weathercock, you know I am honest, howsoever trifles—
 Weath. Now, by my troth, I know no otherwise.
O, your old mother was a dame indeed;
Heaven hath her soul, and my wife's too, I trust:
And your good father, honest gentleman,
He is gone a journey, as I hear, far hence.
 M. Flow. Ay, God be praised, he is far enough;
He is gone a pilgrimage to Paradise,
And left me to cut capers against care.
Luce, look on me, that am as light as air.
 Luce. I' faith, I like not shadows, bubbles, breath;
I hate a *light o' love*, as I hate death.
 Sir Lanc. Girl, hold thee there: look on this De'nshire lad;
Fat, fair, and lovely, both in purse and person.
 Oli. Well, Sir, cham as the Lord hath made me. You know me well ivin; cha have threescore pack of karsey at Blackemhall, and chief credit beside; and my fortunes may be so good as another's, zo it may.
 Luce. 'Tis you I love, whatsoever others say.
                                   [*To Sir Arthur.*
 Sir Arth. Thanks, fairest.
 M. Flow. What, wouldst thou have me quarrel with him?
 Flow. Sen. Do but say he shall hear from you,

Sir Lanc. Yet, gentlemen, howsoever I prefer
This De'nshire suitor, I'll enforce no love:
My daughter shall have liberty to choose
Whom she likes best. In your love-suit proceed;
Not all of you, but only one must speed.
  Weath. You have said well; indeed, right well.

Enter ARTICHOKE.

  Art. Mistress; here's one would speak with you. My fellow Daffodil hath him in the cellar already; he knows him; he met him at Croydon fair.
  Sir Lanc. O, I remember; a little man.
  Art. Ay, a very little man.
  Sir Lanc. And yet a proper man.
  Art. A very proper, very little man.
  Sir Lanc. His name is Monsieur Civet.
  Art. The same, Sir.
  Sir Lanc. Come, gentlemen; if other suitors come,
My foolish daughter will be fitted too:
But Delia my saint, no man dare move.
        [*Exeunt all but M. Flowerdale, Oliver, and*
                Flowerdale Senior.
  M. Flow. Hark you, Sir, a word.
  Oli. What han you say to me now?
  M. Flow. You shall hear from me, and that very shortly.
  Oli. Is that all? vare thee well: che vear thee not a vig.
                                      [*Exit Oliver.*
  M. Flow. What if he should come now? I am fairly
    dress'd.
  Flow Sen. I do not mean that you shall meet with him;
But presently we'll go and draw a will,
Where we'll set down land that we never saw;
And we will have it of so large a sum,
Sir Lancelot shall entreat you take his daughter.
This being fram'd, give it Master Weathercock,
And make Sir Lancelot's daughter heir of all:
And make him swear never to show the will

To any one, until that you be dead.
This done, the foolish changing Weathercock
Will straight discourse unto Sir Lancelot
The form and tenour of your testament.
Ne'er stand to pause of it; be rul'd by me:
What will ensue, that shall you quickly see.

M. Flow. Come, let's about it: if that a will, sweet Kit,
Can get the wench, I shall renown thy wit. [*Exeunt.*

SCENE II. *A room in Sir* LANCELOT'S *house.*

Enter DAFFODIL *and* LUCE.

Daf. Mistress! still froward? No kind looks unto your
Daffodil? Now, by the gods—
Luce. Away, you foolish knave; let go my hand.
Daf. There is your hand; but this shall go with me:
My heart is thine; this is my true love's fee.
[*Takes off her bracelet.*
Luce. I'll have your coat stripp'd o'er your ears for this,
You saucy rascal.

Enter Sir LANCELOT *and* WEATHERCOCK.

Sir Lanc. How now, maid! what is the news with you?
Luce. Your man is something saucy. [*Exit Luce.*
Sir Lanc. Go to, sirrah; I'll talk with you anon.
Daf. Sir, I am a man to be talked withal; I am no horse,
I trow. I know my strength, then, no more than so.
Weath. Ay, by the makins, good Sir Lancelot, I saw him
the other day hold up the bucklers, like an Hercules. I' faith,
God-a-mercy, lad, I like thee well.
Sir Lanc. Ay, ay, like him well. Go, sirrah, fetch me a
    cup of wine,
That, ere I part with Master Weathercock,
We may drink down our farewell in French wine.
[*Exit Daffodil.*
Weath. I thank you, Sir; I thank you, friendly knight.
I'll come and visit you; by the mouse-foot I will:

Meantime, take heed of cutting Flowerdale:
He is a desperate Dick, I warrant you.

Re-enter DAFFODIL.

Sir Lanc. He is, he is. Fill, Daffodil, fill me some wine.
Ha! what wears he on his arm? My daughter Luce's bracelet?
ay, 'tis the same. Ha' to you, Master Weathercock.

Weath. I thank you, Sir. Here, Daffodil; an honest fellow, and a tall, thou art. Well; I'll take my leave, good knight; and I hope to have you and all your daughters at my poor house; in good sooth I must.

Sir Lanc. Thanks, Master Weathercock; I shall be bold to trouble you, be sure.

Weath. And welcome, heartily;—farewell.
[*Exit Weathercock.*

Sir Lanc. Sirrah, I saw my daughter's wrong, and withal her bracelet on your arm. Off with it, and with it my livery too. Have I care to see my daughter matched with men of worship? and are you grown so bold? Go, sirrah, from my house, or I'll whip you hence.

Daf. I'll not be whipp'd, Sir; there's your livery:
This is a serving-man's reward: what care I?
I have means to trust to; I scorn service, I. [*Exit Daffodil.*

Sir Lanc. A lusty knave; but I must let him go:
Our servants must be taught what they should know. [*Exit.*

SCENE III. *Another room in the same.*

Enter Sir ARTHUR *and* LUCE.

Luce. Sir, as I am a maid, I do affect
You above any suitor that I have;
Although that soldiers scarce know how to love.

Sir Arth. I am a soldier, and a gentleman
Knows what belongs to war, what to a lady.
What man offends me, that my sword shall right;
What woman loves me, I'm her faithful knight.

Luce. I neither doubt your valour, nor your love.

But there be some that bear a soldier's form,
That swear by him they never think upon;
Go swaggering up and down from house to house,
Crying, *God pays all.*
　Sir Arth. I' faith, lady, I'll descry you such a man.
Of them there be many which you have spoke of,
That bear the name and shape of soldiers,
Yet, God knows, very seldom saw the war:
That haunt your taverns and your ordinaries,
Your ale-houses sometimes, for all alike,
To uphold the brutish humour of their minds,
Being mark'd down for the bondmen of despair:
Their mirth begins in wine, but ends in blood;
Their drink is clear, but their conceits are mud.
　Luce. Yet these are great gentlemen soldiers.
　Sir Arth. No, they are wretched slaves,
Whose desperate lives doth bring them timeless graves.
　Luce. Both for yourself, and for your form of life,
If I may choose, I'll be a soldier's wife. 　　*[Exeunt.*

SCENE IV. *Another room in the same.*

Enter Sir LANCELOT *and* OLIVER.

　Oli. And tyt trust to it, so then.
　Sir Lanc. 　　　　　　　　Assure yourself
You shall be married with all speed we may:
One day shall serve for Frances and for Luce.
　Oli. Why che would vain know the time, for providing wedding-raiments.
　Sir Lanc. Why no more but this. First get your assurance made touching my daughter's jointure; that despatched, we will in two days make provision.
　Oli. Why, man, chill have the writings made by to-morrow.
　Sir Lanc. To-morrow be it then: let's meet at the King's Head in Fish-street.

Oli. No, fie man, no: let's meet at the Rose at Temple-bar; that will be nearer your counsellor and mine.

Sir Lanc. At the Rose be it then, the hour nine:
He that comes last forfeits a pint of wine.

Oli. A pint is no payment; let it be a whole quart, or nothing.

Enter ARTICHOKE.

Art. Master, here is a man would speak with Master Oliver; he comes from young Master Flowerdale.

Oli. Why, chil speak with him, chil speak with him.

Sir Lanc. Nay, son Oliver, I will surely see what young Flowerdale hath sent unto you. I pray God it be no quarrel.

Oli. Why, man, if he quarrel with me, chil give him his hands full.

Enter FLOWERDALE SENIOR.

Flow. Sen. God save you, good Sir Lancelot.

Sir Lanc. Welcome, honest friend.

Flow. Sen. To you and yours my master wisheth health;
But unto you, Sir, this, and this he sends:
There is the length, Sir, of his rapier;
And in that paper shall you know his mind. [*Delivers a letter.*

Oli. Here? chil meet him, my vriend, chil meet him.

Sir Lanc. Meet him! you shall not meet the ruffian, fie.

Oli. An I do not meet him, chil give you leave to call me cut. Where is't, zirrah? where is't? where is't?

Flow. Sen. The letter showeth both the time and place;
And if you be a man, then keep your word.

Sir Lanc. Sir, he shall not keep his word; he shall not meet.

Flow. Sen. Why, let him choose; he'll be the better known
For a base rascal, and reputed so.

Oli. Zirrah, zirrah, an 'twere not an old fellow, and sent after an errand, chid give thee something, but chud be no money: but hold thee, for I see thou art somewhat testern; hold thee; there's vorty shillings: bring thy master a-veeld, chil give thee vorty more. Look, thou bring him: chil maul him, tell him; chil mar his dancing tressels; chil use him, he was ne'er so used since his dame bound his head; chil mar him for capering any more, che vore thee.

Flow. Sen. You seem a man, Sir, stout and resolute; And I will so report, whate'er befall.

Sir Lanc. And fall out ill, assure thy master this; I'll make him fly the land, or use him worse.

Flow. Sen. My master, Sir, deserves not this of you; And that you'll shortly find.

Sir Lanc. Thy master is an unthrift, you a knave, And I'll attach you first, next clap him up; Or have him bound unto his good behaviour.

Oli. I would you were a sprite, if you do him any harm for this. And you do, chil nere see you, nor any of yours, while chil have eyes open. What do you think, chil bo abaffelled up and down the town for a messel and a scoundrel? No che vore you. Zirrah, chil come; zay no more: chil come, tell him.

Flow. Sen. Well, Sir, my master deserves not this of you; And that you'll shortly find.

Oli. No matter; he's an unthrift; I defy him.
[*Exit Flowerdale Senior.*

Sir Lanc. Now, gentle son, let me know the place.

Oli. No, che vore you.

Sir Lanc. Let me see the note.

Oli. Nay, chil watch you for zutch a trick. But if che meet him, zo; if not, zo: chil make him know me, or chil know why I shall not; chil varo the worse.

Sir Lanc. What! will you then neglect my daughter's love? Venture your state and hers for a loose brawl?

Oli. Why, man, chil not kill him; marry chil veeze him too and again; and zo God bo with you, vather. What, man! we shall meet to-morrow. [*Exit.*

Sir Lanc. Who would have thought he had been so desperate? Come forth, my honest servant Artichoke.

Enter ARTICHOKE.

Arti. Now, what's the matter? some brawl toward, I warrant you.

Sir Lanc. Go get me thy sword bright scoured, thy buckler mended. O, for that knave! that villain, Daffodil, would have done good service. But to thee——

Arti. Ay, this is the tricks of all you gentlemen, when you stand in need of a good fellow. *O, for that Daffodil! O, where is he?* But if you be angry, an it be but for the wagging of a straw, then—*out o' doors with the knave; turn the coat over his ears.* This is the humour of you all.

Sir Lanc. O, for that knave, that lusty Daffodil!

Arti. Why, there 'tis now: our year's wages and our vails will scarce pay for broken swords and bucklers that we use in our quarrels. But I'll not fight if Daffodil be o' t'other side, that's flat.

Sir Lanc. 'Tis no such matter, man. Get weapons ready, And be at London ere the break of day:
Watch near the lodging of the De'nshire youth,
But be unseen; and as he goeth out,
As he will go out, and that very early without doubt——

Arti. What, would you have me draw upon him, as he goes in the street?

Sir Lanc. Not for a world, man.
Into the fields; for to the field he goes,
There to meet the desperate Flowerdale.
Take thou the part of Oliver, my son,
For he shall be my son, and marry Luce:
Dost understand me, knave?

Arti. Ay, Sir, I do understand you; but my young mistress might be better provided in matching with my fellow Daffodil.

Sir Lanc. No more; Daffodil is a knave. That Daffodil is a most notorious knave. [*Exit Artichoke.*

Enter WEATHERCOCK.

Master Weathercock, you come in happy time; the desperate

Flowerdale hath writ a challenge; and who think you must
answer it, but the Devonshire man, my son Oliver?
  Weath. Marry, I am sorry for it, good Sir Lancelot.
But if you will be rul'd by me, we'll stay their fury.
  Sir Lanc. As how, I pray?
  Weath. Marry, I'll tell you; by promising young Flower-
dale the red-lipped Luce.
  Sir Lanc. I'll rather follow her unto her grave.
  Weath. Ay, Sir Lancelot, I would have thought so too;
But you and I have been deceiv'd in him.
Come, read this will, or deed, or what you call it,
I know not: Come, your spectacles, I pray.
                              [*Gives him the will.*
  Sir Lanc. Nay, I thank God, I see very well.
  Weath. Marry, God bless your eyes: mine have been dim
almost this thirty years.
  Sir Lanc. Ha! what is this? what is this?   [*Reads.*
  Weath. Nay, there's true love indeed:
He gave it to me but this very morn,
And bade me keep it unseen from any one.
Good youth! to see how men may be deceiv'd!
  Sir Lanc. Passion of me,
What a wretch am I, to hate this loving youth!
He hath made me, together with my Luce
He loves so dear, executors of all
His wealth.
  Weath. All, all, good man, he hath given you all.
  Sir Lanc. Three ships now in the Straits, and homeward-
                bound;
Two lordships of two hundred pound a year,
The one in Wales, the other in Glostershire:
Debts and accounts are thirty thousand pound;
Plate, money, jewels, sixteen thousand more;
Two houses furnish'd well in Coleman-street;
Beside whatsoe'er his uncle leaves to him,
Being of great domains and wealth at Peckham.

Weath. How like you this, good knight? How like you this?

Sir Lanc. I have done him wrong, but now I'll make amends;
The De'nshire man shall whistle for a wife.
He marry Luce! Luce shall be Flowerdale's.

Weath. Why, that is friendly said. Let's ride to London,
And straight prevent their match, by promising
Your daughter to that lovely lad.

Sir Lanc. We'll ride to London:—or, it shall not need;
We'll cross to Deptford-strand, and take a boat.
Where be these knaves? what, Artichoke! what, fop!

Enter ARTICHOKE.

Art. Here be the very knaves, but not the merry knaves.

Sir Lanc. Here, take my cloak: I'll have a walk to Deptford.

Art. Sir, we have been scouring of our swords and bucklers for your defence.

:Sir Lanc. Defence me no defence; let your swords rust; I'll have no fighting: ay, let blows alone! Bid Delia see all things be in readiness against the wedding: we'll have two at once, and that will save charges, Master Weathercock.

Art. Well, we will do it, Sir. [*Exeunt.*

ACT III.

SCENE I. *A walk before* Sir LANCELOT'S *house.*

Enter CIVET, FRANCES, *and* DELIA.

Civ. By my troth, this is good luck; I thank God for this. In good sooth I have even my heart's desire. Sister Delia— now I may boldly call you so, for your father hath frank and freely given me his daughter Franke.

Franc. Ay, by my troth, Tom, thou hast my good will too; for I thank God I longed for a husband; and, would I might never stir, for one whose name was Tom.

Del. Why, sister, now you have your wish.

Civ. You say very true, sister Delia; and I prithee call me nothing but Tom, and I'll call thee sweetheart, and Franke. Will it not do well, sister Delia?

Del. It will do very well with both of you.

Fran. But, Tom, must I go as I do now, when I am married?

Civ. No, Franke; I'll have thee go like a citizen, in a guarded gown and a French hood.

Fran. By my troth, that will be excellent indeed.

Del. Brother, maintain your wife to your estate.
Apparel you yourself like to your father,
And let her go like to your ancient mother:
He, sparing got his wealth, left it to you.
Brother, take heed; pride soon bids thrift adieu.

Civ. So as my father and my mother went! that's a jest indeed. Why, she went in a fringed gown, a single ruff, and a white cap; and my father in a mocado coat, a pair of red satin sleeves, and a canvas back.

Del. And yet his wealth was all as much as yours.

Civ. My estate, my estate, I thank God, is forty pound a year in good leases and tenements; besides twenty mark a year at Cuckold's Haven; and that comes to us all by inheritance.

Del. That may indeed; 'tis very fitly 'plied.
I know not how it comes, but so it falls out,
That those whose fathers have died wondrous rich,
And took no pleasure but to gather wealth,
Thinking of little that they leave behind
For them they hope will be of their like mind—
But it falls out contrary: forty years' sparing
Is scarce three seven years' spending; never caring
What will ensue; when all their coin is gone,
And, all too late, then thrift is thought upon:
Oft have I heard that Pride and Riot kiss'd,
And then Repentance cries—*for had I wist.*

Civ. You say well, sister Delia, you say well; but I mean

to live within my bounds: for look you, I have set down my rest thus far, but to maintain my wife in her French hood and her coach, keep a couple of geldings and a brace of greyhounds; and this is all I'll do.

Del. And you'll do this with forty pounds a year?

Civ. Ay, and a better penny, sister.

Fran. Sister, you forget that at Cuckhold's Haven.

Civ. By my troth well remember'd, Franke; I'll give thee that to buy thee pins.

Del. Keep you the rest for points. Alas the day! Fools shall have wealth, though all the world say nay. Come, brother, will you in? Dinner stays for us.

Civ. Ay, good sister, with all my heart.

Fran. Ay, by my troth, Tom, for I have a good stomach.

Civ. And I the like, sweet Franke. No, sister, do not think I'll go beyond my bounds.

Del. God grant you may not. [*Exeunt.*

SCENE II. *London. The street before young* FLOWERDALE'S *house.*

Enter M. FLOWERDALE, *and* FLOWERDALE SENIOR, *with foils in their hands.*

Flow. Sirrah, Kit, tarry thou there; I have spied Sir Lancelot and old Weathercock coming this way: they are hard at hand; I will by no means be spoken withal.

Flow. Sen. I'll warrant you: go, get you in.

[*Exit M. Flowerdale.*

Enter Sir LANCELOT *and* WEATHERCOCK.

Sir Lanc. Now, my honest friend, thou dost belong to Master Flowerdale?

Flow. Sen. I do, Sir.

Sir Lanc. Is he within, my good fellow?

Flow. Sen. No, Sir, he is not within.

Sir Lanc. I prithee, if he be within, let me speak with him.

Flow. Sen. Sir, to tell you true, my master is within, but

indeed would not be spoke withal. There be some terms
that stand upon his reputation, therefore he will not admit
any conference till he hath shook them off.

Sir Lanc. I prithee tell him, his very good friend, Sir
Lancelot Spurcock, entreats to speak with him.

Flow. Sen. By my troth, Sir, if you come to take up the
matter between my master and the Devonshire man, you do
but beguile your hopes, and lose your labour.

Sir Lanc. Honest friend, I have not any such thing to
him. I come to speak with him about other matters.

Flow. Sen. For my master, Sir, hath set down his resolution, either to redeem his honour, or leave his life behind
him.

Sir Lanc. My friend, I do not know any quarrel touching
thy master or any other person. My business is of a dif-
ferent nature to him: and I prithee so tell him.

Flow. Sen. For howsoever the Devonshire man is, my
master's mind is bloody, that's a round O [*aside*], and therefore, Sir, entreaty is but vain.

Sir Lanc. I have no such thing to him, I tell thee once
again.

Flow. Sen. I will then so signify to him.

[*Exit Flowerdale Senior.*

Sir Lanc. A sirrah! I see this matter is hotly carried: but
I'll labour to dissuade him from it.

Enter M. FLOWERDALE *and* FLOWERDALE SENIOR.

Good morrow, Master Flowerdale.

M. Flow. Good morrow, good Sir Lancelot; good morrow,
Master Weathercock. By my troth, gentlemen, I have been
reading over Nick Machiavel; I find him good to be known,
not to be followed. A pestilent inhuman fellow! I have made
certain annotations on him, such as they be. And how is't,
Sir Lancelot? ha! how is't? A mad world! men cannot live
quiet in it.

Sir Lanc. Master Flowerdale, I do understand there is
some jar between the Devonshire man and you.

Flow. Sen. They, Sir? they are as good friends as can be.

M. Flow. Who, Master Oliver and I? as good friends as can be.

Sir Lanc. It is a kind of safety in you to deny it, and a generous silence, which too few are endued withal: but, Sir, such a thing I hear, and I could wish it otherwise.

M. Flow. No such thing, Sir Lancelot; on my reputation, as I am an honest man.

Sir Lanc. Now, then, I do believe you, if you do engage your reputation, there is none.

M. Flow. Nay, I do not engage my reputation there is none. You shall not bind me to any condition of hardness; but if there be anything between us, then there is; if there be not, then there is not. Be, or be not, all is one.

Sir Lanc. I do perceive by this, that there is something between you; and I am very sorry for it.

M. Flow. You may be deceived, Sir Lancelot. The Italian hath a pretty saying. *Questo*—I have forgot it, too; 'tis out of my head; but in my translation, if it hold, thus: If thou hast a friend, keep him; if a foe, trip him.

Sir Lanc. Come, I do see by this, there is somewhat between you; and, before God, I could wish it otherwise.

M. Flow. Well, what is between us can hardly be altered. Sir Lancelot, I am to ride forth to-morrow. That way which I must ride, no man must deny me the sun: I would not by any particular man be denied common and general passage. If any one saith, Flowerdale, thou passest not this way; my answer is, I must either on or return; but return is not my word; I must on: if I cannot then make my way, nature hath done the last for me; and there's the fine.

Sir Lanc. Master Flowerdale, every man hath one tongue, and two ears. Nature, in her building, is a most curious workmaster.

M. Flow. That is as much as to say, a man should hear more than he should speak.

Sir Lanc. You say true; and indeed I have heard more han at this time I will speak.

M. Flow. You say well.

Sir Lanc. Slanders are more common than truths, Master Flowerdale; but proof is the rule for both.

M. Flow. You say true. What-do-you-call-him, hath it there in his third canton.

Sir Lanc. I have heard you have been wild; I have believed it.

M. Flow. 'Twas fit, 'twas necessary.

Sir Lanc. But I have seen somewhat of late in you, that hath confirmed in me an opinion of goodness toward you.

M. Flow. I' faith, Sir, I'm sure I never did you harm:
Some good I have done, either to you or yours,
I am sure you know not; neither is it my will
You should.

Sir Lanc. Ay, your will, Sir.

M. Flow. Ay, my will, Sir. 'Sfoot, do you know aught of my will? By God, an you do, Sir, I am abused.

Sir Lanc. Go, Master Flowerdale; what I know, I know: and know you thus much out of my knowledge, that I truly love you. For my daughter, she's yours. And if you like a marriage better than a brawl, all quirks of reputation set aside, go with me presently; and where you should fight a bloody battle, you shall be married to a lovely lady.

M. Flow. Nay, but, Sir Lancelot—

Sir Lanc. If you will not embrace my offer, yet assure yourself thus much; I will have order to hinder your encounter.

M. Flow. Nay, but hear me, Sir Lancelot.

Sir Lanc. Nay, stand not you upon putative honour. 'Tis merely unsound, unprofitable, and idle inference. Your business is to wed my daughter; therefore give me your present word to do it. I'll go and provide the maid; therefore give me your present resolution; either now or never.

M. Flow. Will you so put me to it?

Sir Lanc. Ay, afore God, either take me now, or take me never. Else what I thought should be our match shall be our parting: so fare you well for ever.

M. Flow. Stay; fall out what may fall, my love is above all: I will come.

Sir Lanc. I expect you; and so fare you well.

[*Exeunt Sir Lancelot and Weathercock.*

Flow. Sen. Now, Sir, how shall we do for wedding-apparel?

M. Flow. By the mass, that's true. Now help, Kit: the marriage ended, we'll make amends for all.

Flow. Sen. Well, well, no more; prepare you for your bride:
We will not want for clothes, whate'er betide.

M. Flow. And thou shalt see, when once I have my dower,
In mirth we'll spend full many a merry hour:
As for this wench, I not regard a pin,
It is her gold must bring my pleasures in. [*Exit.*

Flow. Sen. Is't possible he hath his second living?
Forsaking God, himself to the devil giving?
But that I knew his mother firm and chaste,
My heart would say, my head she had disgrac'd;
But her fair mind so foul a deed did shun:
Else would I swear, he never was my son.

Enter FLOWERDALE JUNIOR.

Flow. Jun. How now, brother! how do you find your son?

Flow. Sen. O brother, heedless as a libertine;
Even grown a master in the school of vice:
One that doth nothing, but invent deceit;
For all the day he humours up and down,
How he the next day may deceive his friend;
He thinks of nothing but the present time.
For one groat ready down he'll pay a shilling;
But then the lender must needs stay for it.
When I was young I had the scope of youth,
Both wild and wanton, careless and desperate;
But such mad strains as he's possess'd withal
I thought it wonder for to dream upon.

Flow. Jun. I told you so, but you would not believe it.

Flow. Sen. Well, I have found it: but one thing comforts me,
Brother, to-morrow he is to be married
To beauteous Luce, Sir Lancelot Spurcock's daughter.
Flow. Jun. Is't possible?
Flow. Sen. 'Tis true, and thus I mean to curb him.
Brother, that day I will you shall arrest him:
If anything will tame him, it must be that;
For he is rank in mischief, chain'd to a life
That will increase his shame, and kill his wife.
Flow. Jun. What! arrest him on his wedding-day? That
Were an unchristian, and inhuman part.
How many couple even for that very day
Have purchas'd seven years' sorrow afterward!
Forbear it then to-day; do it the morrow;
And that day mingle not his joy with sorrow.
Flow. Sen. Brother, I'll have it done the very day,
And in the view of all, as he comes from church.
Do but observe the course that he will take;
Upon my life he will forswear the debt.
And, for we'll have the sum shall not be slight,
Say that he owes you near three thousand pound:
Good brother, let it be done immediately.
Flow. Jun. Well, brother, seeing you will have it so,
I will do it, and straight provide the sheriff.
Flow. Sen. So, brother, by this means shall we perceive
What 'tis Sir Lancelot in this pinch will do,
And how his wife doth stand affected to him
(Her love will then be tried to the uttermost),
And all the rest of them. What I will do,
Shall harm him much, and much avail him too. [*Exeunt.*

SCENE III. *A high-road near London.*

Enter OLIVER; *afterwards* Sir ARTHUR GREENSHIELD.

Oli. Cham assured thick be the place that the scoundrel appointed to meet me. If 'a come, zo: if 'a come not, zo.

And che were avise he would make a coystrel on us, ched
veese him, and ched vang him in hand; che would hoyst him,
and give it him to and again, zo chud. Who been 'a there?
Sir Arthur? chil stay aside.

[Goes aside.

Sir Arth. I have dogg'd the De'nshire man into the field,
For fear of any harm that should befall him.
I had an inkling of that yesternight,
That Flowerdale and he should meet this morning.
Though, of my soul, Oliver fears him not,
Yet for I'd see fair play on either side,
Made me to come, to see their valours tried.—
Good morrow to Master Oliver.

Oli. God and good morrow.

Sir Arth. What, Master Oliver, are you angry?

Oli. What an it be, tyt and grieven you?

Sir Arth. Not me at all, Sir; but I imagine by
Your being here thus arm'd, you stay for some
That you should fight withal.

Oli. Why, an he do? che would not dezire you to take his
part.

Sir Arth. No, by my troth, I think you need it not;
For he you look for, I think, means not to come.

Oli. No! an che were assure of that ched veeze him in
another place.

Enter DAFFODIL.

Daf. O, Sir Arthur, Master Oliver, ah me!
Your love, and yours, and mine, sweet Mistress Luce,
This morn is married to young Flowerdale.

Sir Arth. Married to Flowerdale! 'tis impossible.

Oli. Married, man? che hope thou dost but jest, to make
a vlowten merriment of it.

Daf. O, 'tis too true! here comes his uncle.

Enter FLOWERDALE JUNIOR, *with* Sheriff *and* Officers.

Flow. Jun. Good morrow, Sir Arthur; good morrow, Master Oliver.

Oli. God and good morn, Master Flowerdale. I pray you tellen us, is your scoundrel kinsman married?

Flow. Jun. Master Oliver, call him what you will, but he is married to Sir Lancelot's daughter here.

Sir Arth. Unto her?

Oli. Ay, ha' the old yellow zerved me thick a trick? why, man, he was a promise, chil chud 'a had her: is 'a zutch a vox? chil look to his water, che vore him.

Flow. Jun. The music plays; they are coming from the church.

Sheriff, do your office: fellows, stand stoutly to it. '

Enter Sir LANCELOT SPURCOCK, M. FLOWERDALE, WEATHERCOCK, CIVET, LUCE, FRANCES, FLOWERDALE SENIOR, *and* Attendants.

Oli. God give you joy, as the old zaid proverb is, and some zorrow among! You met us well, did you not?

Sir Lanc. Nay, be not angry, Sir; the fault is in me. I have done all the wrong; kept him from coming to the field to you, as I might, Sir; for I am a justice, and sworn to keep the peace.

Weath. Ay, marry is he, Sir, a very justice, and sworn to keep the peace: you must not disturb the weddings.

Sir Lanc. Nay, never frown nor storm, Sir; if you do, I'll have an order taken for you.

Oli. Well, well, chil be quiet.

Weath. Master Flowerdale, Sir Lancelot; look you, who here is? Master Flowerdale.

Sir Lanc. Master Flowerdale, welcome with all my heart.

M. Flow. Uncle, this is she, i' faith!—Master Undersheriff, arrest me? At whose suit?—Draw, Kit.

Flow. Jun. At my suit, Sir.

Sir Lanc. Why, what's the matter, Master Flowerdale?

Flow. Jun. This is the matter, Sir: this unthrift here

hath cozen'd you, and hath had of me in several sums three thousand pound.

M. Flow. Why, uncle, uncle!

Flow. Jun. Cousin, cousin, you have uncled me; and if you be not now stayed, you will prove a cozener unto all that know you.

Sir Lanc. Why, Sir, suppose he be to you in debt
Ten thousand pound, his state to me appears
To be at least three thousand by the year.

Flow. Jun. O, Sir, I was too late informèd of that plot;
How that he went about to cozen you,
And form'd a will, and sent it
To your good friend there, Master Weathercock,
In which was nothing true, but brags and lies.

Sir Lanc. Ha! hath he not such lordships, lands, and ships?

Flow. Jun. Not worth a groat, not worth a halfpenny, he.

Sir. Lanc. Pray, tell us true; be plain, young Flowerdale.

M. Flow. My uncle here's mad, and disposed to do me wrong; but here's my man, by the lord, an honest fellow, and of good credit, knows all is true.

Flow. Sen. Not I, Sir; I am too old to lie. I rather know
You forg'd a will, where every line you writ,
You studied where to quote your lands might lie.

Weath. I prithee where be they, my honest friend?

Flow. Sen. I' faith, nowhere, Sir; for he hath none at all.

Weath. Benedicite! We are o'erreach'd, I believe.

Sir Lanc. I am cozen'd, and my hopefull'st child undone.

M. Flow. You are not cozen'd, nor is she undone;
They slander me; by this light, they slander me.
Look you, my uncle here's an usurer,
And would undo me; but I'll stand in law;
Do you but bail me, you shall do no more:
You, brother Civet, and Master Weathercock, do but bail me,
And let me have my marriage-money paid me,

And we'll ride down, and your own eyes shall see
How my poor tenants there will welcome me.
You shall but bail me, you shall do no more:—
And you, you greedy gnats, their bail will serve?
   Flow. Jun. Ay, Sir, I'll ask no better bail.
   Sir Lanc. No, Sir, you shall not take my bail, nor his,
Nor my son Civet's: I'll not be cheated, I.
Shrieve, take your prisoner; I'll not deal with him;
Let his uncle make false dice with his false bones;
I will not have to do with him: mock'd, gull'd, and wrong'd!
Come, girl, though it be late, it falls out well;
Thou shalt not live with him in beggar's hell.
   Luce. He is my husband, and high heaven doth know
With what unwillingness I went to church;
But you enforc'd me, you compell'd me to it.
The holy church pronounc'd these words but now:
I must not leave my husband in distress;
Now I must comfort him, not go with you.
   Sir Lanc. Comfort a cozener! on my curse forsake him!
   Luce. This day you caus'd me on your curse to take him.
Do not, I pray, my grieved soul oppress:
God knows my heart doth bleed at his distress.
   Sir Lanc. O Master Weathercock,
I must confess I forc'd her to this match,
Led with opinion his false will was true.
   Weath. Ah, he hath o'erreach'd me too.
   Sir Lanc.   She might have liv'd
Like Delia, in a happy virgin's state.
   Del. Father, be patient: sorrow comes too late.
   Sir Lanc. And on her knees she begg'd and did entreat,
If she must needs taste a sad marriage-life,
She crav'd to be Sir Arthur Greenshield's wife.
   Sir Arth. You have done her and me the greater wrong.
   Sir Lanc. O, take her yet.
   Sir Arth.   Not I.
   Sir Lanc.   Or, Master Oliver,
Accept my child, and half my wealth is yours.

Oli. No, Sir, chil break no laws.

Luce. Never fear, she will not trouble you.

Del. Yet, sister, in this passion
Do not run headlong to confusion:
You may affect him, though not follow him.

Fran. No, sister; hang him, let him go.

Weath. Do 'faith, Mistress Luce; leave him.

Luce. You are three gross fools; pray, let me alone:
I swear, I'll live with him in all his moan.

Oli. But an he have his legs at liberty,
Cham aveard he will never live with you.

Sir Arth. Ay, but he is now in huckster's handling for running away.

Sir Lanc. Huswife, you hear how you and I are wrong'd,
And if you will redress it yet, you may:
But if you stand on terms to follow him,
Never come near my sight, nor look on me;
Call me not father, look not for a groat;
For all thy portion I will this day give
Unto thy sister Frances.

Fran. How say you to that, Tom [*to Civet*]? I shall have a good deal: besides, I'll be a good wife; and a good wife is a good thing, I can tell.

Civ. Peace, Franke. I would be sorry to see thy sister cast away, as I am a gentleman.

Sir Lanc. What, are you yet resolv'd?

Luce.   Yes, I 'm resolv'd.

Sir Lanc. Come, then away; or now, or never come.

Luce. This way I turn; go you unto your feast;
And I to weep, that am with grief oppress'd.

Sir Lanc. For ever fly my sight!—Come, gentlemen,
Let's in; I'll help you to far better wives than her.
Delia, upon my blessing talk not to her;
Base baggage, in such haste to beggary!

Flow. Jun. Sheriff, take your prisoner to your charge.

M. Flow. Uncle, by God, you have used me very hardly;
by my troth, upon my wedding-day.
*[Exeunt Sir Lancelot, Civet, Weathercock, Frances,
Delia, and their Attendants.*
Luce. O Master Flowerdale, but hear me speak.
[To Flowerdale Junior.
Stay but a little while, good master sheriff;
If not for him, for my sake pity him.
Good Sir, stop not your ears at my complaint;
My voice grows weak, for women's words are faint.
M. Flow. Look you, uncle, she kneels to you.
Flow. Jun. Fair maid, for you, I love you with my hear,
And grieve, sweet soul, thy fortune is so bad,'
That thou shouldst match with such a graceless youth.
Go to thy father, think not upon him,
Whom hell hath mark'd to be the son of shame.
Luce. Impute his wildness, Sir, unto his youth,
And think that now's the time he doth repent.
Alas, what good or gain can you receive,
To imprison him that nothing hath to pay?
And where naught is, the king doth lose his due:
O, pity him, as God shall pity you.
Flow. Jun. Lady, I know his humours all too well;
And nothing in the world can do him good,
But misery itself to chain him with.
Luce. Say that your debt were paid, then is he free?
Flow. Jun. Ay, virgin; that being answer'd, I have done.
But that to him is as impossible,
As 'twere with me to scale the pyramids.
Sheriff, take your prisoner: maiden, fare thee well.
Luce. O, go not yet, good Master Flowerdale:
Take my word for the debt, my word, my bond.
M. Flow. Ay, by God, uncle, and my bond too.
Luce. Alas, I ne'er ow'd nothing but I paid it;
And I can work: alas, he can do nothing.
I have some friends perhaps will pity me:
His chiefest friends do seek his misery.

All that I can, or beg, get, or receive,
Shall be for you. O, do not turn away:
Methinks, that one with face so reverend,
So well experienc'd in this tottering world,
Should have some feeling of a maiden's grief:
For my sake, for his father's, your brother's sake,
Ay, for your soul's sake, that doth hope for joy,
Pity my state, do not two souls destroy.

Flow. Jun. Fair maid, stand up; not in regard of him,
But in deep pity of thy hapless choice,
I do release him.—Master Sheriff, I thank you;
And officers, there is for you to drink.—
Here, maid, take this money; there is a hundred angels:
And, for I will be sure he shall not have it,
Here, Kester, take it you, and use it sparingly;
But let not her have any want at all.
Dry your eyes, niece, do not too much lament
For him whose life hath been in riot spent:
If well he useth thee, he gets him friends;
If ill, a shameful end on him depends.

[Exit Flowerdale Junior.

M. Flow. A plague go with you for an old fornicator! Come, Kit, the money; come, honest Kit.

Flow. Sen. Nay, by my faith, Sir, you shall pardon me.

M. Flow. And why, Sir, pardon you? Give me the money, you old rascal, or I will make you.

Luce. Pray, hold your hands;—give it him, honest friend.

Flow. Sen. If you be so content, with all my heart.

[Gives the money.

M. Flow. Content, Sir? 'sblood, she shall be content whether she will or no. A rattle-baby come to follow me! Go, get you gone to the greasy chuff, your father: bring me your dowry, or never look on me.

Flow. Sen. Sir, she hath forsook her father, and all her friends for you.

M. Flow. Hang thee, her friends and father, altogether!

Flow. Sen. Yet part with something to provide her lodging.

M. Flow. Yes, I mean to part with her and you; but if I part with one angel, hang me at a post. I'll rather throw them at a cast of dice, as I have done a thousand of their fellows.

Flow. Sen. Nay, then, I will be plain: degenerate boy, Thou hadst a father would have been asham'd—

M. Flow. My father was an ass, an old ass.

Flow. Sen. Thy father? O thou proud licentious villain! What are you at your foils? I'll foil with you.

Luce. Good Sir, forbear him.

Flow. Sen. Did not this whining woman hang on me, I'd teach thee what it was to abuse thy father. Go hang, beg, starve, dice, game; that when all's gone, Thou mayst after despair and hang thyself.

Luce. O, do not curse him.

Flow. Sen. I do not; but to pray for him were vain: It grieves me that he bears his father's name.

M. Flow. Well, you old rascal, I shall meet with you. Sirrah, get you gone: I will not strip the livery over your ears, because you paid for it: but do not use my name, sirrah, do you hear? Look you do not use my name, you were best.

Flow. Sen. Pay me the twenty pound then that I lent you, Or give me security when I may have it.

M. Flow. I'll pay thee not a penny, And for security, I'll give thee none. Minckins, look you do not follow me; look you, do not: If you do, beggar, I shall slit your nose.

Luce. Alas, what shall I do?

M. Flow. Why turn where: that's a good trade; And so perhaps I'll see thee now and then.

[*Exit M. Flowerdale.*

Luce. Alas the day that ever I was born!

Flow. Sen. Sweet mistress, do not weep; I'll stick to you.

Luce. Alas, my friend, I know not what to do.
My father and my friends, they have despis'd me;
And I, a wretched maid, thus cast away,
Know neither where to go, nor what to say.

Flow. Sen. It grieves me to the soul, to see her tears [*Aside.*
Thus stain the crimson roses of her cheeks.—
Lady, take comfort, do not mourn in vain;
I have a little living in this town,
The which I think comes to a hundred pound;
All that and more shall be at your dispose.
I'll straight go help you to some strange disguise,
And place you in a service in this town,
Where you shall know all, yet yourself unknown.
Come, grieve no more, where no help can be had;
Weep not for him, that is more worse than bad.

Luce. I thank you, Sir. [*Exeunt.*

ACT IV.

SCENE I. *A room in* Sir LANCELOT SPURCOCK's *house in Kent.*

Enter Sir LANCELOT, SIR ARTHUR, OLIVER, WEATHERCOCK, CIVET, FRANCES, *and* DELIA.

Oli. Well, cha 'a bin zarved many a sluttish trick, but zutch a lerripoop as thick ich was ne'er yzarved.

Sir Lanc. Son Civet, daughter Frances, bear with me:
You see how I'm press'd down with inward grief.
About that luckless girl, your sister Luce.
But 'tis fallen out
With me, as with many families beside:
They are most unhappy that are most belov'd.

Civ. Father, 'tis so, 'tis even fallen out so.
But what the remedy? set hand to heart,
And let it pass. Here is your daughter Frances
And I; and we'll not say, we will bring forth
As witty children, but as pretty children
As ever she was, though she had the prick

And praise for a pretty wench: But, father,
Dun is the mouse: you'll come?

Sir Lanc. Ay, son Civet, I'll come.

Civ. And you, Master Oliver?

Oli. Ay, for che a vext out this veast, chil see if a gan make a better veast there.

Civ. And you, Sir Arthur?

Sir Arth. Ay, Sir, although my heart be full, I'll be a partner at your wedding-feast.

Civ. And welcome all indeed, and welcome. Come, Franke, are you ready?

Fran. Jesu, how hasty these husbands are! I pray, father, pray to God to bless me.

Sir Lanc. God bless thee! and I do. God make thee wise! Send you both joy! I wish it with wet eyes.

Fran. But, father, shall not my sister Delia go along with us? she is excellent good at cookery, and such things.

Sir Lanc. Yes, marry shall she: Delia, make you ready.

Del. I am ready, Sir. I will first go to Greenwich; from thence to my cousin Chesterfield's, and so to London.

Civ. It shall suffice, good sister Delia, it shall suffice; but fail us not, good sister: give order to cooks and others; for I would not have my sweet Franke to soil her fingers.

Fran. No, by my troth, not I. A gentlewoman, and a married gentlewoman too, to be companion to cooks and kitchen-boys! Not I, i' faith; I scorn that.

Civ. Why, I do not mean thou shalt, sweetheart; thou seest I do not go about it. Well, farewell to you.—God's pity, Master Weathercock! we shall have your company too?

Weath. With all my heart, for I love good cheer.

Civ. Well, God be with you all.—Come, Franke.

Fran. God be with you, father; God be with you. Sir Arthur, Master Oliver, and Master Weathercock, sister, God be with you all: God be with you, father; God be with you, every one.   [*Exeunt Civet and Frances.*

Weath. Why, how now, Sir Arthur? all a-mort?
Master Oliver, how now, man?
Cheerily, Sir Lancelot; and merrily say,
Who can hold that will away?

Sir Lanc. Ay, she is gone indeed, poor girl, undone;
But when they'll be self-will'd, children must smart.

Sir Arth. But, Sir,
That she is wrong'd, you are the chiefest cause;
Therefore, 'tis reason you redress her wrong.

Weath. Indeed you must, Sir Lancelot, you must.

Sir Lanc. Must? who can compel me, Master Weathercock?
I hope I may do what I list.

Weath. I grant you may; you may do what you list.

Oli. Nay, but an you be well avisen, it were not good, by this vrampolness and vrowardness, to cast away as pretty a Dowsabel as an chould chance to see in a summer's day. Chil tell you what chall do; chil go spy up and down the town, and see if I can hear any tale or tydings of her, and take her away from thick a messel; vor cham assured, he'll but bring her to the spoil; and so vare you well. We shall meet at your son Civet's.

Sir Lanc. I thank you, Sir; I take it very kindly.

Sir Arth. To find her out, I'll spend my dearest blood;
So well I lov'd her, to effect her good.

[Exeunt Civet and Sir Arthur.

Sir Lanc. O Master Weathercock, what hap had I,
To force my daughter from Master Oliver,
And this good knight, to one that hath no goodness
In his thought?

Weath. Ill luck; but what remedy?

Sir Lanc. Yes, I've almost devis'd a remedy:
Young Flowerdale is sure a prisoner.

Weath. Sure; nothing more sure.

Sir Lanc. And yet perhaps his uncle hath releas'd him.

Weath. It may be very like; no doubt he hath.

Sir Lanc. Well, if he be in prison, I'll have warrants

T'attach my daughter till the law be tried;
For I will sue him upon cozenage.
　Weath. Marry, you may, and overthrow him too.
　Sir Lanc. Nay, that's not so; I may chance to be scoff'd
And sentence pass'd with him.
　Weath. Believe me, so it may; therefore take heed.
　Sir Lanc. Well howsoever, yet I will have warrants;
In prison, or at liberty, all's one:
You 'll help to serve them, Master Weathercock?
　　　　　　　　　　　　　　　　　　　[*Exeunt.*

Scene II. *A street in London.*

Enter Matthew Flowerdale.

　M. Flow. A plague of the devil! the devil take the dice! the dice and the devil and his dam go together! Of all my hundred golden angels, I have not left me one denier. A pox of *come a five!* What shall I do? I can borrow no more of my credit: there's not any of my acquaintance, man nor boy, but I have borrowed more or less of. I would I knew where to take a good purse, and go clear away; by this light, I'll venture for it. God's lid, my sister Delia! I'll rob her, by this hand.

Enter Delia *and* Artichoke.

　Del. I prithee, Artichoke, go not so fast;
The weather's hot, and I am something weary.
　Art. Nay, I warrant you, Mistress Delia, I'll not tire you with leading; we'll go an extreme moderate pace.
　M. Flow. Stand; deliver your purse.
　Art. O Lord, thieves, thieves! 　　　　[*Exit Artichoke.*
　M. Flow. Come, come, your purse, lady; your purse.
　Del. That voice I have heard often before this time;
What, brother Flowerdale become a thief?
　M. Flow. Ay, plague on't, I thank your father: but sister,
Come, your money, come. What!
'The world must find me; I am born to live;
'Tis not a sin to steal, where none will give.

Del. O God, is all grace banish'd from thy heart?
Think of the shame that doth attend this fact.

M. Flow. Shame me no shames. Come, give me your
    purse;
I'll bind you, sister, lest I fare the worse.

Del. No, bind me not: hold, there is all I have;
And would that money would redeem thy shame.

Enter OLIVER, SIR ARTHUR, *and* ARTICHOKE.

Art. Thieves, thieves, thieves!

Oli. Thieves! where man? why, how now, Mistress Delia.
Ha' you yliked to been yrobbed?

Del. No, Master Oliver; 'tis Master Flowerdale; he did
but jest with me.

Oli. How, Flowerdale, that scoundrel? Sirrah, you meten
us well; vang thee that.   [*Strikes him.*

M. Flow. Well, Sir, I'll not meddle with you, because I
have a charge.

Del. Here, brother Flowerdale, I'll lend you this same
money.

M. Flow. I thank you, sister.

Oli. I wad you were ysplit, an you let the messel have a
penny; but since you cannot keep it, chil keep it myself.

Sir Arth. "Tis pity to relieve him in this sort,
Who makes a trompant life his daily sport.

Del. Brother, you see how all men censure you:
Farewell; and I pray God amend your life.

Oli. Come, chil bring you along, and you, safe enough
from twenty such scoundrels as thick a one is. Farewell, and
be hanged, zyrrah, as I think so thou wilt be shortly. Come,
Sir Arthur.   [*Exeunt all but M. Flowerdale.*

M. Flow. A plague go with you for a kersey rascal.
This Devonshire man I think is made all of pork:
His hands made only for to heave up packs;
His heart as fat and big as is his face;
As differing far from all brave gallant minds,
As I to serve the hogs, and drink with hinds;

As I am very near now. Well, what remedy?
When money, means, and friends, do grow so small,
Then farewell life, and there's an end of all. [*Exit.*

SCENE III. *Another street. Before* CIVET'S *house.*

Enter FLOWERDALE SENIOR, LUCE, *like a Dutch frow,* CIVET, *and* FRANCES.

Civ. By my troth, God-a-mercy for this, good Christopher. I thank thee for my maid; I like her very well. How dost thou like her, Frances?

Fran. In good sadness, Tom, very well, excellent well; she speaks so prettily:—I pray, what's your name?

Luce. My name, forsooth, be called Tanikin.

Fran. By my troth, a fine name. O Tanikin, you are excellent for dressing one's head a new fashion.

Luce. Me sall do every ting about de head.

Civ. What countrywoman is she, Kester?

Flow. Sen. A Dutch woman, Sir.

Civ. Why, then, she is outlandish, is she not?

Flow. Sen. Ay, Sir, she is.

Fran. O, then, thou canst tell how to help me to cheeks and ears.

Luce. Yes, mistress, very well.

Flow. Sen. Cheeks and ears! why, Mistress Frances, want you cheeks and ears? methinks you have very fair ones.

Fran. Thou art a fool, indeed. Tom, thou knowest what I mean.

Civ. Ay, ay, Kester; 'tis such as they wear a' their heads. I prithee, Kit, have her in, and show her my house.

Flow. Sen. I will, Sir.—Come, Tanikin.

Fran. O Tom, you have not bussed me to-day, Tom.

Civ. No, Frances, we must not kiss afore folks. God save me, Franke. See yonder; my sister Delia is come.

Enter DELIA *and* ARTICHOKE.

Welcome, good sister.

Fran. Welcome, good sister. How do you like the tire of my head?

Del. Very well, sister.

Civ. I am glad you're come, sister Delia, to give order for supper; they will be here soon.

Art. Ay, but if good luck had not served, she had not been here now. Filching Flowerdale had like to have peppered us; but for Master Oliver, we had been robbed.

Del. Peace, sirrah, no more.

Flow. Sen. Robbed! by whom?

Art. Marry, by none but by Flowerdale; he is turned thief.

Civ. By my faith, but that is not well; but, God be praised for your escape. Will you draw near, sister?

Flow. Sen. Sirrah, come hither. Would Flowerdale, he that was my master, have robbed you? I prithee tell me true.

Art. Yes, i' faith, even that Flowerdale that was thy master.

Flow. Sen. Hold thee; there is a French crown, and speak no more of this. [*Aside.*

Art. Not I, not a word. [Aside] Now do I smell knavery: in every purse Flowerdale takes, he is half; and gives me this to keep counsel.—Not a word, I.

Flow. Sen. Why, God-a-mercy.

Fran. Sister, look here; I have a new Dutch maid, and she speaks so fine, it would do your heart good.

Civ. How do you like her, sister?

Del. I like your maid well.

Civ. Well, dear sister, will you draw near, and give directions for supper? The guests will be here presently.

Del. Yes, brother; lead the way; I'll follow you.

[*Exeunt all except Delia and Luce.*

Hark you, Dutch frow, a word?
 Luce. Vat is your vill vit me?
 Del. Sister Luce, 'tis not your broken language,
Nor this same habit, can disguise your face
From I that know you. Pray, tell me, what means this?
 Luce. Sister, I see you know me; yet be secret:
This borrow'd shape that I have ta'en upon me,
Is but to keep myself a space unknown,
Both from my father, and my nearest friends;
Until I see how time will bring to pass
The desperate course of Master Flowerdale.
 Del. O, he is worse than bad; I prithee leave him,
And let not once thy heart to think on him.
 Luce. Do not persuade me once to such a thought.
Imagine yet that he is worse than naught;
Yet one hour's time may all that ill undo
That all his former life did run into.
Therefore, kind sister, do not disclose my estate;
If e'er his heart doth turn, 'tis ne'er too late.
 Del. Well, seeing no counsel can remove your mind,
I'll not disclose you that are wilful blind.
 Luce. Delia, I thank you. I now must please her eyes,
My sister Franke, who's neither fair nor wise. [*Exeunt.*

ACT V.

SCENE I. *A street before* CIVET's *house.*

Enter MATTHEW FLOWERDALE.

M. Flow. On goes he that knows no end of his journey.
I have passed the very utmost bounds of shifting; I have no
course now but to hang myself. I have lived since yesterday
two o'clock on a spice-cake I had at a burial; and for drink,
I got it at an ale-house among porters, such as will bear out
a man if he have no money indeed; I mean—out of their

companies, for they are men of good carriage. Who comes here? the two coney-catchers that won all my money of me. I'll try if they'll lend me any.

Enter DICK *and* RALPH.

What, Master Richard, how do you? How dost thou, Ralph? By God, gentlemen, the world grows bare with me; will you do as much as lend me an angel between you both? You know, you won a hundred of me the other day.

Ralph. How! an angel? God damn us if we lost not every penny within an hour after thou wert gone.

M. Flow. I prithee lend me so much as will pay for my supper. I'll pay you again, as I am a gentleman.

Ralph. I' faith, we 've not a farthing, not a mite.
I wonder at it, Master Flowerdale,
You will so carelessly undo yourself.
Why, you will lose more money in an hour,
Than any honest man spends in a year.
For shame! betake you to some honest trade,
And live not thus so like a vagabond.

[*Exeunt Dick and Ralph.*

M. Flow. A vagabond, indeed! more villains you:
They give me counsel that first cozen'd me.
Those devils first brought me to this I am,
And being thus, the first that do me wrong.
Well, yet I have one friend left me in store:
Not far from hence there dwells a cockatrice,
One that I first put in a satin gown;
And not a tooth that dwells within her head,
But stands me at the least in twenty pound:
Her will I visit now my coin is gone;
And as I take it here dwells the gentlewoman. [*Knocks.*
What ho, is Mistress Apricock within?

Enter RUFFIAN.

Ruf. What saucy rascal 's that which knocks so bold?

O, is it you, old spendthrift? Are you here?
One that 's turn'd cozener about the town?
My mistress saw you, and sends this word by me;
Either be packing quickly from the door,
Or you shall have such greeting sent you straight
As you will little like: you had best be gone. *[Exit.*
  M. Flow. Why, so, this is as it should be; being poor,
Thus art thou serv'd by a vile painted whore.
Well, since thy damned crew do so abuse me,
I'll try of honest men, how they will use me.

Enter an ancient Citizen.

Sir, I beseech you to take compassion of a man; one whose fortunes have been better than at this instant they seem to be; but if I might crave of you so much little portion as would bring me to my friends, I would rest thankful until I had requited so great a courtesy.
  Cit. Fie, fie, young man! this course is very bad.
Too many such have we about this city;
Yet, for I have not seen you in this sort,
Nor noted you to be a common beggar,
Hold; there's an angel to bear your charges down.
Go to your friends; do not on this depend:
Such bad beginnings oft have worser end. *[Exit Citizen.*
  M. Flow. Worser end! nay, if it fall out no worse than in old angels, I care not. Nay, now I have had such a fortunate beginning, I'll not let a sixpenny purse escape me:—By the mass, here comes another.

Enter a Citizen's Wife, *and a* Servant, *with a torch before her.*

God bless you, fair mistress. Now would it please you, gentlewoman, to look into the wants of a poor gentleman, a younger brother: I doubt not but God will treble restore it

back again; one that never before this time demanded penny,
halfpenny, nor farthing.

Cit. Wife. Stay, Alexander. Now, by my troth, a very
proper man; and 'tis great pity. Hold, my friend; there's
all the money I have about me, a couple of shillings; and
God bless thee.

M. Flow. Now, God thank you, sweet lady. If you have
any friend, or garden-house where you may employ a poor
gentleman as your friend, I am yours to command in all
secret service.

Cit. Wife. I thank you, good friend; I prithee let me
see that again I gave thee; there is one of them a brass shilling:
give me them, and here is half a crown in gold. [*He
gives the money to her.*] Now, out upon thee, rascal! Secret
service—what dost thou make of me? It were a good deed
to have thee whipped! Now I have my money again, I'll see
thee hanged before I give thee a penny. Secret service!—
On, good Alexander. [*Exeunt Citizen's Wife and Servant.*

M. Flow. This is villanous luck; I perceive dishonesty
will not thrive. Here comes more. God forgive me, Sir
Arthur and Master Oliver. Afore God, I'll speak to them.

Enter Sir ARTHUR *and* OLIVER.

God save you, Sir Arthur; God save you, Master Oliver.

Oli. Been you there, zirrah? come, will you ytaken yourself
to your tools, coystrel?

M. Flow. Nay, Master Oliver, I'll not fight with you.
Alas, Sir, you know it was not my doings;
It was only a plot to get Sir Lancelot's daughter:
By God, I never meant you harm.

Oli. And where is the gentlewoman thy wife, messel?
where is she, zirrah, ha!

M. Flow. By my troth, Master Oliver, sick, very sick:
and God is my judge, I know not what means to take for
her, good gentlewoman.

Oli. Tell me true; is she sick? tell me true, ich 'vise thee.

M. Flow. Yes, 'faith, I tell you true, Master Oliver; if you would do me the small kindness but to lend me forty shillings, so God help me, I will pay you so soon as my ability shall make me able;—as I am a gentleman.

Oli. Well, thou zaist thy wife is zick; hold, there's vorty shillings; give it to thy wife. Look thou, give it her, or I shall zo veeze thee, thou wert not zo veezed this zeven year; look to it.

Sir Arth. I' faith, Master Oliver, 'tis in vain
To give to him that never thinks of her.

Oli. Well, would che could yvind it.

M. Flow. I tell you true, Sir Arthur, as I am a gentleman.

Oli. Well, farewell zirrah: come, Sir Arthur.
[*Exeunt Sir Arthur and Oliver.*

M. Flow. By the Lord, this is excellent;
Five golden angels compass'd in an hour:
If this trade hold, I'll never seek a new;
Welcome, sweet gold, and beggary adieu.

Enter FLOWERDALE SENIOR *and* FLOWERDALE JUNIOR.

Flow. Jun. See, Kester, if you can find the house.

M. Flow. Who's here? My uncle and my man Kester? By the mass, 'tis they. How do you, uncle? how dost thou, Kester? By my troth, uncle, you must needs lend me some money. The poor gentlewoman my wife, so God help me, is very sick: I was robbed of the hundred angels you gave me; they are gone.

Flow. Jun. Ay, they are gone indeed. Come, Kester, away.

M. Flow. Nay, uncle; do you hear, good uncle?

Flow. Jun. Out, hypocrite, I will not hear thee speak: Come, leave him, Kester.

M. Flow.   Kester, honest Kester!

Flow. Sen. Sir, I have naught to say to you.—Open the door to me, 'Kin: thou hadst best lock it fast, for there's a false knave without.

[*Flowerdale Senior and Flowerdale Junior go in.*
M. Flow. You are an old lying rascal, so you are.

Enter LUCE *from* CIVET's *house.*
Luce. Vat is de matter? Vat be you, yonker?
M. Flow. By this light, a Dutch frow; they say they are called kind. By this light, I'll try her.
Luce. Vat bin you, yonker? why do you not speak?
M. Flow. By my troth, sweetheart, a poor gentleman, that would desire of you, if it stand with your liking, the bounty of your purse.

Re-enter FLOWERDALE SENIOR.
Luce. O hear, God! so young an armin!
M. Flow. Armin, sweetheart? I know not what you mean by that; but I am almost a beggar.
Luce. Are you not a married man? vere bin your vife? Here is all I have; take dis.
M. Flow. What, gold, young frow? this is brave.
Flow. Sen. If he have any grace, he'll now repent. [*Aside.*
Luce. Why speak you not? vere be your vife?
M. Flow. Dead, dead, she's dead; 'tis she hath undone me. Spent me all I had, and kept rascals under my nose to brave me.
Luce. Did you use her vell?
M. Flow. Use her! there's never a gentlewoman in England could be better used than I did her. I could but coach her; her diet stood me in forty pound a month: but she is dead; and in her grave my cares are buried.
Luce. Indeed, dat vas not shoen.
Flow. Sen. He is turn'd more devil than he was before.
[*Aside.*
M. Flow. Thou dost belong to Master Civet here: dost thou not?

Luce. Yes, me do.

M. Flow. Why, there's it! There's not a handful of plate but belongs to me. God's my judge, if I had such a wench as thou art, there's never a man in England would make more of her than I would do—so she had any stock.

[*Voice within,* Tanikin!

Luce. Stay; one doth call: I shall come by-and-by again.

[*Call within. Exit Luce.*

M. Flow. By this hand, this Dutch wench is in love with me. Were it not admirable to make her steal all Civet's plate, and run away?

Flow. Sen. It were beastly. O Master Flowerdale,
Have you no fear of God, nor conscience?
What do you mean by this vile course you take?

M. Flow. What do I mean? why, to live; that I mean.

Flow. Sen. To live in this sort? Fie upon the course:
Your life doth show, you are a very coward.

M. Flow. A coward! I pray, in what?

Flow. Sen. Why, you will borrow sixpence of a boy.

M. Flow. 'Snails, is there such cowardice in that? I dare borrow it of a man, ay, and of the tallest man in England,— if he will lend it me: let me borrow it how I can, and let them come by it how they dare. And it is well known, I might have rid out a hundred times if I would, so I might.

Flow. Sen. It was not want of will, but cowardice.
There is none that lends to you, but know they gain:
And what is that but only stealth in you?
Delia might hang you now, did not her heart
Take pity of you for her sister's sake.
Go, get you hence, lest ling'ring here your stay,
You fall into their hands you look not for.

M. Flow. I'll tarry here, till the Dutch frow comes, if all the devils in hell were here.

[*Flowerdale Senior goes into Civet's house.*

Enter Sir LANCELOT, Master WEATHERCOCK, *and* ARTICHOKE.

Sir Lanc. Where is the door? are we not past it, Artichoke?

Art. By the mass, here's one; I'll ask him. Do you hear, Sir? What, are you so proud? Do you hear? Which is the way to Master Civet's house? What, will you not speak? O me! this is filching Flowerdale.

Sir Lanc. O wonderful! is this lewd villain here?
You cheating rogue, you cut-purse, coney-catcher!
What ditch, you villain, is my daughter's grave?
A cozening rascal that must make a will,
Take on him a strict habit, feigning that,
When he should turn to angel, dying grace.
I'll father-in-law you, Sir, I'll make a will;
Speak, villain, where's my daughter?
Poison'd, I warrant you, or knock'd o' the head:
And to abuse good Master Weathercock,
With his forged will; make
To shake my grounded resolution.
Then to abuse the De'nshire gentleman:
Go; away with him to prison.

M. Flow. Wherefore to prison? Sir, I will not go.

Enter CIVET *and his* Wife, OLIVER, Sir ARTHUR, FLOWERDALE SENIOR, FLOWERDALE JUNIOR, *and* DELIA.

Sir Lanc. O, here's his uncle: welcome, gentlemen, welcome all. Such a cozener, gentlemen, a murderer too, for anything I know! My daughter is missing; hath been looked for; cannot be found.—A vild upon thee!

Flow. Jun. He is my kinsman, though his life be vile: Therefore, in God's name, do with him what you will.

Sir Lanc. Marry, to prison.

M. Flow. Wherefore to prison? snick-up; I owe you nothing.

Sir Lanc. Bring forth my daughter, then; away with him.
M. Flow. Go seek your daughter. What do you lay to my charge?
Sir Lanc. Suspicion of murder. Go; away with him.
M. Flow. Murder your dogs! I murder your daughter? Come, uncle, I know you'll bail me.
Flow. Jun. Not I, were there no more than I the gaoler, thou the prisoner.
Sir Lanc. Go; away with him.

Enter LUCE.

Luce. O' my life, hear: where will you ha' de man? Vat ha' do yonker done?
Weath. Woman, he hath killed his wife.
Luce. His wife! dat is not good; dat is not shoen.
Sir Lanc. Hang not upon him, huswife; if you do, I'll lay you by him.
Luce. Have me no oder way dan you have him: He tell me dat he love me heartily.
Fran. Lead away my maid to prison; why, Tom, will you suffer that?
Civ. No, by your leave, father, she is no vagrant; she is my wife's chamber-maid, and as true as the skin between any man's brows here.
Sir Lanc. Go to, you're both fools.
Son Civet, of my life, this is a plot;
Some straggling counterfeit preferr'd to you,
No doubt to rob you of your plate and jewels:—
I'll have you led away to prison, trull.
Luce. I am no trull, neither outlandish frow:
Nor he nor I shall to the prison go.
Know you me now? nay, never stand amaz'd.
            [*Throws off her Dutch dress.*
Father, I know I have offended you;
And though that duty wills me bend my knees
To you in duty and obedience,

Yet this way do I turn, and to him yield
My love, my duty, and my humbleness.
   Sir Lanc. Bastard in nature! yield to such a slave?
   Luce. O Master Flowerdale, if too much grief
Have not stopp'd up the organs of your voice,
Then speak to her that is thy faithful wife;
Or doth contempt of me thus tie thy tongue?
Turn not away; I am no Æthiop,
No wanton Cressid, nor a changing Helen;
But rather one made wretched by thy loss.
What! turn'st thou still from me? O, then,
I guess thee wofull'st among hapless men.
   M. Flow. I am, indeed, wife, wonder among wives!
Thy chastity and virtue hath infus'd
Another soul in me, red with defame,
For in my blushing cheeks is seen my shame.
   Sir Lanc. Out, hypocrite! I charge thee, trust him not.
   Luce. Not trust him? By the hopes of after-bliss,
I know no sorrow can be compar'd to his.
   Sir Lanc. Well, since thou wert ordain'd to beggary,
Follow thy fortune: I defy thee, I.
   Oli. I wood che were so well ydoussed as was ever white cloth in a tocking mill, an che ha' not made me weep.
   Flow. Sen. If he hath any grace, he'll now repent.
   Sir Arth. It moves my heart.
   Weath. By my troth, I must weep, I cannot choose.
   Flow. Jun. None but a beast would such a maid misuse.
   M. Flow. Content thyself, I hope to win his favour,
And to redeem my reputation lost:
And, gentlemen, believe me, I beseech you;
I hope your eyes shall soon behold such change
As shall deceive your expectation.
   Oli. I would che were ysplit now, but che believe him.
   Sir Lanc. How, believe him?
   Weath. By the mackins, I do.
   Sir Lanc. What, do you think that e'er he will have grace?

Weath. By my faith, it will go hard.

Oli. Well, che vore ye, he is changed. And, Master Flowerdale, in hope you been so, hold, there's vorty pound toward your zetting up. What! be not ashamed; vang it, man, vang it: be a good husband, loven to your wife; and you shall not want for vorty more, I che vore thee.

Sir Arth. My means are little, but, if you'll follow me,
I will instruct you in my ablest power;
But, to your wife I give this diamond,
And prove true diamond-fair in all your life.

M. Flow. Thanks, good Sir Arthur: Master Oliver,
You being my enemy, and grown so kind,
Binds me in all endeavour to restore—

Oli. What! restore me no restorings, man; I have vorty pound more for Luce here; vang it: zooth chil devy London else. What, do you think me a messel or a scoundrel, to throw away my money? Che have an hundred pound more to pace of any good spotation. I hope your under and your uncle will vollow my zamples.

Flow. Jun. You have guess'd right of me; if he leave off
This course of life, he yet shall be mine heir.

Sir Lanc. But he shall never get a groat of me.
A cozener, a deceiver, one that kill'd
His painful father, honest gentleman,
That pass'd the fearful danger of the sea,
To get him living, and maintain him brave.

Weath. What, hath he kill'd his father?

Sir Lanc. Ay, Sir, with conceit of his vile courses.

Flow. Sen. Sir, you are misinform'd.

Sir Lanc. Why, thou old knave, thou told'st me so thyself.

Flow. Sen. I wrong'd him, then: and towards my master's stock
There's twenty nobles for to make amends.

M. Flow. No, Kester, I have troubled thee, and wrong'd thee more;
What thou in love giv'st, I in love restore.

18*

Fran. Ha, ha, sister! there you played bo-peep with Tom. What shall I give her toward household? sister Delia, shall I give her my fan?

Del. You were best ask your husband.

Fran. Shall I, Tom?

Civ. Ay, do, Franke; I'll buy thee a new one with a longer handle.

Fran. A russet one, Tom.

Civ. Ay, with russet feathers.

Fran. Here, sister; there's my fan toward household, to keep you warm.

Luce. I thank you, sister.

Weath. Why, this is well: and toward fair Luce's stock, Here's forty shillings: and forty good shillings more, I'll give her, marry. Come, Sir Lancelot, I must have you friends.

Sir Lanc. Not I: all this is counterfeit; he will consume it, were it a million.

Flow. Sen. Sir, what is your daughter's dower worth?

Sir Lanc. Had she been married to an honest man, It had been better than a thousand pound.

Flow. Sen. Pay it to him, and I'll give you my bond To make her jointure better worth than three.

Sir Lanc. Your bond, Sir! why, what are you?

Flow. Sen. One whose word in London, though I say it, Will pass there for as much as yours.

Sir Lanc. Wert not thou late that unthrift's serving-man?

Flow. Sen. Look on me better, now my scar is off: Ne'er muse, man, at this metamorphosis.

[*Discovers himself.*

Sir Lanc. Master Flowerdale!

M. Flow. My father! O, I shame to look on him. Pardon, dear father, the follies that are past.

Flow. Sen. Son, son, I do; and joy at this thy change, And applaud thy fortune in this virtuous maid, Whom heaven hath sent to thee to save thy soul.

Luce. This addeth joy to joy; high heaven be prais'd.
Weath. Welcome from death, good Master Flowerdale!
'Twas said so here, 'twas said so here, good faith.
Flow. Sen. I caus'd that rumour to be spread myself,
Because I'd see the humours of my son,
Which to relate the circumstance is needless.—
And, sirrah, see
You run no more into that same disease:
For he that's once cur'd of that malady,
Of riot, swearing, drunkenness, and pride,
And falls again into the like distress,
That fever's deadly, doth till death endure:
Such men die mad, as of a calenture.
 M. Flow. Heaven helping me, I'll hate the course as
   hell.
 Flow. Jun. Say it, and do it, cousin, all is well.
 Sir Lanc. Well, being in hope you'll prove an honest man,
I take you to my favour. Brother Flowerdale,
Welcome with all my heart: I see your care
Hath brought these acts to this conclusion,
And I am glad of it. Come, let's in, and feast.
 Oli. Nay, zoft you a while. You promised to make Sir
Arthur and me amends: here is your wisest daughter; see
which on us she'll have.
 Sir Lanc. A God's name, you have my good will; get hers.
 Oli. How say you, then, damsel?
 Del. I, Sir, am yours.
 Oli. Why, then, send for a vicar, and chil have it de-
spatched in a trice; so chil.
 Del. Pardon me, Sir; I mean that I am yours
In love, in duty, and affection;
But not to love as wife: it shall ne'er be said,
Delia was buried married, but a maid.
 Sir Arth. Do not condemn yourself for ever thus,
Most virtuous fair; for you were born to love.
 Oli. Why, you say true, Sir Arthur; she was ybore to it,

so well as her mother:—but, I pray you, show us some zamples
or reasons why you will not marry?

Del. Not that I do condemn a married life
(For 'tis, no doubt, a sanctimonious thing):
But for the care and crosses of a wife,
The trouble in this world that children bring;
My vow's in heaven, on earth to live alone;
Husbands, however good, I will have none.

Oli. Why, then, che will live a bachelor too. Che zet not
a vig by a wife, if a wife zet not a vig by me.—Come, shall's
go to dinner?

Flow. Sen. To-morrow I crave your companies in Mark-
lane:
To-night we'll frolic in Master Civet's house,
And to each health drink down a full carouse.   [*Exeunt.*

THE BIRTH OF MERLIN,

OR,

THE CHILD HATH FOUND HIS FATHER.

DRAMATIS PERSONÆ.

AURELIUS, king of Britain.
VORTIGER, king of Britain.
UTER PENDRAGON, the Prince, brother to AURELIUS.
DONOBERT, a nobleman, and father to CONSTANTIA and MODESTIA.
The Earl of GLOSTER, father to EDWIN.
EDOL, Earl of Chester, and general to King AURELIUS.
CADOR, Earl of Cornwal, and Sutor to CONSTANTIA.
EDWIN, son to the Earl of Gloster, and suitor to MODESTIA.
TOCLIO and OSWALD, two noblemen.
MERLIN, the prophet.
ANSELME, the hermit, after bishop of Winchester.
Clown, brother to JOAN, mother of MERLIN.
Sir NICODEMUS Nothing, a courtier.
The Devil, father of MERLIN.
OSTORIUS, a Saxon general.
OCTA, the Saxon nobleman.
PROXIMUS, a Saxon magician.
Two bishops.
Two Saxon lords.
Two of EDOL's captains.
Two gentlemen.
A little antick spirit.

ARTESIA, sister to OSTORIUS the Saxon general.
CONSTANTIA, } daughters to
MODESTIA, } DONOBERT.
JOAN Go-to-'t, mother of MERLIN.
A waiting-woman to ARTESIA.
LUCINA, Queen of the Shades.

SCENE.—*Britain.*

ACT I.

SCENE I. *Enter* DONOBERT, GLOSTER, CADOR, EDWIN, CONSTANTIA *and* MODESTIA.

Cador. You teach me language, sir, as one that knows
The debt of love I owe unto their virtues;

Wherein like a true courtier I have fed
Myself with hope of fair success, and now
Attend your wish'd consent to my long suit.
   Dono. Believe me, youthful lord,
'Time could not give an opportunity
More fitting your desires; always provided,
My daughter's love be suited with my grant.
   Cador. 'Tis the condition, sir, her promise seal'd.
   Dono. Is't so, Constantia?
   Const. I was content to give him words for oaths,
He swore so oft he lov'd me.
   Dono. That thou believest him?
   Const. He is a man, I hope.
   Dono. That's in the trial, girl.
   Const. However, I am a woman, sir.
   Dono. The law's on thy side then, sha't have a husband,
Ay, and a worthy one.—Take her, brave Cornwal,
And make our happiness great as our wishes.
   Cador. Sir, I thank you.
   Glost. Double the fortunes of the day, my lord,
And crown my wishes too: I have a son here,
Who in my absence would protest no less
Unto your other daughter.
   Dono. Ha, Gloster, is it so? what says Lord Edwin?
Will she protest as much to thee?
   Edw. Else must she want some of her sister's faith, sir.
   Mod. Of her credulity much rather, sir.
My lord, you are a soldier, and methinks
The height of that profession should diminish
All heat of love's desires,
Being so late employ'd in blood and ruin.
   Edw. The more my conscience ties me to repair
The world's losses in a new succession.
   Mod. Necessity, it seems, ties your affections then,
And at that rate I would unwillingly
Be thrust upon you; a wife's a dish soon cloys, sir.
   Edw. Weak and diseasèd appetites it may.

Mod. Most of your making have dull stomachs, sir.
Dono. If that be all, girl, thou shalt quicken him,
Be kind to him, Modestia.—Noble Edwin,
Let it suffice, what's mine in her, speaks yours;
For her consent, let your fair suit go on,
She is a woman, sir, and will be won.
   Edw. You give me comfort, sir.

Enter TOCLIO.

Dono. Now, Toclio?
Toclio. The King, my honour'd lords, requires your presence,
And calls a council for return of answer
Unto the parling enemy, whose ambassadors
Are on the way to court.
   Dono.   So suddenly?
Chester, it seems, has plied them hard at war,
They sue so fast for peace, which by my advice
They ne'er shall have, unless they leave the realm.
Come, noble Gloster, let's attend the king;
It lies, sir, in your son to do me pleasure,
And save the charges of a wedding-dinner;
If you'll make haste to end your love-affairs,
One cost may give discharge to both my cares.
[*Exeunt Donobert and Gloster.*

   Edw. I'll do my best.
   Cador. Now, Toclio, what stirring news at court?
   Toclio. O my lord, the court's all filled with rumour, the city with news, and the country with wonder, and all the bells i' the kingdom must proclaim it, we have a new holy-day a coming.
   Const. A holy-day! for whom? for thee?
   Toclio. Me, Madam! 'sfoot! I'd be loath that any man should make a holy-day for me yet:
In brief, 'tis thus: There's here arriv'd at court,
Sent by the Earl of Chester to the king,
A man of rare esteem for holiness,

A reverend hermit, that by miracle
Not onely sav'd our army,
But without aid of man o'erthrew
The pagan host, and with such wonder, sir,
As might confirm a kingdom to his faith.
 Edw. This is strange news, indeed; where is he?
 Toclio. In conference with the king, that much respects
  him.
 Mod. Trust me, I long to see him.
 Toclio. 'Faith, you will find no great pleasure in him', for aught that I can see, lady; they say, he is half a prophet too. 'Would he could tell me any news of the lost prince, there's twenty talents offer'd to him that finds him.
 Cador. Such news was breeding in the morning.
 Toclio. And now it has birth and life, sir. If fortune bless me, I'll once more search those woods where then we lost him; I know not yet what fate may follow me. [*Exit.*
 Cador. Fortune go with you, sir.—Come, fair mistress,
Your sister and Lord Edwin are in game,
And all their wits at stake to win the set.
 Const. My sister has the hand yet, we had best leave them,
She will be out anon, as well as I:
He wants but cunning to put in a die. [*Exeunt Cador and Const.*
 Edw. You are a cunning gamester, Madam.
 Mod. It is a desperate game, indeed, this marriage,
Where there's no winning without loss to either.
 Edw. Why, what but your perfection, noble lady,
Can bar the worthiness of this my suit?
If so you please, I count my happiness,
From difficult obtaining, you shall see
My duty and observance.
 Mod. There shall be place to neither, noble sir:
I do beseech you, let this mild reply
Give answer to your suit; for here I vow,
If e'er I change my virgin name, by you
It gains or loses.
 Edw. My wishes have their crown.

Mod. Let them confine you then.
As to my promise, you give faith and credence?
Edw. In your command, my willing absence speaks it.
[*Exit.*
Mod. Noble and virtuous! could I dream of marriage,
I should affect thee, Edwin: O, my soul,
Here's something tells me, that these best of creatures,
These models of the world, weak man and woman,
Should have their souls, their making, life and being,
To some more excellent use: if what the sense
Calls pleasure were our ends, we might justly blame
Great nature's wisdom, who rear'd a building
Of so much art and beauty, to entertain
A guest so far incertain, so imperfect:
If only speech distinguish us from beasts,
Who know no inequality of birth or place,
But still to fly from goodness: O, how base
Were life at such a rate! No, no, that Power
That gave to man his being, speech, and wisdom,
Gave it for thankfulness. To him alone
That made me thus, may I thence truly know,
I'll pay to him, not man, the love I owe. [*Exit.*

SCENE II. *Flourish Cornets. Enter* AURELIUS, DONOBERT,
GLOSTER, CADOR, EDWIN, TOCLIO, OSWALD, *and* Attendants.

Aur. No tiding of our brother yet? 'Tis strange,
So near the court, and in our own land too,
And yet no news of him: O, this loss
Tempers the sweetness of our happy conquests
With much untimely sorrow.
Dono. Royal sir,
His safety, being unquestion'd, should to time
Leave the redress of sorrow. Were he dead,
Or taken by the foe, our fatal loss
Had wanted no quick herald to disclose it.
Aur. That hope alone sustains me,

Nor will we be so ungrateful unto heaven,
To question what we fear with what we enjoy.
Is answer of our message yet return'd
From that religious man, the holy hermit,
Sent by the Earl of Chester to confirm us
In that miraculous act? For 'twas no less,
Our army being in rout, nay, quite o'erthrown,
As Chester writes; even then this holy man
Arm'd with his cross and staff, went smiling on,
And boldly fronts the foe; at sight of whom
The Saxons stood amaz'd; for, to their seeming,
Above the hermit's head appear'd such brightness,
Such clear and glorious beams, as if our men
March'd all in fire, wherewith the pagans fled
And by our troops were all to death pursu'd.

    Glost. 'Tis full of wonder, sir.

    Aur. O Gloster, he's a jewel worth a kingdom.
Where's Oswald with his answer?

    Osw. 'Tis here, my royal lord.

    Aur.   In writing?
Will he not sit with us?

    Osw. His orizons perform'd, he bad me say,
He would attend with all submission.

    Aur. Proceed to council then, and let some give order,
The ambassadors being come, to take our answer,
They have admittance. Oswald, Toclio,
Be it your charge: And now, my lords, observe
The holy counsel of this reverend hermit: [*reads*]
"As you respect your safety, limit not
That only power that hath protected you;
Trust not an open enemy too far,
He's yet a loser, and knows you have won,
Mischiefs not ended, are but then begun.
                              Anselme the Hermit."

    Dono. Powerful and pithy, which my advice confirms:
No man leaves physic when his sickness slakes,
But doubles the receipts. The word of peace

Seems fair to blood-shot eyes, but being applied
With such a medicine as blinds all the sight,
Argues desire of cure, but not of art.
 Aur. You argue from defects; if both the name
And the condition of the peace be one,
It is to be preferr'd, and in the offer
Made by the Saxon, I see naught repugnant.
 Glost. The time of truce requir'd for thirty days,
Carries suspicion in it, since half that space
Will serve to strength their weaken'd regiment.
 Cador. Who in less time will undertake to free
Our country from them?
 Edw.   Leave that unto our fortune.
 Dono. Is not our bold and hopeful general
Still master of the field, their legions fallen,
The rest intrench'd for fear, half starv'd, and wounded,
And shall we now give o'er our fair advantage?
'Fore heaven, my lord, the danger is far more,
In trusting to their words than to their weapons.

      Enter OSWALD.

 Osw. The ambassadors are come, sir.
 Aur.   Conduct them in;
We are resolv'd, my lords, since policy fail'd
In the beginning, it shall have no hand
In the conclusion.
That heavenly power that hath so well begun
Their fatal overthrow, I know, can end it:
From which fair hope myself will give them answer.

  Flourish Cornets. *Enter* ARTESIA *with the* Saxon *lords.*

 Dono. What's here, a woman orator?
 Aur. Peace, Donobert.—Speak, what are you, lady?
 Art. The sister of the Saxon general,
Warlike Ostorius, the East-Angles king.
My name Artesia, who in terms of love
Brings peace and health to great Aurelius,

Wishing she may return as fair a present,
As she makes tender of.

Aur. The fairest present e'er mine eyes were blest with!
Command a chair there for this Saxon beauty:—
Sit, lady, we'll confer: your warlike brother
Sues for a peace, you say?

Art. With endless love unto your state and person.

Aur. He's sent a moving orator, believe me.—
What think'st thou, Donobert?

Dono. Believe me, sir, were I but young again,
This gilded pill might take my stomach quickly.

Aur. True, thou art old: How soon we do forget
Our own defects! Fair damsel,—O, my tongue
Turns traitor, and will betray my heart,—sister to
Our enemy:—'sdeath! her beauty mazes me,
I cannot speak if I but look on her.—
What's that we did conclude?

Dono.   This, royal lord—

Aur. Pish, thou canst not utter it.—
Fairest of creatures, tell the king, your brother,
That we in love, ha! and honour to our country,
Command his armies to depart our realm.
But if you please, fair soul—Lord Donobert,
Deliver you our pleasure.

Dono.   I shall, sir:
Lady, return, and certify your brother—

Aur. Thou art too blunt, and rude: Return so soon?
Fie, let her stay, and send some messenger
To certify our pleasure.

Dono.   What means your grace?

Aur. To give her time of rest to her long journey;
We would not willingly be thought uncivil.

Art. Great king of Britain, let it not seem strange,
To embrace the princely offers of a friend,
Whose virtues with thine own, in fairest merit
Both states in peace and love may now inherit.

Aur. She speaks of love again!
Sure, 'tis my fear, she knows I do not hate her.
   Art. Be then thyself, most great Aurelius,
And let not envy, nor a deeper sin
In these thy counsellors, deprive thy goodness
Of that fair honour. We, in seeking peace,
Give first to thee, who never use to sue,
But force our wishes. Yet, if this seem light,
O, let my sex, though worthless your respect,
Take the report of thy humanity.
Whose mild and virtuous life loud fame displays,
As being o'ercome by one so worthy praise.
   Aur. She has an angel's tongue.—Speak still.
   Dono. This flattery is gross, sir; hear no more on 't.—
Lady, these childish compliments are needless:
You have your answer, and believe it, madam,
His grace, though young, doth wear within his breast
Too grave a counsellor, to be seduc'd
By smoothing flattery, or oily words.
   Art. I come not, sir, to woo him.
   Dono. 'Twere folly if you should; you must not wed
     him.
   Aur. Shame take thy tongue! being old and weak thyself,
Thou dot'st, and looking on thine own defects,
Speak'st what thou 'dst wish in me. Do I command
The deeds of others, mine own act not free?
Be pleas'd to smile or frown, we respect neither:
My will and rule shall stand and fall together.—
Most fair Artesia, see, the king descends
To give thee welcome with these warlike Saxons,
And now on equal terms both sues and grants.
Instead of truce, let a perpetual league
Seal our united bloods in holy marriage;
Send the East-Angles' king this happy news,
That thou with me hast made a league for ever,
And added to his state a friend and brother:
Speak, dearest love, dare you confirm this title?

Art. I were no woman, to deny a good
So high and noble to my fame and country.
Aur. Live then a queen in Britain.
Glost. He means to marry her?
Dono. Death! he shall marry the devil first!
Marry a pagan, an idolatress?
Cador. He has won her quickly.
Edw. She was woo'd afore she came, sure,
Or came of purpose to conclude the match.
Aur. Who dares oppose our will? My Lord of Gloster,
Be you ambassador unto our brother,
The brother of our queen Artesia.
Tell him for such our entertainment looks him,
Our marriage adding to the happiness
Of our intended joys; man's good or ill,
In this like waves agree, come double still.—

Enter the Hermit.

Who's this? the Hermit? Welcome, my happiness!
Our country's hope, most reverend holy man,
I wanted but thy blessing to make perfect
The infinite sum of my felicity.
Herm. Alack, sweet prince, that happiness is yonder,
Felicity and thou art far asunder;
This world can never give it.
Aur. Thou art deceiv'd, see here, what I have found,
Beauty, alliance, peace, and strength of friends,
All in this all-exceeding excellence:
The league's confirm'd.
Herm. With whom, dear lord?
Aur. With the great brother of this beauteous woman,
The royal Saxon king.
Herm. O! then I see,
And fear thou art too near thy misery.
What magic could so link thee to this mischief?
By all the good that thou hast reap'd by me,
Stand further from destruction.

Aur. Speak as a man, and I shall hope to obey thee.
Herm. Idolaters, get hence!—Fond king, let go,
Thou hugg'st thy ruin, and thy country's woe.
Dono. Well spoke, old father; to him! bait him soundly.
Now, by heaven's blest lady, I can scarce keep patience.
First Sax. Lord. What devil is this?
Sec. Sax. Lord. That cursèd Christian, by whose hellish
charms
Our army was o'erthrown.
Herm. Why do you dally, sir? O, tempt not heaven,
Warm not a serpent in your naked bosom:
Discharge them from your court.
Aur. Thou speak'st like madness.
Command the frozen shepherd to the shade,
When he sits warm i' the sun; the fever-sick,
To add more heat unto his burning pain:
These may obey, 'tis less extremity
Than thou enjoin'st to me. Cast but thine eye
Upon this beauty, do it, I'll forgive thee,
Though jealousy in others finds no pardon.
Then say thou dost not love; I shall then swear
Thou art immortal, and no earthly man.
O, blame then my mortality, not me.
Herm. It is thy weakness brings thy misery,
Unhappy prince.
Aur. Be milder in thy doom.
Herm. "Tis you that must indure heaven's doom, which
fall'n,
Remember's just.
Art. [*aside*] Thou shalt not live to see it.—
How fares my lord?
If my poor presence breed dislike, great prince,
I am no such neglected soul, will seek
To tie you to your word.
Aur. My word, dear love! May my religion,
Crown, state, and kingdom fail, when I fail thee!—
Command Earl Chester to break up the camp,

Without disturbance to our Saxon friends;
Send every hour swift posts, to hasten on
The king her brother, to conclude this league,
This endless happy peace of love and marriage;
Till when provide for revels, and give charge
That naught be wanting which may make our triumphs
Sportful and free to all. If such fair blood
Engender ill, man must not look for good.
[*Exeunt all but the Hermit. Flourish.*

Enter MODESTIA, *reading in a book.*

Mod. How much the oft report of this bless'd hermit
Hath won on my desires: I must behold him,
And, sure, this should be he. O, the world's folly,
Proud earth and dust, how low a price bears goodness!
All that should make man absolute, shines in him.—
Much reverend Sir, may I without offence
Give interruption to your holy thoughts?

Herm. What would you, lady?

Mod. That which till now ne'er found a language in me:
I am in love.

Herm.   In love, with what?

Mod.   With virtue.

Herm. There is no blame in that.

Mod. Nay, sir, with you, with your religious life,
Your virtue, goodness. If there be a name,
To express affection greater than that word,
That would I learn and utter. Reverend sir,
If there be any thing to bar my suit,
Be charitable and expose it, your prayers
Are the same orisons, which I will number.
Holy Sir,
Keep not instruction back from willingness,
Possess me of that knowledge, leads you on
To this humility, for well I know,
Were greatness good, you would not live so low.

Herm. Are you a virgin?

Mod.   Yes, Sir.
Herm.   Your name?
Mod.   Modestia.
   Herm. Your name and virtues meet, a modest virgin:
Live ever in the sanctimonious way
To heaven and happiness. There's goodness in you;
I must instruct you further; come, look up,
Behold yon firmament, there sits a power,
Whose footstool is this earth. O, learn this lesson,
And practise it: he that will climb so high,
Must leave no joy beneath to move his eye.   [*Exit.*
   Mod. I apprehend you, sir; on heaven I fix my love,
Earth gives us grief, our joys are all above,
For this was man in innocence naked born,
To show us wealth hinders our sweet return.   [*Exit.*

ACT II.

SCENE 1. *Enter* Clown, *and his sister* JOAN *great with child.*

   Clown. Away, follow me no further, I am none of thy brother. What, with child? great with child? and knows not who's the father on 't! I am ashamed to call thee sister.
   Joan. Believe me, brother, he was a gentleman.
   Clown. Nay, I believe that, he gives arms, and legs too, and has made you the herald to blaze 'em. But, Joan, Joan, sister Joan, can you tell me his name that did it? how shall we name my cousin, your bastard, when we have it?
   Joan. Alas, I know not the gentleman's name, brother,
I met him in these woods, the last great hunting;
He was so kind and proffer'd me so much,
As I had not the heart to ask him more.
   Clown. Not his name? Why, this shows your country breeding. Now, had you been brought up i' the city, you'd have got a father first, and the child afterwards. Hast thou no marks to know him by?

19*

Joan. He had most rich attire, a fair hat and feather, a gilt sword, and most excellent hangers.

Clown. Pox on his hangers! 'would he had been gelt for his labour.

Joan. Had you but heard him swear you would have thought—

Clown. Ay, as you did: Swearing and lying goes together still. Did his oaths get you with child, we shall have a roaring boy then, i' faith. Well, sister, I must leave you.

Joan. Dear brother, stay, help me to find him out; I'll ask no further.

Clown. 'Sfoot, who should I find? Who should I ask for?

Joan. Alas, I know not; he uses in these woods, And these are witness of his oaths and promise.

Clown. We are like to have a hot suit on 't, when our best witness's but a knight o' the post.

Joan. Do but inquire this forest, I'll go with you; Some happy fate may guide us till we meet him.

Clown. Meet him? and what name shall we have for him, when we meet him? 'Sfoot! thou neither know'st him, nor canst tell what to call him. Was ever man tired with such a business, to have a sister got with child, and know not who did it? Well, you shall see him, I'll do my best for you; I'll make proclamation; if these woods and trees, as you say, will bear any witness, let them answer; Oyes! If there be any man that wants a name, will come in for conscience' sake, and acknowledge himself to be a whore-master, he shall have that laid to his charge in an hour, he shall not be rid on in an age; if he have lands, he shall have an heir; if he have patience, he shall have a wife; if he have neither lands nor patience, he shall have a whore. So ho, boy, so ho, so so!

Within Prince Uter. So ho, boy, so, ho, illo ho, illo ho!

Clown. Hark, hark, sister, there's one halloes to us. What a wicked world's this! A man cannot so soon name a whore but a knave comes presently; and see where he is; stand close a while, sister.

Enter Prince UTER.

Prince. How like a voice that echo spake, but O!
My thoughts are lost for ever in amazement.
Could I but meet a man to tell her beauties,
These trees would bend their tops to kiss the air,
That from my lips should give her praises up.
    Clown. He talks of a woman, sister.
    Joan. This may be he, brother.
    Clown. View him well, you see he has a fair sword: but his hangers are fallen.
    Prince. Here did I see her first, here view her beauty:
O, had I known her name, I had been happy.
    Clown. Sister, this is he; sure, he knows not thy name either. A couple of wise fools, i' faith, to get children, and know not one another.
    Prince. You weeping leaves, upon whose tender cheeks
Doth stand a flood of tears at my complaint,
You heard my vows and oaths—
    Clown. La, la, he has been a great swearer too; 'tis he, sister.
    Prince. For having overtook her;
As I have seen a forward blood-hound strip
The swifter of the cry, ready to seize
His wishèd hopes, upon the sudden view,
Struck with astonishment at his arrivèd prey,
Instead of seizure stands at fearful bay;
Or like to Marius' soldier, whom o'ertook
The eyesight-killing Gorgon, at one look
Made everlasting stand: so fear'd, my power,
Whose cloud aspir'd the sun, dissolv'd a shower.
Pygmalion, then I tasted thy sad fate,
Whose ivory picture and my fair were one:
Our dotage past imagination,
I saw and felt desire—
    Clown. Pox a' your fingering! Did he feel, sister?
    Prince. But enjoy'd not.

O fate, thou hadst thy days and nights to feed
On calm affection; one poor sight was all,
Converts my pleasure to perpetual thrall.
Embracing thine, thou lostest breath and desire:
So I relating mine, will here expire;
For here I vow to you, ye mournful plants,
Who were the first made happy by her fame,
Never to part hence, till I know her name.

Clown. Give me thy hand, sister; the child hath found his father. This is he, sure, as I am a man; had I been a woman, these kind words would have won me, I should have had a great belly too, that's certain. Well, I'll speak to him. —Most honest and fleshly-minded gentleman, give me your hand, sir.

Prince. Ha, what art thou, that thus rude and boldly
Darest take notice of a wretch
So much allied to misery as I am?

Clown. Nay, sir, for our alliance, I shall be found to be a poor brother-in-law of your worship's. The gentlewoman you spake on, is my sister: You see what a clew she spreads, her name is Joan Go-to-'t, I am her elder, but she has been at it before me: 'tis a woman's fault.—Pox a' this bashfulness! come forward, Jug, prithee, speak to him.

Prince. Have you e'er seen me, lady?

Clown. Seen ye? ha, ha! it seems she has felt you too; here's a young Go-to-'t a coming, sir; she is my sister, we all love to go to 't, as well as your worship. She's a maid yet, but you may make her a wife, when you please, sir.

Prince. I am amaz'd with wonder: tell me, woman,
What sin have you committed worthy this?

Joan. Do you not know me, sir?

Prince. Know thee! as I do thunder, hell and mischief,
Witch, scullion, hag!

Clown. I see, he will marry her; he speaks so like a husband.

Prince. Death, I will cut their tongues

Out for this blasphemy.—Strumpet, villain,
Where have you ever seen me?
　Clown. Speak for yourself with a pox to ye.
　Prince. Slaves,
I'll make you curse yourselves for this temptation.
　Joan. O sir, if ever you did speak to me,
It was in smoother phrase, in fairer language.
　Prince. Lightning consume me, if I ever saw thee:
My rage o'erflows my blood, all patience flies me.
　　　　　　　　　　　　　　　　　　[*Beats her.*
　Clown. Hold! I beseech you, sir, I have nothing to say
　　to you.
　Joan. Help, help, murder, murder!

　　　　　　Enter TOCLIO *and* OSWALD.

　Toclio. Make haste, sir, this way the sound came, it was
　　i' the wood.
　Osw. See where she is, and the prince, the price of all
　　our wishes.
　Clown. The prince, say ye? he's made a poor subject of
me, I am sure.
　Toclio. Sweet prince, noble Uter, speak, how fare you,
　　sir?
　Osw. Dear sir, recall yourself, your fearful absence
Hath won too much already on the grief
Of our sad king, from whom our labouring search
Hath had this fair success in meeting you.
　Toclio. His silence and his looks argue distraction.
　Clown. Nay, he's mad, sure, he will not acknowledge my
sister, nor the child neither.
　Osw. Let us entreat your grace along with us;
Your sight will bring new life to the king your brother.
　Toclio. Will you go, sir?
　Prince. Yes, any whither; guide me, all's hell; I see,
Man may change air, but not his misery.
　　　　　　　　　　　　　　　[*Exeunt Prince and Toclio.*
　Joan. Lend me one word with you, sir.

Clown. Well said, sister, he has a feather, and fair hangers too, this may be he.
Osw. What would you, fair one?
Clown. Sure, I have seen you in these woods ere this.
Osw. Trust me, never; I never saw this place,
Till at this time my friend conducted me.
Joan. The more 's my sorrow then.
Osw. 'Would I could comfort you:
I am a bachelor, but it seems you have
A husband, you have been foully o'ershot else.
Clown. A woman's fault, we are all subject to go to 't, sir.

Enter Toclio.

Toclio. Oswald, away, the prince will not stir a foot without you.
Osw. I am coming. Farewell, woman.
Toclio. Prithee, make haste.
Joan. Good sir, but one word with you ere you leave us.
Toclio. With me, fair soul?
Clown. She'll have a fling at him too, the child must have a father.
Joan. Have you ne'er seen me, sir?
Toclio. Seen thee?
'Sfoot, I have seen many fair faces in my time,
Prithee, look up; and do not weep so;
Sure, pretty wanton, I have seen this face before.
Joan. It is enough, though you ne'er see me more.

(*Sinks down.*)

Toclio. 'Sfoot, she's fallen.
This place is enchanted, sure, look to the woman, fellow.

[*Exit.*

Clown. O, she's dead! she's dead! As you are a man, stay and help, sir.—Joan, Joan, sister Joan, why, Joan Go-to't, I say; will you cast away yourself, and your child, and me too? what do you mean, sister?
Joan. O, give me pardon, sir, 'twas too much joy,

Oppress'd my loving thought. I know you were
Too noble to deny me,—Ha! where is he?
 Clown. Who, the gentleman? he's gone, sister
 Joan. O! I'm undone then: run, tell him I did
But faint for joy, dear brother, haste: why dost thou stay?
O, never cease, till he give answer to thee.
 Clown. He: which he? what do you call him, trow?
 Joan. Unnatural brother, show me the path he took
Why dost thou dally? speak, O, which way went he?
 Clown. This way, that way, through the bushes there.
 Joan. Were it through fire,
The journey 's easy, wing'd with sweet desire. [*Exit.*
 Clown. Heyday, there's some hope of this yet. I'll follow her for kindred's sake, if she miss of her purpose now, she'd challenge all she finds, I see; for if ever we meet with a two-legged creature in the whole kingdom, the child shall have a father, that's certain. [*Exit.*

SCENE II. *Loud music. Enter two with the sword and mace,* CADOR, EDWIN, *two* Bishops, AURELIUS, OSTORIUS *leading* ARTESIA *crowned,* CONSTANTIA, MODESTIA, OCTA, PROXIMUS *a Magician,* DONOBERT, GLOSTER, OSWALD, TOCLIO, *all pass over the stage. Manent* DONOBERT, GLOSTER, EDWIN, CADOR.

 Dono. Come, Gloster,
I do not like this hasty marriage.
 Glost. She was quickly woo'd and won: not six days since
Arriv'd an enemy to sue for peace,
And now crown'd Queen of Britain; this is strange.
 Dono. Her brother too made as quick speed in coming,
Leaving his Saxons, and his starvèd troops,
To take the advantage, whilst 'twas offerèd.
'Fore heaven, I fear the king 's too credulous;
Our army is dischargèd too.
 Glost. Yes, and our general commanded home.—
Son Edwin, have you seen him since?

Edw. He's come to court, but will not view the presence,
Nor speak unto the king, he is so discontent
At this so strange alliance with the Saxon,
As nothing can persuade his patience.
    Cador. You know, his humour will endure no check,
No if the king oppose it;
All crosses feed both his spleen and his impatience:
Those affections are in him like powder,
Apt to inflame with every little spark,
And blow up all his reason.
    Glost. Edol of Chester is a noble soldier.
    Dono. So is he', by the rood, ever most faithful
To the king and kingdom, howe'er his passions guide him.

    Enter EDOL *with* Captains.

    Cador. See where he comes, my lord.
    All. Welcome to court, brave Earl.
    Edol. Do not deceive me by your flatteries;
Is not the Saxon here? the league confirm'd?
The marriage ratified? the court divided
With pagan infidels? the least part Christians,
At least in their commands? O, the gods!
It is a thought that takes away my sleep,
And dulls my senses so, I scarcely know you:
Prepare my horses, I'll away to Chester.
    Capt. What shall we do with our companies, my lord?
    Edol. Keep them at home to increase cuckolds,
And get some cases for your captainships;
Smooth up your brows, tho wars has spoil'd your faces,
And few will now regard you.
    Dono. Preserve your patience, sir.
    Edol. Preserve your honours, lords, your country's safety,
Your lives, and lands, from strangers. What black devil
Could so bewitch the king, so to discharge
A royal army in the height of conquest,
Nay, even already made victorious,
To give such credit to an enemy,

A starvèd foe, a struggling fugitive,
Beaten beneath our feet, so low dejected,
So servile and so base, as hope of life
Had won them all, to leave the land for ever?
    Dono. It was the king's will.
    Edol. It was your want of wisdom,
That should have laid before his tender youth
The dangers of a state, where foreign powers
Bandy for sovereignty with lawful kings,
Who being settled once, to assure themselves,
Will never fail to seek the blood and life
Of all competitors.
    Dono. Your words sound well, my lord, and point at safety,
Both for the realm and us; but why did you,
Within whose power it lay, as general,
With full commission to dispose the war,
Lend ear to parley with the weaken'd foe?
    Edol. O, the good gods!
    Cador. And on that parley came this embassy.
    Edol. You will hear me?
    Edw. Your letters did declare it to the king,
Both of the peace, and all conditions,
Brought by this Saxon lady, whose fond love
Has thus bewitchèd him.
    Edol. I will curse you all as black as hell,
Unless you hear me; your gross mistake would make
Wisdom herself run madding through the streets,
And quarrel with her shadow. Death!
Why kill'd you not that woman?
    Dono., Glost.   O, my lord!
    Edol. The great devil take me quick, had I been by,
And all the women of the world were barren,
She should have died ere he had married her
On these conditions.
    Cador. It is not reason that directs you thus.
    Edol. Then have I none, for all I have directs me.

Never was man so palpably abus'd,
So basely marted, bought and sold to scorn.
My honour, fame, and hopeful victories,
The loss of time, expenses, blood and fortunes,
All vanish'd into nothing.
   Edw. This rage is vain, my lord:
What the king does, nor they, nor you can help.
   Edol. My sword must fail me then.
   Cador. 'Gainst whom will you oppose it?
   Edol. What's that to you? 'Gainst all the devils in hell
To guard my country.
   Edw.   These are airy words.
   Edol. Sir, you tread too hard upon my patience.
   Edw. I speak the duty of a subject's faith,
And say again, had you been here in presence,
What the king did, you had not dar'd to cross it.
   Edol. I'll trample on his life and soul that says it.
   Cador. My lord—
   Edw.   Come, come.
   Edol.   Now before heaven!
   Cador.   Dear sir.
   Edol. Not dare? Thou liest beneath thy lungs.
   Gloster. No more, son Edwin.
   Edw. I have done, sir; I take my leave.
   Edol. But thou shalt not; you shall take no leave of me,
        sir.
   Dono. For wisdom's sake, my lord—
   Edol. Sir, I'll leave him, and you, and all of you,
The court and king, and let my sword, and friends,
Shuffle for Edol's safety. Stay you here,
And hug the Saxons, till they cut your throats,
Or bring the land to servile slavery.
Such yokes of baseness Chester must not suffer!
Go, and repent betimes these foul misdeeds,
For in this league all our whole kingdom bleeds,
Which I'll prevent, or perish.   *[Exeunt Edol and Captains.*
   Glost. See, how his rage transports him!

Cador. These passions set apart, a braver soldier
Breathes not i' the world this day.
　　Dono. I wish his own worth do not court his ruin.
The king must rule, and we must learn to obey;
True virtue still directs the noble way.
　　Loud music. Enter AURELIUS, ARTESIA, OSTORIUS, OCTA,
　　　　PROXIMUS, OSWALD, *the* Hermit.
　　Aur. Why is the court so dull? methinks, each room
And angle of our palace should appear
Stock full of objects fit for mirth and triumphs,
To show our high content. Oswald, fill wine.
Must we begin the revels? be it so then!
Reach me the cup: I'll now begin a health
To our lov'd queen, the bright Artesia,
The royal Saxon king, our warlike brother.
Go and command all the whole court to pledge it;
Fill to the Hermit there.—Most reverend Anselme,
We'll do thee honour first, to pledge my queen.
　　Herm. I drink no healths, great king, and if I did,
I would be loath to part with health to those
That have no power to give it back again.
　　Aur. Mistake not, 'tis the argument of love
And duty to our queen and us.
　　Art. But he owes none, it seems.
　　Herm. I do to virtue, madam; temperate minds
Covet that health to drink, which nature gives
In every spring to man. He that doth hold
His body but a tenement at will,
Bestows no cost but to repair what's ill.
Yet if your healths or heat of wine, fair princess,
Could this old frame, or these craz'd limbs restore,
Or keep out death, or sickness, then fill more;
I'll make fresh way for appetite; if no,
On such a prodigal who would wealth bestow?
　　Ostor. He speaks not like a guest to grace a wedding.

Art. No, sir, but like an envious impostor.
Octa. A Christian slave, a cynic.

Enter Toclio.

Ostor. What virtue could decline your kingly spirit,
To such respect of him whose magic spells
Met with your vanquish'd troops, and turn'd your arms
To that necessity of fight, when the despair
Of any hope to stand but by his charms,
Had been defeated in a bloody conquest?
Octa. 'Twas magic, hellbred magic did it, sir,
And that's a course, my lord, which we esteem,
In all our Saxon wars, unto the last
And lowest ebb of servile treachery.
Aur. Sure, you are deceiv'd, it was the hand of heaven,
That in his virtue gave us victory.
Is there a power in man that can strike fear
Thorough a general camp, or create spirits,
In recreant bosoms above present sense?
Ostor. To blind the sense there may, with apparition
Of well-arm'd troops, within themselves are air,
Form'd into human shapes; and such that day
Were by that sorcerer rais'd to cross our fortunes.
Aur. There is a law tells us, that words want force
To make deeds void; examples must be shown
By instances alike, ere I believe it.
Ostor. 'Tis easily perform'd, believe me, sir:
Propose your own desires, and give but way
To what our magic here shall straight perform,
And then let his or our deserts be censur'd.
Aur. We could not wish a greater happiness,
Than what this satisfaction brings with it.
Let him proceed, fair brother.
Ostor. He shall, sir.
Come, learnèd Proximus, this task be thine;
Let thy great charms confound the opinion,
This Christian by his spells has falsely won.

Prox. Great king, propound your wishes then,
What persons, of what state, what numbers, or how arm'd—
Please your own thoughts, they shall appear before you.
  Aur. Strange art! What think'st thou, reverend Hermit?
  Herm. Let him go on, sir.
  Aur. Wilt thou behold his cunning?
  Herm. Right gladly, sir; 'twill be my joy to tell,
That I was here to laugh at him and hell.
  Aur. I like thy confidence.
  Art. His saucy impudence!—Proceed to the trial.
  Prox. Speak your desires, my lord, and be it plac'd
In any angle underneath the moon,
The center of the earth, the sea, the air,
The region of the fire, nay, hell itself,
And I'll present it.
  Aur. We'll have no sight so fearful, only this:
If all thy art can reach it, show me here
The two great champions of the Trojan war,
Achilles and brave Hector, our great ancestor,
Both in their warlike habits, armour, shields
And weapons then in use for fight.
  Prox. 'Tis done, my lord, command a halt and silence,
As each man will respect his life or danger!—
Armel! Plesgeth!

Enter Spirits.

Spir.   Quid vis?
Prox.   Attend me.
  Aur. The Apparition comes; on our displeasure,
Let all keep place and silence.
                [*Within drums beat marches.*

Enter PROXIMUS *bringing in* HECTOR *attired and armed after the Trojan manner, with target, sword, and battle-axe, a trumpet before him, and a spirit in flame-colours with a torch; at the other door* ACHILLES *with his spear and falchion, a trumpet and a spirit in black before him; trumpets sound alarm, and they manage their weapons to begin the fight: and after some charges, the Hermit steps between them, at which seeming amazed the spirits tremble.*

[*Thunder within.*

Prox. What means this stay, bright Armel, Plesgeth?
Why fear you and fall back?
Renew the alarums, and enforce the combat,
Or hell or darkness circles you for ever.
Armel. We dare not.
Prox. Ha!
Plesgeth. Our charms are all dissolv'd; Armel, away!
'Tis worse than hell to us, whilst here we stay.

[*Exeunt Spirits.*

Herm. What! at a non-plus, sir? Command them back, for shame!
Prox. What power o'erawes my spells? return, you hell-hounds:
Armel, Plesgeth, double damnation seize you!
By all the infernal powers, the prince of devils
Is in this Hermit's habit: What else could force
My spirits quake or tremble thus?
Herm. Weak argument to hide your want of skill:
Does the devil fear the devil, or war with hell?
They have not been acquainted long, it seems.
Know, misbelieving pagan, even that power,
That overthrew your forces, still lets you see,
He only can control both hell and thee.
Prox. Disgrace and mischief! I'll enforce new charms,
New spells, and spirits rais'd from the low abyss
Of hell's unbottom'd depths.
Aur. We have enough, sir;
Give o'er your charms, we'll find some other time
To praise your art. I dare not but acknowledge
That heavenly power my heart stands witness to.—
Be not dismay'd, my lords, at this disaster,
Nor thou, my fairest queen: we'll change the scene
To some more pleasing sports. Lead to your chamber.—

Howe'er in this thy pleasures find a cross,
Our joy's too fixèd here to suffer loss.
  Toclio. Which I shall add to, sir, with news I bring:
The prince your brother lives—
  Aur. Ha!
  Toclio. And comes to grace this high and heaven-knit
       marriage.
  Aur. Why dost thou flatter me, to make me think,
Such happiness attends me?

  Enter Prince UTER *and* OSWALD.

  Toclio. His presence speaks my truth, sir.
  Dono. 'Fore me, 'tis he: Look, Gloster.
  Glost. A blessing beyond hope, sir.
  Aur. Ha! it is he: welcome, my second comfort.
Artesia, dearest love, it is my brother,
My princely brother, all my kingdom's hope:
O, give him welcome, as thou lov'st my health.
  Art. You have so free a welcome, sir, from me
As this your presence has such power, I swear,
O'er me, a stranger, that I must forget
My country, name, and friends, and count this place
My joy and birth-right.
  Prince. 'Tis she!
'Tis she, I swear! O, ye good gods, 'tis she!
That face within those woods, where first I saw her,
Captiv'd my senses, and thus many months
Barr'd me from all society of men.
How came she to this place?
Brother Aurelius, speak that angel's name,
Her heaven-blest name, O, speak it quickly, sir.
  Aur. It is Artesia, the royal Saxon princess.
  Prince. A woman, and no deity? no feign'd shape,
To mock the reason of admiring sense,
On whom a hope as low as mine may live,
Love, and enjoy, dear brother, may it not?

Shakspeare, Doubtful Plays.

Aur. She is all the good, or virtue, thou canst name,
My wife, my queen.
 Prince. Ha! your wife!
 Art. Which you shall find, sir, if that time and fortune
May make my love but worthy of your trial.
 Prince. O!
 Aur. What troubles you, dear brother?
Why with so strange and fix'd an eye dost thou
Behold my joys?
 Art. You are not well, sir?
 Prince. Yes, yes. O, you immortal powers,
Why has poor man so many entrances
For sorrow to creep in at, when our sense
Is much too weak to hold his happiness?
O, say I was born deaf: and let your silence
Confirm in me the knowing my defect.
At least be charitable to conceal my sin,
For hearing is no less in me, dear brother.
 Aur. No more!
I see thou art a rival in the joys
Of my high bliss. Come, my Artesia;
The day 's most prais'd, when 'tis eclips'd by night:
Great good must have as great ill opposite.
 Prince. Stay, hear but a word; yet now I think on 't,
This is your wedding-night, and were it mine,
I should be angry with least loss of time.
 Art. Envy speaks no such words, has no such looks.
 Prince. Sweet rest unto you both.
 Aur. Lights to our nuptial chamber!
 Art. Could you speak so, [*Aside to the Prince.*
I would not fear how much my grief did grow.
 Aur. Lights to our chamber; on, on, set on.
       [*Exeunt all except Prince.*
 Prince. "Could you speak so,
I would not fear how much my grief did grow."
Those were her very words, sure! I am waking,
She wrung me by the hand, and spoke them to me

With a most passionate affection.
Perhaps she loves, and now repents her choice
In marriage with my brother. O, fond man,
How dar'st thou trust thy traitorous thoughts, thus to
Betray thyself? 'Twas but a waking dream
Wherein thou mad'st thy wishes speak, not her,
In which thy foolish hopes strive to prolong
A wretched being. So sickly children play
With health-lov'd toys, which for a time delay,
But do not cure the fit. Be then a man,
Meet that destruction which thou canst not fly
From, not to live, make it thy hest to die;
And call her now, whom thou didst hope to wed,
Thy brother's wife: thou art too near a kin,
And such an act above all name 's a sin
Not to be blotted out, heaven pardon me!
She's banish'd from my bosom now for ever;
To lowest ebbs men justly hope a flood;
When vice grows barren, all desires are good.

Enter Waiting-Gentlewoman *with a jewel.*

Gent. The noble prince, I take it, sir?
Prince. You speak me, what I should be, lady.
Gent. Know, by that name, sir, queen Artesia greets
    you—
Prince. Alas, good virtue, how is she mistaken!
Gent. Commending her affection in this jewel, sir.
Prince. She binds my service to her: Ha! a jewel, 'tis
A fair one, trust me, and methinks, it much
Resembles something I have seen with her.
Gent. It is an artificial crab, sir.
Prince. A creature that goes backward.
Gent. True, from the way it looks.
Prince. There is no moral in it alludes to herself?
Gent. 'Tis your construction gives you that, sir, she 's a
    woman.

Prince. And, like this, may use her legs, and eyes two several ways.

Gent. Just like the sea-crab, which on the mistle preys, whilst he bills at a stone.

Prince. Pretty in truth; prithee, tell me, art thou honest?

Gent. I hope I seem no other, sir.

Prince. And those that seem so,
Are sometimes bad enough.

Gent. If they will accuse themselves for want of witness, let them; I am not so foolish.

Prince. I see th' art wise; come, speak me truly:
What is the greatest sin?

Gent. That which man never acted; what has been done Is, at the least, common to all as one.

Prince. Dost think thy lady is of thy opinion?

Gent. She's a bad scholar else, I have brought her up, And she dares owe me still.

Prince. Ay, 'tis a fault in greatness, they dare owe
Many, ere they pay one. But dar'st thou expose
Thy scholar to my examining?

Gent. Yes, in good troth, sir, and pray, put her to 't too; 'tis a hard lesson, if she answer it not.

Prince. Thou know'st the hardest.

Gent. As far as a woman may, sir.

Prince. I commend thy plainness.
When wilt thou bring me to thy lady?

Gent. Next opportunity I attend you, sir.

Prince. Thanks, take this and commend me to her.

Gent. Think of your sea-crab, sir, I pray. [*Exit.*

Prince. O, by any means, lady—
What should all this tend to?
If it be love or lust that thus incites her,
The sin is horrid and incestuous;
If to betray my life, what hopes she by it?
Yes, it may be a practice 'twixt themselves,
To expel the Britons and ensure the state

Through our destructions, all this may be
Veil'd with a deeper reach in villany,
Than all my thoughts can guess at. However,
I will confer with her, and if I find
Lust hath given life to envy in her mind,
I may prevent the danger; so men wise
By the same step by which they fell, may rise.
Vices are virtues, if so thought and seen,
And trees, with foulest roots, branch soonest green. [*Exit.*

ACT III.

Scene I. *Enter* Clown *and his sister* Joan.

Clown. Come, sister, thou art all fool, all madwoman.

Joan. Prithee, have patience, we are now at court.

Clown. At court! ha, ha, that proves thy madness; was there ever any woman in thy taking travell'd to court for a husband? 'Slid, 'tis enough for them to get children, and the city to keep 'em, and the country to find nurses: every thing must be done in his due place, sister.

Joan. Be but content a while; for, sure, I know
This journey will be happy. O, dear brother,
This night my sweet friend came to comfort me;
I saw him, and embrac'd him in mine arms.

Clown. Why did you not hold him, and call me to help you?

Joan. Alas, I thought I had been with him still,
But when I wak'd—

Clown. A pox of all logger-heads! Then you were but in a dream all this while, and we may still go look him. Well, since we are come to court, cast your cat's eyes about you, and either find him out you dreamt on, or some other, for I'll trouble myself no further.

Enter Donobert, Cador, Edwin *and* Toclio.

See, see, here comes more courtiers, look about you, come,

pray, view 'em all well; the old man has none of the marks about him, the other have both swords and feathers: what thinkest thou of that tall young gentleman?

Joan. He much resembles him; but, sure, my friend, Brother, was not so high of stature.

Clown. O beast, wast thou got a child with a short thing too?

Dono. Come, come, I'll hear no more on 't: go, lord Edwin,
Tell her, this day her sister shall be married
To Cador, Earl of Cornwal; so shall she
To thee, brave Edwin, if she'll have my blessing.

Edw. She is addicted to a single life,
She will not hear of marriage.

Dono. Tush, fear it not: go you from me to her,
Use your best skill, my lord, and if you fail,
I have a trick shall do it: haste, haste about it.

Edw. Sir, I am gone;
My hope is in your help more than my own.

Dono. And worthy Toclio, to your care I must
Commend this business,
For lights and music, and what else is needful.

Toclio. I shall, my lord.

Clown. We would entreat a word, sir; come forward, sister.

[*Exeunt Donobert, Toclio, Cador.*

Edw. What lack'st thou, fellow?

Clown. I lack a father for a child, sir.

Edw. How! a god-father?

Clown. No, sir, we mean the own father: it may be you, sir, for any thing we know: I think the child is like you.

Edw. Like me! prithee, where is it?

Clown. Nay, 'tis not born yet sir, 'tis forth-coming; you see, the child must have a father: what do you think of my sister?

Edw. Why, I think, if she ne'er had husband, she's a whore, and thou a fool; farewell. [*Exit.*

Clown. I thank you, sir. Well, pull up thy heart, sister; if there be any law i' the court, this fellow shall father it, 'cause he uses me so scurvily. There's a great wedding towards, they say. We'll amongst them for a husband for thee.

Enter Sir Nicodemus *with a letter.*

If we miss there, I'll have another bout with him that abus'd me. See, look, there comes another hat and feather, this should be a close letcher, he's reading of a love-letter.

Sir Nic. Earl Cador's marriage, and a masque to grace it, So, so.

This night shall make me famous for presentments.—
How now, what are you?

Clown. A couple of Great Britons, you may see by our bellies, sir.

Sir Nic. And what of this, sir?

Clown. Why, thus the matter stands, sir: there's one of your courtiers' hunting nags, has made a gap through another man's inclosure. Now, sir, here's the question, who should be at charge of a fur-bush to stop it?

Sir Nic. Ha, ha, this is out of my element: the law must end it.

Clown. Your worship says well; for, surely, I think some lawyer had a hand in the business, we have such a troublesome issue.

Sir Nic. But what's thy business with me now?

Clown. Nay, sir, the business is done already, you may see by my sister's belly.

Sir Nic. O, now I find thee. This gentlewoman, it seems, has been humbled.

Clown. As low as the ground would give her leave, sir, and your worship knows this: though there be many fathers without children, yet to have a child without a father, were most unnatural.

Sir Nic. That's true, i' faith, I never heard of a child yet that e'er begot his father.

Clown. Why, true, you say wisely, sir.

Sir Nic. And therefore I conclude, that he that got the child, is without all question the father of it.

Clown. Ay, now you come to the matter, sir; and our suit is to your worship for the discovery of this father.

Sir Nic. Why, lives he in the court here?

Joan. Yes, sir, and I desire but marriage.

Sir Nic. And does the knave refuse it? Come, come, be merry, wench, he shall marry thee, and keep the child too, if my knighthood can do any thing; I am bound by mine orders to help distressed ladies, and can there be a greater injury to a woman with child, than to lack a father for 't? I am ashamed of simpleness: come, come, give me a courtier's fee for my pains, and I'll be thy advocate myself, and justice shall be found; nay, I'll sue the law for it; but give me my fee first.

Clown. If all the money I have i' the world will do it, you shall have it, sir.

Sir Nic. An angel does it.

Clown. Nay, there's two, for your better eyesight, sir.

Sir Nic. Why, well said! give me thy hand, wench, I'll teach thee a trick for all this, shall get a father for thy child presently, and this it is, mark now: you meet a man, as you meet me now, thou claimest marriage of me, and layest the child to my charge; I deny it: pish, that's nothing, hold thy claim fast, thy word carries it, and no law can withstand it.

Clown. Is 't possible?

Sir Nic. Past all opposition; her own word carries it. Let her challenge any man, the child shall call him father; there's a trick for your money, now.

Clown. Troth, sir, we thank you, we'll make use of your trick, and go no further to seek the child a father, for we challenge you, sir. Sister, lay it to him, he shall marry thee, I shall have a worshipful old man to my brother.

Sir Nic. Ha, ha, I like thy pleasantness.

Joan. Nay, indeed, sir, I do challenge you.

Clown. You think we jest, sir?

Sir Nic. Ay, by my troth do I, I like thy wit, i' faith, thou shalt live at court with me; didst never hear of Nicodemus Nothing? I am the man.

Clown. Nothing? 'Slid, we are out again. Thou wast never got with child with nothing, sure?

Joan. I know not what to say.

Sir Nic. Never grieve, wench, show me the man, and process shall fly out.

Clown. 'Tis enough for us to find the children, we look that you should find the father, and therefore either do us justice, or we'll stand to our first challenge.

Sir Nic. Would you have justice without an adversary? Unless you can show me the man, I can do [you no good in it.

Clown. Why, then I hope you'll do us no harm, sir, you'll restore my money.

Sir Nic. What, my fee?
Marry, law forbid it, and all shall be amended,
The child find his father, and the law ended. [*Exit.*

Clown. Well, he has deserved his fee, indeed, for he has brought our suit to a quick end, I promise you, and yet the child has never a father; nor we have no more money to seek after him, a shame of all lecherous plackets! Now you look like a cat had newly kitten'd; what will you do now, trow? Follow me no further, lest I beat your brains out.

Joan. Impose upon me any punishment,
Rather than leave me now.

Clown. Well, I think I am bewitched with thee; I cannot find in my heart to forsake her, there was never sister would have abused a poor brother as thou hast done. I am even pined away with fretting, there's nothing but flesh and bones about me. Well, an I had my money again, it were some comfort; hark, sister, does it not thunder? (*Thunder.*)

Joan. O yes, most fearfully: what shall we do, brother?

Clown. Marry, e'en get some shelter ere the storm catch us: away, let 's away, I prithee.

Enter the Devil *in man's habit, richly attired, his feet and his head horrid.*

Joan. Ha, 'tis he: stay, brother, dear brother, stay.
Clown. What's the matter now?
Joan. My love, my friend is come, yonder he goes.
Clown. Where, where? Show me, where, I'll stop him, if the devil be not in him.
Joan. Look there, look yonder.—O, dear friend, pity my distress,
For heaven and goodness, do but speak to me.
Devil. She calls me, and yet drives me headlong from her.— [*Aside.*
Poor mortal, thou and I are much uneven,
Thou must not speak of goodness, nor of heaven,
If I confer with thee: but be of comfort,
Whilst men do breathe and Britain's name be known,
The fatal print thou bear'st within thy womb,
Shall here be famous till the day of doom.
Clown. 'Slid, who's that talks so? I can see nobody.
Joan. Then art thou blind, or mad; see where he goes,
And beckons me to come; O, lead me forth,
I'll follow thee in spite of fear or death. [*Exit.*
Clown. O brave! she'll run to the devil for a husband, she's stark mad, sure, and talks to a shadow, for I could see no substance: well, I'll after her, the child was got by chance, and the father must be found at all adventure.
[*Exit.*

SCENE II. *Enter the* Hermit, MODESTIA *and* EDWIN.

Mod. O, reverend sir, by you my heart hath reach'd
At the large hopes of holy piety,
And for this have I crav'd your company,
Here in your sight religiously to vow,
My chaste thoughts up to heaven, and make you now
The witness of my faith.

Herm. Angels assist thy hopes.
Edw. What means my love? thou art my promis'd wife.
Mod. To part with willingly what friends and life
Can make no good assurance of.
Edw. O, find remorse, fair soul, to love and merit,
And yet recant thy vow.
Mod. Never:
This world and I are parted now for ever.
Herm. To find the way to bliss, O, happy woman,
Thou'st learn'd the hardest lesson well, I see;
Now show thy fortitude and constancy,
Let these thy friends thy sad departure weep,
Thou shalt but lose the wealth thou could'st not keep—
My contemplation calls me, I must leave ye.
Edw. O, reverend sir, persuade not her to leave me.
Herm. My lord, I do not, nor to cease, to love ye;
I only pray, her faith may fixèd stand,
Marriage was blest, I know, with heaven's own hand.
[*Exit.*
Edw. You hear him, lady, 'tis not a virgin's state,
But sanctity of life, must make you happy.
Mod. Good sir, you say you love me, gentle Edwin,
Even by that love I do beseech you leave me.
Edw. Think of your father's tears, your weeping friends,
Whom cruel grief makes pale and bloodless for you.
Mod. 'Would I were dead to all.
Edw. Why do you weep?
Mod. O, who would live to see
How men with care and cost seek misery.
Edw. Why do you seek it then? What joy, what pleasure,
Can give you comfort in a single life?
Mod. The contemplation of a happy death,
Which is to me so pleasing that I think
No torture could divert me: what's this world,
Wherein you'd have me walk, but a sad passage
To a dread judgment-seat, from whence even now

We are but bail'd, upon our good abearing,
Till that great sessions come, when death, the crier,
Will surely summon us, and all to appear,
To plead us guilty or our bail to clear:
What music 's this?   [*Soft music.*

Enter two Bishops, Edwin, Donobert, Gloster, Cador,
        Constantia, Oswald, Toclio.

   Edw. O, now resolve and think upon my love.
This sounds the marriage of your beauteous sister,
Virtuous Constantia, with the noble Cador;
Look, and behold this pleasure.
   Mod. Cover me with night;
It is a vanity not worth the sight.
   Dono. See, see, she's yonder!—
Pass on, son Cador, daughter Constantia;
I beseech you all, unless the first move speech,
Salute her not.—Edwin, what good success?
   Edw. Nothing as yet, unless this object take her.
   Dono. See, see, her eye is fix'd upon her sister—
Seem careless all, and take no notice of her—
On, afore there, come, my Constantia;
   Mod. Not speak to me, nor deign to cast an eye,
To look on my despisèd poverty?
I must be more charitable,—pray, stay, lady,
Are not you she whom I did once call sister?
   Const. I did acknowledge such a name to one
Whilst she was worthy of it, in whose folly,
Since you neglect your fame and friends together,
In you I drown'd a sister's name for ever.
   Mod. Your looks did speak no less.
   Glost. It now begins to work, this sight has mov'd her.
   Dono. I know this trick would take, or nothing.
   Mod. Though you disdain in me a sister's name,
Yet charity, methinks, should be so strong
To instruct ere you reject. I am a wretch,
Even folly's instance, who perhaps have err'd,

Not having known the goodness bears so high
And fair a show in you; which being express'd,
I may recant this low despisèd life
And please those friends whom I have mov'd to grief.
 Cador. She is coming, i' faith; be merry, Edwin.
 Const. Since you desire instruction, you shall have it.
What is 't should make you thus desire to live,
Vow'd to a single life?
 Mod. Because I know I cannot fly from death.
O, my good sister, I beseech you, hear me:
This world is but a masque, catching weak eyes,
With what is not ourselves, but our disguise,
A vizard that falls off, the dance being done,
And leaves death's glass for all to look upon.
Our best happiness here lasts but a night,
Whose burning tapers make false wares seem right;
Who knows not this, and will not now provide,
Some better shift before his shame be spied,
And knowing this vain world at last will leave him,
Shake off these robes that help but to deceive him!
 Const. Her words are powerful, I am amaz'd to hear her!
 Dono. Her soul's enchanted with infected spells.
Leave her, best girl, for now in thee
I'll seek the fruits of age, posterity.—
Out o' my sight! sure; I was half asleep,
Or drunk, when I begot thee.
 Const. Good sir, forbear. What say you to that, sister?
The joy of children, a blest mother's name?
O, who without much grief can lose such fame!
 Mod. Who can enjoy it without sorrow rather?
And that most certain where the joy's unsure,
Seeing the fruit that we beget, endure
So many miseries, that oft we pray
The heavens to shut up their afflicted day:
At best we do but bring forth heirs to die,
And fill the coffins of our enemy.
 Const. O, my soul!

Dono. Hear her no more, Constantia,
She's sure bewitch'd with error; leave her, girl.
  Const. Then must I leave all goodness, sir: away,
Stand off, I say.
  Dono. How's this?
  Const. I have no father, friend, no husband now;
All are but borrow'd robes, in which we mask
To waste and spend the time, when all our life
Is but one good betwixt two ague-days,
Which from the first, ere we have time to praise,
A second fever takes us: O, my best sister,
My soul's eternal friend, forgive the rashness
Of my distemper'd tongue; for how could she,
Knew not herself, know thy felicity?
From which worlds cannot now remove me.
  Dono. Art thou mad too, fond woman? what's thy meaning?
  Const. To seek eternal happiness in heaven,
Which all this world affords not.
  Cador. Think of thy vow, thou art my promis'd wife.
  Const. Pray, trouble me no further.
  All. Strange alteration!
  Cador. Why do you stand at gaze, you sacred priests?
You holy men, be equal to the gods,
And consummate my marriage with this woman.
  Bishop. Herself gives bar, my lord, to your desires,
And our performance; 'tis against the law
And orders of the church, to force a marriage.
  Cador. How am I wrong'd! Was this your trick, my lord?
  Dono. I am abus'd past sufferance;
Grief and amazement strive which sense of mine
Shall lose her being first; yet let me call thee daughter.
  Cador. Me, wife.
  Const. Your words are air, you speak of want to wealth,
And wish her sickness, newly rais'd to health.
  Dono. Bewitched girls, tempt not an old man's fury,
That hath no strength to uphold his feeble age,

But what your sights give life to; O, beware,
And do not make me curse you.
   Mod. [*kneeling*] Dear father,
Here at your feet we kneel, grant us but this,
That in your sight and hearing the good Hermit
May plead our cause; which if it shall not give
Such satisfaction as your age desires,
We will submit to you.
   Const.   You gave us life:
Save not our bodies, but our souls, from death.
   Dono. This gives some comfort yet: rise with my bless-
                ings.—
Have patience, noble Cador, worthy Edwin;
Send for the Hermit that we may confer;
For, sure, religion ties you not to leave
Your careful father thus. If so it be,
Take you content, and give all grief to me.   [*Exeunt.*

      Scene III. *Thunder and lightning. Enter* Devil.

   Devil. Mix light and darkness, earth and heaven dissolve,
Be of one piece again, and turn to chaos;
Break all your works, you powers, and spoil the world,
Or, if you will maintain earth still, give way
And life to this abortive birth now coming,
Whose fame shall add unto your oracles.
Lucina, Hecate, dreadful queen of night,
Bright Proserpine, be pleas'd for Ceres' love,
From Stygian darkness summon up the Fates,
And in a moment bring them quickly hither,
Lest death do vent her birth and her together.   [*Thunder.*
Assist, you spirits of infernal deeps,
Squint-ey'd Erictho, midnight Incubus,
Rise, rise to aid this birth prodigious.

      Enter Lucina, *and the three* Fates.
Thanks, Hecate, hail, sister to the gods!
There lies your way, haste with the Fates, and help,

Give quick dispatch unto her labouring throes,
To bring this mixture of infernal seed
To human being; [*Exeunt Fates.*
And to beguile her pains, till back you come,
Anticks shall dance, and music fill the room.— [*Dance.*
Thanks, queen of shades.
　Lucina. Farewell, great servant to th' infernal king.
In honour of this child, the Fates shall bring
All their assisting powers of knowledge, arts,
Learning, and wisdom, all the hidden parts
Of all-admiring prophecy, to foresee
The event of times to come. His art shall stand
A wall of brass to guard the Britain land.
Even from this minute, all his art appears
Manlike in judgment, person, state, and years.
Upon his breast the Fates have fix'd his name,
And since his birthplace was this forest here,
They now have nam'd him Merlin Silvester.
　Devil. And Merlin's name in Britany shall live,
Whilst men inhabit here, or Fates can give
Power to amazing wonder; envy shall weep,
And mischief sit and shake her ebon wings,
Whilst all the world of Merlin's magic sings. [*Exeunt.*

SCENE IV. *Enter* Clown.

　Clown. Well, I wonder how my poor sister does, after all this thundering. I think she's dead, for I can hear no tidings of her. Those woods yield small comfort for her; I could meet nothing but a swineherd's wife keeping hogs by the forestside, but neither she nor none of her sows would stir a foot to help us. Indeed, I think she durst not trust herself amongst the trees with me, for I must needs confess I offer'd some kindness to her. Well, I would fain know what's become of my sister. If she have brought me a young cousin, his face may be a picture to find his father by. So ho! sister Joan, Joan Go-to-'t, where art thou?

[*Within* Joan. Here, here, brother, stay but a while, I come to thee.

Clown. O brave! she's alive still, I know her voice, she speaks, and speaks cheerfully, methinks. How now, what moon-calf has she got with her?

Enter JOAN *and* MERLIN *with a book.*

Joan. Come, my dear Merlin, why dost thou fix thine eye
So deeply on that book?
Merl.   To sound the depth
Of arts, of learning, wisdom, knowledge.
Joan. O, my dear, dear son,
Those studies fit thee when thou art a man.
Merl. Why, mother, I can be but half a man at best,
And that is your mortality; the rest
In me is spirit; 'tis not meat, nor time,
That gives this growth and bigness; no, my years
Shall be more strange than yet my birth appears.
Look, mother, there's my uncle.
Joan. How dost thou know him, son? thou never saw'st him.
Merl. Yes, I know him, and know the pains he has taken for ye, to find out my father.—Give me your hand, good uncle.

Clown. Ha, ha, I'd laugh at that, i' faith. Do you know me, sir?

Merl. Yes, by the same token that even now you kissed the swineherd's wife l' the woods, and would have done more, if she would have let you, uncle.

Clown. A witch, a witch, a witch, sister! Rid him out of your company, he is either a witch or a conjurer; he could never have known this else.

Joan. Pray, love him, brother; he is my son.

Clown. Ha, ha, this is worse than all the rest, i' faith; by his beard he is more like your husband. Let me see, is your great belly gone?

Joan. Yes, and this the happy fruit.

Clown. What, this artichoke? A child born with a beard on his face?

Merl. Yes, and strong legs to go, and teeth to eat.

Clown. You can nurse up yourself then? There's some charges saved for soap and caudle. 'Slid, I have heard of some that has been born with teeth, but never none with such a talking tongue before.

Joan. Come, come, you must use him kindly, brother; did you but know his worth, you would make much of him.

Clown. Make much of a monkey? This is worse than Tom Thumb, that let a fart in his mother's belly; a child to speak, eat, and go the first hour of his birth, nay, such a baby as had need of a barber before he was born too! Why, sister, this is monstrous, and shames all our kindred.

Joan. That thus 'gainst nature and our common births
He comes thus furnish'd, to salute the world,
Is power of Fates, and gift of his great father.

Clown. Why, of what profession is your father, sir?

Merl. He keeps a hot-house i' the Low Countries; will you see him, sir?

Clown. See him? why, sister, has the child found his father?

Merl. Yes, and I'll fetch him, uncle. [*Exit.*

Clown. Do not uncle me, till I know your kindred. For my conscience, some baboon begot thee.—Surely thou art horribly deceived, sister, this urchin cannot be of thy breeding; I shall be ashamed to call him cousin, though his father be a gentleman.

Enter MERLIN *and* Devil.

Merl. Now, my kind uncle, see;
The child has found his father, this is he.

Clown. The devil it is; ha, ha, is this your sweetheart, sister? have we run through the country, haunted the city, and examined the court to find out a gallant with a hat and feather, and a silken sword, and golden hangers, and do you now bring me to a ragamuffin with a face like a frying-pan?

Joan. Fie, brother, you mistake; behold him better.

Clown. How's this? do you juggle with me, or are mine eyes matches? Hat and feather, sword, and hangers, and all! This is a gallant, indeed, sister; this has all the marks of him we look for.

Devil. And you have found him now, sir:
Give me your hand, I now must call you brother.

Clown. Not till you have married my sister, for all this while she's but your whore, sir.

Devil. Thou art too plain, I'll satisfy that wrong
To her, and thee, and all, with liberal hand:
Come, why art thou fearful?

Clown. Nay, I am not afraid, an you were the devil, sir.

Devil. Thou needest not; keep with thy sister still,
And I'll supply your wants, you shall lack nothing
That gold and wealth can purchase.

Clown. Thank you, brother. We have gone many a weary step to find you; you may be a husband for a lady, for you are far-fetched and dear-bought, I assure you. Pray, how should I call your son, my cousin here?

Devil. His name is Merlin.

Clown. Merlin? Your hand, cousin Merlin; for your father's sake I accept you unto my kindred; if you grow in all things as your beard does, you will be talk'd on. By your mother's side, cousin, you come of the Go-to-'ts, Suffolk-bred, but our standing house is at Hocklye i' th' Hole, and Layton-Buzzard. For your father, no doubt you may from him claim titles of worship, but I cannot describe it; I think his ancestors came first from Hell-broe in Wales, cousin.

Devil. No matter whence we do derive our name:
All Britany shall ring of Merlin's fame,
And wonder at his acts. Go hence to Wales,
There live a while, there Vortiger the king

Builds castles and strong holds, which cannot stand,
Unless supported by young Merlin's hand.
There shall thy fame begin, wars are a breeding.
The Saxons practise treason, yet unseen,
Which shortly shall break out.—Fair love, farewell;
Dear son and brother, here I must leave you all,
Yet still I will be near at Merlin's call. [*Exit.*
   Merl. Will you go, uncle?
   Clown. Yes, I'll follow you, cousin.—Well, I do most horribly begin to suspect my kindred; this brother-in-law of mine is the devil, sure, and though he hide his horns with his hat and feather, I spied his cloven foot for all his cunning.
                                       [*Exeunt.*

       Scene V. *Enter* Ostorius, Octa, *and* Proximus.

   Ostor. Come, come, time calls our close complots to action:
Go, Proximus, with wingèd speed fly hence,
Hie thee to Wales, salute great Vortiger
With these our letters; bid the king to arms,
Tell him we have new friends, more forces landed
In Norfolk and Northumberland; bid him
Make haste to meet us; if he keep his word,
We'll part the realm between us.
   Octa. Bend all thine art to quit that late disgrace
The christian Hermit gave thee; make thy revenge
Both sure and home.
   Prox.   That thought, sir, spurs me on,
Till I have wrought their swift destruction. [*Exit.*
   Ostor. Go then and prosper.—Octa, be vigilant:
Speak, are the forts possess'd? the guards made sure?
Revolve, I pray, on how large consequence
The bare event and sequel of our hopes
Jointly consists, that have embark'd our lives
Upon the hazard of the least miscarriage.
   Octa. All's sure, the queen your sister hath contriv'd

The cunning plot so sure, as at an instant
The brothers shall be both surpris'd and taken.
　Ostor. And both shall die, yet one a while must live,
Till we by him have gather'd strength and power
To meet bold Edol, their stern general,
That now, contrary to the king's command,
Hath re-united all his cashier'd troops,
And this way beats his drums to threaten us.
　Octa. Then our plot is discover'd.
　Ostor. Come, th' art a fool, his army and his life
Is given unto us. Where is the queen my sister?
　Octa. In conference with the prince.
　Ostor. Bring the guards nearer, all is fair and good;
This conference, I hope, shall end in blood.　　[*Exeunt.*

Scene VI. *Enter* Prince *and* Artesia.

　Art. Come, come, you do but flatter;
What you term love, is but a dream of blood,
Wakes with enjoying, and with open eyes
Forgot, contemn'd, and lost.
　Prince. [*aside.*] I must be wary, her words are danger-
　　　　　　ous.—
True, we'll speak of love no more then.
　Art. Nay, if you will, you may;
'Tis but in jest, and yet so children play
With fiery flames, and covet what is bright,
But, feeling his effects, abhor the light.
Pleasure is like a building, the more high,
The narrower still it grows; cedars do die
Soonest at top.
　Prince.　　How does your instance suit?
　Art. From art and nature to make sure the root,
And lay a fast foundation, ere I try
The incertain changes of a wavering sky.
Make your example thus: you have a kiss;　　[*Kisses him.*
Was it not pleasing?

Prince. Above all name to express it.
Art. Yet now the pleasure 's gone,
And you have lost your joy's possession.
Prince. Yet when you please, this flood may ebb again.
Art. But where it never ebbs, there runs the main.
Prince. Who can attain such hopes?
Art. I'll show the way to 't. Give me
A taste once more of what you may enjoy.   [*Kisses him.*
Prince. [*aside.*] Impudent whore!—
I were more false than atheism can be,
Should I not call this high felicity.
Art. If I should trust your faith, alas, I fear,
You soon would change belief.
Prince. I'd covet martyrdom to make 't confirm'd.
Art. Give me your hand on that you'll keep your word.
Prince. I will.
Art. Enough.—Help, husband, king Aurelius, help!
Rescue betray'd Artesia.
Prince. Nay then 'tis I that am betray'd, I see;
Yet with thy blood I'll end thy treachery.
Art. How now? what troubles you? Is this you, sir,
That but even now would suffer martyrdom
To win your hopes, and is there now such terror
In names of men to fright you? Nay, then I see
What mettle you are made of.
Prince. Ha! was't but trial? then I ask your pardon:
What a dull slave was I to be so fearful!
[*Aside.*] I'll trust her now no more, yet try the utmost.—
I am resolv'd, no brother, no man breathing,
Were he my blood's begetter, should withhold
Me from your love; I'd leap into his bosom,
And from his breast pull forth that happiness
Heaven had reserv'd in you for my enjoying.
Art. Ay, now you speak a lover like a prince!—
Treason, treason!
    Prince.   Again?
    Art.   Help, Saxon princes, treason!

Enter Ostorius, Octa, *and others.*

Ostor. Rescue the queen; strike down the villain!

Enter Edol, Aurelius, Donobert, Cador, Edwin, Toclio, Oswald, *at the other door.*

Edol. Call in the guards; the prince in danger!—
Fall back, dear sir, my breast shall buckler you.
  Aur. Beat down their weapons!
  Edol. Slave, wert thou made of brass, my sword shall bite thee.
  Aur. Withdraw on pain of death! Where is the traitor?
  Art. O, save your life; my lord, let it suffice
My beauty forc'd mine own captivity.
  Aur. Who did attempt to wrong thee?
  Prince.   Hear me, sir.
  Aur. O my sad soul! was't thou?
  Art. O, do not stand to speak; one minute's stay
Prevents a second speech for ever.
  Aur. Make our guards strong:
My dear Artesia, let us know thy wrongs,
And our own dangers.
  Art. The prince your brother, with these Briton lords,
Have all agreed to take me hence by force,
And marry me to him.
  Prince. The devil shall wed thee first;
Thy baseness and thy lust confound and rot thee!
  Art. He courted me even now, and in mine ear
Sham'd not to plead his most dishonest love,
And their attempts to seize your sacred person,
Either to shut you up within some prison,
Or, which is worse, I fear, to murder you.
  All Britons. 'Tis all as false as hell.
  Edol.   And as foul as she is.
  Art. You know me, sir?
  Edol.   Yes, deadly sin, we know you,
And shall discover all your villany.

Aur. Chester, forbear.
Ostor. Their treasons, sir, are plain:
Why are their soldiers lodg'd so near the court?
Octa. Nay, why came he in arms so suddenly?
Edol. You fleering anticks, do not wake my fury.
Octa. Fury?
Edol. Ratsbane, do not urge me.
Art. Good sir, keep farther from them.
Prince. O my sick heart!
She is a witch by nature, devil by art.
Aur. Bite thine own slanderous tongue, 'tis thou art false;
I have observ'd your passions long ere this.
Ostor. Stand on your guard, my lord, we are your friends,
And all our force is yours.
Edol. To spoil and rob the kingdom.
Aur. Sir, be silent.
Edol. Silent! how long? till doomsday? shall I stand by,
And hear mine honour blasted with foul treason,
The state half lost, and your life endanger'd, yet be silent?
Art. Yes, my blunt lord, unless you speak your treasons.—
Sir, let your guards, as traitors, seize them all,
And then let tortures and divulsive racks
Force a confession from them.
Edol. Wildfire and brimstone eat thee! Hear me, sir.
Aur. Sir, I'll not hear you.
Edol. But you shall! Not hear me?
Were the world's monarch, Cæsar, living, he
Should hear me.
I tell you, sir, these serpents have betray'd
Your life and kingdom. Does not every day
Bring tidings of more swarms of lousy slaves,
The offal fugitives of barren Germany,
That land upon our coasts, and by our neglect
Settled in Norfolk and Northumberland?
Ostor. They come as aids and safeguards to the king.

Octa. Has he not need, when Vortiger's in arms,
And you raise powers, 'tis thought, to join with him?
  Edol. Peace, you pernicious rat.
  Dono.   Prithee, forbear.
  Edol. Away, suffer a gilded rascal,
A low-bred despicable creeper, an insulting toad,
To spit his poison'd venom in my face!
  Octa. Sir, sir.
  Edol. Do not reply, you cur; for, by the gods,
Though the king's presence guard thee, I shall break all
    patience,
And, like a lion rous'd to spoil, shall run
Foul-mouth'd upon thee, and devour thee quick.—
Speak, sir, will you forsake these scorpions,
Or stay, till they have stung you to the heart?
  Aur. You are traitors all, this is our wife, our queen.
Brother Ostorius, troop your Saxons up,
We'll hence to Winchester, and raise more powers,
To man with strength the castle Camilot.—
Go hence, false men, join you with Vortiger,
The murderer of our brother Constantine:
We'll hunt both him and you with dreadful vengeance.
Since Britain fails, we'll trust to foreign friends,
And guard our person from your traitorous ends.
      [*Exeunt Aur., Ostor., Octa., Art., Tocl., Osw.*
  Edw. He's sure bewitch'd.
  Glost.   What counsel now for safety?
  Dono. Only this, sir: with all the speed we can,
Preserve the person of the king and kingdom.
  Cador. Which to effect, 'tis best march hence to Wales,
And set on Vortiger before he join
His forces with the Saxons.
  Edw. On then with speed for Wales and Vortiger!
That tempest once o'erblown, we come, Ostorius,
To meet thy traitorous Saxons, thee and them,
That with advantage thus have won the king,
To back your factions, and to work our ruins,

This, by the gods and my good sword, I'll set
In bloody lines upon thy burgonet. [*Exeunt.*

ACT IV.

SCENE I. *Enter* Clown, MERLIN, *and a little antick* Spirit.

Merl. How now, uncle? Why do you search your pockets so? do you miss any thing?

Clown. Ha! cousin Merlin, I hope your beard does not overgrow your honesty; I pray, remember, you are made up of my sister's thread, I am your mother's brother, whosoever was your father.

Merl. Why, wherein can you task my duty, uncle?

Clown. Yourself, or your page it must be; I have kept no other company, since your mother bound your head to my protectorship; I do feel a fault of one side; either it was that sparrowhawk, or a cast of Merlin's, for I find a covey of cardecu's sprung out of my pocket.

Merl. Why, do you want any money, uncle?—Sirrah, had you any from him?

Clown. Deny it not, for my pockets are witness against you.

Spirit. Yes, I had, to teach you better wit to look to it.

Clown. Pray, use your fingers better, and my wit may serve as it is, sir.

Merl. Well, restore it.

Spirit. There it is.

Clown. Ay, there's some honesty in this; 'twas a token from your invisible father, cousin, which I would not have to go invisibly from me again.

Merl. Well, you are sure you have it now, uncle?

Clown. Yes, and mean to keep it now from your page's filching fingers too.

Spirit. If you have it so sure, pray, show it me again.

Clown. Yes, my little juggler, I dare show it.—Ha, cleanly conveyance again! ye have no invisible fingers, have ye? 'Tis gone, certainly.

Spirit. Why, sir, I touch'd you not.

Merl. Why, look you, uncle, I have it now. How ill do you look to it. Here, keep it safer.

Clown. Ha, ha, this is fine, i' faith. I must keep some other company, if you have these sleights of hand.

Merl. Come, come, uncle, 'tis all my art which shall not offend you, sir, only I give you a taste of it, to show you sport.

Clown. O, but 'tis all jesting with a man's pocket, though.—But I am glad to see your cunning, cousin, for now will I warrant thee a living till thou diest. You have heard the news in Wales here?

Merl. Uncle, let me prevent your care and counsel,
'Twill give you better knowledge of my cunning;
You would prefer me now, in hope of gain,
To Vortiger, king of the Welsh Britons,
To whom are all the artists summon'd now,
That seek the secrets of futurity,
The bards, the druids, wizards, conjurers,
Not an Aruspex with his whistling spells,
No Capnomancer with his musty fumes,
No witch or juggler, but is thither sent,
To calculate the strange and fear'd event
Of his prodigious castle, now in building,
Where all the labours of the painful day,
Are ruin'd still i' the night, and to this place
You would have me go.

Clown. Well, if thy mother were not my sister, I would say she was a witch that begot thee; but this is thy father, not thy mother wit. Thou hast taken my tale into thy mouth, and spoke my words before me; therefore away, shuffle thyself amongst the conjurers, and be a made man before thou comest to age.

Merl. Nay, but stay, uncle, you overslip my dangers:
The prophecies and all the cunning wizards,
Have certified the king, that this his castle
Can never stand, till the foundation 's laid

With mortar temper'd with the fatal blood
Of such a child, whose father was no mortal.

Clown. What's this to thee? If the devil were thy father, was not thy mother born at Carmarthen? Diggon for that then; and then it must be a child's blood, and who will take thee for a child with such a beard of thy face? Is there not diggon for that too, cousin?

Merl. I must not go: lend me your ear a while, I'll give you reasons to the contrary.

Enter two Gentlemen.

First Gent. Sure, this is an endless piece of work, the king has sent us about!

Sec. Gent. Kings may do it, man; the like has been done to find out the unicorn.

First Gent. Which will be sooner found, I think, than this fiend-begotten child we seek for.

Sec. Gent. Pox of those conjurers that would speak of such a one, and yet all their cunning could not tell us where to find him.

First Gent. In Wales they say assuredly he lives; come, let's enquire further.

Merl. Uncle, your persuasions must not prevail with me: I know mine enemies better than you do.

Clown. I say th' art a bastard then, if thou disobey thine uncle. Was not Joan Go-to-'t, thy mother, my sister? If the devil were thy father, what kin art thou to any man alive, but baileys and brokers? and they are but brothers-in-law to thee neither.

First Gent. How's this? I think we shall speed here.

Sec. Gent. Ay, and unlook'd for to. Go near and listen to them.

Clown. Hast thou a beard to hide it? Wilt then show thyself a child? Wilt thou have more hair than wit? Wilt thou deny thy mother, because nobody knows thy father? Or shall thine uncle be an ass?

First Gent. Bless ye, friend: pray, what call you this small gentleman's name?

Clown. Small, sir? A small man may be a great gentleman; his father may be of an ancient house, for aught we know, sir.

Sec. Gent. Why, do you not know his father?

Clown. No, nor you neither, I think, unless the devil be in ye.

First Gent. What is his name, sir?

Clown. His name is my cousin, sir; his education is my sister's son, but his manners are his own.

Merl. Why ask ye, gentlemen? My name is Merlin.

Clown. Yes, and a goshawk was his father, for aught we know; for I am sure his mother was a wind-sucker.

Sec. Gent. He has a mother then?

Clown. As sure as I have a sister, sir.

First Gent. But his father you leave doubtful.

Clown. Well, sir, as wise men as you doubt, whether he had a father or no.

First Gent. Sure, this is he we seek for.

Sec. Gent. I think no less; and, sir, we let you know the king hath sent for you.

Clown. The more child he; an he had been rul'd by me, he should have gone before he was sent for.

First Gent. May we not see his mother?

Clown. Yes, and feel her too, if you anger her. A devilish thing, I can tell ye, she has been. I'll go fetch her to ye. [*Exit.*

Sec. Gent. Sir, it were fit you did resolve for speed, You must unto the king.

Merl.   My service, sir,
Shall need no strict command, it shall obey
Most peaceably; but needless 'tis to fetch
What is brought home. My journey may be staid,
The king is coming hither
With the same quest you bore before him.—Hark,
'This drum will tell ye.   [*Within drums beat a low march.*

First Gent. This is some cunning, indeed, sir.

Flourish. Enter VORTIGER *reading a letter,* PROXIMUS, *with drum and soldiers, and others.*

Vort. Still in our eye your message, Proximus,
We keep to spur our speed:
Ostorius and Octa we shall salute
With succour 'gainst prince Uter and Aurelius,
Whom now we hear encamp'd at Winchester.
There's nothing interrupts our way so much,
As doth the erection of this fatal castle,
That spite of all our art and daily labour,
The night still ruins.

Prox. As erst I did affirm, still I maintain,
The fiend-begotten child must be found out,
Whose blood gives strength to the foundation,
It cannot stand else.

Enter Clown, MERLIN, *and* JOAN.

Vort. Ha! is't so?
Then, Proximus, by this intelligence
He should be found: speak, is this he you tell of?

Clown. Yes, sir, and I his uncle, and she his mother.

Vort. And who is his father?

Clown. Why, she his mother can best tell you that, and yet I think the child be wise enough, for he has found his father.

Vort. Woman, is this thy son?

Joan. It is, my lord.

Vort. What was his father? Or where lives he?

Merl. Mother, speak freely and unastonish'd;
That which you dar'd to act, dread not to name.

Joan. In which I shall betray my sin and shame,
But since it must be so, then know, great king,
All that myself yet knows of him, is this:
In pride of blood and beauty I did live,
My glass the altar was, my face the idol;
Such was my peevish love unto myself,

That I did hate all other; such disdain
Was in my scornful eye, that I suppos'd
No mortal creature worthy to enjoy me.
Thus with the peacock I beheld my train,
But never saw the blackness of my feet,
Oft have I chid the winds for breathing on me,
And curs'd the sun, fearing to blast my beauty.
In midst of this most leperous disease,
A seeming fair young man appear'd unto me,
In all things suiting my aspiring pride,
And with him brought along a conquering power,
To which my frailty yielded; from whose embraces
This issue came. What more he is, I know not.

Vort. Some Incubus, or spirit of the night
Begot him then; for, sure, no mortal did it.

Merl. No matter who, my lord; leave further quest,
Since 'tis as hurtful as unnecessary
More to enquire: go to the cause, my lord,
Why you have sought me thus?

Vort. I have no doubt but thou know'st; yet, to be plain,
I sought thee for thy blood.

Merl.   By whose direction?

Prox. By mine.
My art infallible instructed me,
Upon thy blood must the foundation rise
Of the king's building, it cannot stand else.

Merl. Hast thou such leisure to enquire my fate,
And let thine own hang careless over thee?
Know'st thou what pendulous mischief roofs thy head,
How fatal, and how sudden?

Prox. Pish!
Bearded abortive, thou foretell my danger?—
My lord, he trifles to delay his own.

Merl. No,
I yield myself; and here before the king
Make good thine augury, as I shall mine.
If thy fate fall not, thou hast spoke all truth,

And let my blood satisfy the king's desires:
If thou thyself wilt write thine epitaph,
Dispatch it quickly, there's not a minute's time
'Twixt thee and thy death.
    Prox. Ha, ha, ha!   [*A stone falls and kills Proximus.*
    Merl. Ay, so thou mayst die laughing.
    Vort. Ha! This is above admiration. Look, is he dead?
    Clown. Yes, sir, here's brains to make mortar of, if you'll use them.—Cousin Merlin, there's no more of this stone fruit ready to fall, is there? I pray, give your uncle a little fair warning.
    Merl. Remove that shape of death; and now, my lord,
For clear satisfaction of your doubts, Merlin will show
The fatal cause that keeps your castle down,
And hinders your proceedings.
Stand there, and by an apparition see
The labour and end of all your destiny.—
Mother and uncle, you must be absent.
    Clown. Is your father coming, cousin?
    Merl. Nay, you must be gone.
    Joan. Come, you'll offend him, brother.
    Clown. I would fain see my brother-in-law; if you were married, I might lawfully call him so.
                            [*Exeunt Joan and Clown.*

Merlin *strikes his wand. Thunder and lightning. Two dragons appear, a white and a red; they fight a while and pause.*
    Vort. What means this stay?
    Merl. Be not amaz'd, my lord, for on the victory
Of loss or gain, as these two champions' ends,
Your fate, your life, and kingdom all depends;
Therefore observe it well.
    Vort. I shall; heaven be auspicious to us.

    Thunder. The two dragons fight again, and the white dragon drives off the red.
    Vort. The conquest is on the white dragon's part.
Now, Merlin, faithfully expound the meaning.

Merl. Your grace must then not be offended with me.
Vort. Is it the weakest part I found in thee,
To doubt of me so slightly? Shall I blame
My prophet that foretells me of my dangers?
Thy cunning I approve most excellent.
Merl. Then know, my lord, there is a dampish cave,
The nightly habitation of these dragons,
Vaulted beneath where you would build your castle,
Whose enmity and nightly combats there
Maintain a constant ruin of your labours.
To make it more plain, the dragons then
Yourself betoken, and the Saxon king;
'The vanquish'd red is, sir, your dreadful emblem.
Vort. O my fate!
Merl. Nay, you must bear with patience, royal sir:
You slew the lawful king Constantius;
'Twas a red deed, your crown his blood did cement.
The English Saxon, first brought in by you,
For aid against Constantius' brethren,
Is the white horror; who now, knit together,
Have driven and shut you up in these wild mountains.
And though they now seek to unite with friendship,
It is to wound your bosom, not embrace it,
And with an utter extirpation
To rout the Britons out, and plant the English.
Seek for your safety, sir, and spend no time
To build the airy castles; for prince Uter
Armèd with vengeance for his brother's blood
Is hard upon you. If you mistrust me,
And to my words crave witness, sir, then know,
Here comes a messenger to tell you so. [*Exit Merlin.*

Enter Messenger.

Mess. My lord! prince Uter!
Vort. And who else, sir?
Mess. Edol, the great general.

Vort. The great devil!
They are coming to meet us.
  Mess. With a full power, my lord.
  Vort. With a full vengeance
They mean to meet us; so we are ready
To their confront, at full march double footing.
We'll lose no ground, nor shall their numbers fright us:
If it be fate, it cannot be withstood:
We got our crown so, be it lost in blood. [*Exeunt.*

SCENE II. *Enter Prince* UTER, EDOL, CADOR, EDWIN, TOCLIO,
  and soldiers with drum.

  Prince. Stay, and advice; hold, drum,
  Edol. Beat, slave, why do you pause?
Why make a stand? where are our enemies?
Or do you mean we fight amongst ourselves?
  Prince. Nay, noble Edol, let us here take counsel;
It cannot hurt,
It is the surest garrison to safety.
  Edol. Fie on such slow delays! so fearful men,
That are to pass over a flowing river,
Stand on the bank to parley of the danger,
Till the tide rise, and then be swallowed.
Is not the king in field?
  Cador. Proud Vortiger, the traitor, is in field.
  Edw. The murderer, and usurper.
  Edol. Let him be the devil,
So I may fight with him. For heaven's love, sir, march on.
O my patience! will you delay
Until the Saxons come to aid his party? [*A tucket.*
  Prince. There's no such fear: Prithee, be calm a while.
Hark!
It seems by this; he comes or sends to us.
  Edol. If it be for parley, I will drown the summons,
If all our drums and hoarseness choke me not.

Enter Captain.

Prince. Nay, prithee, hear.—From whence art thou?
Capt. From the king Vortiger.
Edol. Traitor, there's none such:
Alarum drum, strike, slave, or by mine honour
I'll break thy head, and beat thy drumsticks both
About thine ears.
  Prince. Hold, noble Edol,
Let's hear what articles he can enforce.
  Edol. What articles, or what conditions
Can you expect to value half your wrong,
Unless he kill himself by thousand tortures,
And send his carcass to appease your vengeance,
For the foul murder of Constantius,
And that's not a tenth part neither.
  Prince.   'Tis true,
My brother's blood is crying to me now;
I do applaud thy counsels.—Hence, be gone!
                                    [*Exit Captain.*
We'll hear no parley now but by our swords.
  Edol. And those shall speak home in death-killing
              words.—
Alarum to the fight, sound, sound the alarum.   [*Exeunt.*
  Alarum. Re-enter Edol *driving all* Vortiger's *force before him; then exit.*

Scene III. *Enter* Prince Uter *pursuing* Vortiger.

Vort. Dost follow me?
Prince.   Yes, to thy death I will.
Vort. Stay, be advis'd!
It would not be the only fall of princes,
I slew thy brother.
  Prince. Thou didst, black traitor,
And in that vengeance I pursue thee.
  Vort. Take mercy for thyself, and fly my sword,

22*

Save thine own life as satisfaction,
Which here I give thee for thy brother's death.
    Prince. Give what 's thine own: a traitor's heart and
        head,
That's all thou art right lord of; the kingdom
Which thou usurp'st, thou most unhappy tyrant,
Is leaving thee; the Saxons which thou brought'st
To back thy usurpations, are grown great,
And where they seat themselves, do hourly seek
To blot the records of old Brute and Britons
From memory of men, calling themselves
Hingest-men, and Hingest-land, that no more
The Briton name be known; all this by thee,
Thou base destroyer of thy native country.

               Enter EDOL.
    Edol. What, stand you talking? Fight!
    Prince. Hold, Edol.
    Edol.   Hold out, my sword,
And listen not to king or prince's word,
There's work enough abroad, this task is mine.   [*Alarum.*
    Prince. Prosper thy valour, as thy virtues shine.
                                                    [*Exeunt.*

       SCENE IV. *Enter* CADOR *and* EDWIN.

    Cador. Bright victory herself fights on our part,
And, buckled in a golden beaver, rides
Triumphantly before us.
    Edw.   Justice is with her,
Who ever takes he true and rightful cause;
Let us not lag behind them.

               Enter Prince.
    Cador. Here comes the prince; how go our fortunes, sir?
    Prince. Hopeful, and fair, brave Cador;
Proud Vortiger, beat down by Edol's sword,
Was rescu'd by the following multitudes,
And now for safety 's fled unto a castle

Here standing on the hill; but I have sent
A cry of hounds as violent as hunger,
To break his stony walls; or if they fail,
We'll send in wildfire to dislodge him thence,
Or burn them all with flaming violence. [*Exeunt.*

SCENE V. *Blazing star appears. Flourish. Enter* Prince UTER,
EDOL, CADOR, EDWIN, TOCLIO, *and soldiers with drum.*

Prince. Look, Edol: Still this fiery exhalation shoots
His frightful horrors on th' amazèd world;
See, in the beam that 'bout his flaming ring,
A dragon's head appears, from out whose mouth
Two flaming flakes of fire stretch east and west.
   Edol. And see, from forth the body of the star
Seven smaller blazing streams directly point
On this affrighted kingdom.
   Cador. 'Tis a dreadful meteor.
   Edw. And doth portend strange fears.
   Prince. This is no crown of peace; this angry fire
Hath something more to burn than Vortiger;
If it alone were pointed at his fall,
It would pull in his blazing pyramids,
And be appeas'd, for Vortiger is dead.
   Edol. These never come without their large effects.
   Prince. The will of heaven be done! Our sorrow's this,
We want a mystic Python to expound
This fiery oracle.
   Cador.   O no, my lord,
You have the best that ever Britain bred;
And durst I prophecy of your prophet, sir,
None like him shall succeed him.
   Prince.   You mean Merlin?
   Cador. True, sir, wonderous Merlin,
He met us in the way, and did foretell
The fortunes of this day successful to us.
   Edw. He's sure about the camp; send for him, sir.

Cador. He told the bloody Vortiger his fate,
And truly too, and if I could give faith
To any wizard's skill, it should be Merlin.

Enter MERLIN *and* Clown.

And see, my lord,
As if to satisfy your highness' pleasure,
Merlin is come.
    Prince. See,
The comet's in his eye, disturb him not.
    Edol. With what a piercing judgment he beholds it!
    Merl. Whither will heaven and fate translate this kingdom?
What revolutions, rise and fall of nations
Is figur'd yonder in that star, that sings
The change of Britain's state, and death of kings?
Ha! He's dead already, how swiftly mischief creeps!
Thy fatal end, sweet prince, even Merlin weeps.
    Prince. He does foresee some evil, his action shows it,
For, ere he does expound, he weeps the story.
    Edol. There is another weeps too.—
Sirrah, dost thou understand what thou lament'st for?
    Clown. No, sir, I am his uncle, and weep because my cousin weeps; flesh and blood cannot forbear.
    Prince. Gentle Merlin, speak thy prophetic knowledge,
In explanation of this fiery horror,
By which we gather from thy mournful tears,
Much sorrow and disaster in it.
    Merl.   'Tis true,
Fair prince, but you must hear the rest with patience.
    Prince. I vow I will, tho' it portend my ruin.
    Merl. There's no such fear,
This brought the fiery fall of Vortiger,
And yet not him alone: This day is fall'n
A king more good, the glory of our land,
The mild, and gentle, sweet Aurelius.
    Prince. Our brother?

Edw. Forefend it, heaven!
Merl. He at his palace royal, sir,
At Winchester, this day is dead and poison'd.
Cador. By whom? or what means, Merlin?
Merl. By the traitorous Saxons.
Edol. I ever fear'd as much: that devil Ostorius,
And the damn'd witch Artesia, sure, have done it.
Prince. Poisoned! O, look further, gentle Merlin,
Behold the star again, and do but find
Revenge for me, though it cost thousand lives,
And mine the foremost.
Merl. Comfort yourself, the heavens have given it fully;
All the portentous ills to you are told.
Now hear a happy story, sir, from me,
To you and to your fair posterity.
Clown. Methinks, I see something like a peeled onion, it makes me weep again.
Merl. Be silent, uncle, you'll be forced else.
Clown. Can you not find in the star, cousin, whether I can hold my tongue or no?
Edol. Yes, I must cut it out.
Clown. O, ha, you speak without book, sir, my cousin Merlin knows.
Merl. True, I must tie it up.—Now speak your pleasure, uncle.
Clown. Hum, hum, hum, hum.
Merl. So, so.—Now observe, my lord, and there behold
Above yon flame-hair'd beam that upwards shoots,
Appears a dragon's head, out of whose mouth
Two streaming lights point their flame-feather'd darts
Contrary ways, yet both shall have their aims.
Again behold from the igniferous body,
Seven splendent and illustrious rays are spread,
All speaking heralds to this Briton isle,
And thus they are expounded: the dragon's head
Is the hieroglyphic that figures out
Your princely self that here must reign a king;

'Those by-form'd fires that from the dragon's mouth
Shoot east and west, emblem two royal babes,
Which shall proceed from you, a son and daughter:
Her pointed constellation northwest tending,
Crowns her a queen in Ireland, of whom first springs
That kingdom's title to the Briton kings.
    Clown. Hum, hum, hum.
    Merl. But of your son, thus fate and Merlin tells:
All after-times shall fill their chronicles
With fame of his renown, whose warlike sword
Shall pass through fertile France and Germany,
Nor shall his conquering foot be forc'd to stand,
Till Rome's imperial wreath hath crown'd his fame
With monarch of the west, from whose seven hills
With conquest, and contributary kings,
He back returns to enlarge the Briton bounds,
His heraldry adorn'd with thirteen crowns.
    Clown. Hum, hum, hum.
    Merl. He to the world shall add another worthy,
And, as a loadstone for his prowess, draw
A train of martial lovers to his court.
It shall be then the best of knighthood's honour,
At Winchester to fill his castle hall,
And at his royal table sit and feast
In warlike orders, all their arms round hurl'd,
As if they meant to circumscribe the world.
            [*He touches the Clown's mouth with his wand.*
    Clown. Hum, hum, hum. O, that I could speak a little!
    Merl. I know your mind, uncle; again be silent.
                            [*Strikes him again.*
    Prince. Thou speak'st of wonders, Merlin, prithee, go on,
Declare at full this constellation.
    Merl. Those seven beams pointing downward, sir, betoken
The troubles of this land, which then shall meet
With other fate; war and dissension strives
To make division, till seven kings agree
To draw this kingdom to a heptarchy.

Prince. Thine art hath made such proof, that we believe
Thy words authentical; be ever near us,
My prophet, and the guide of all my actions.
 Merl. My service shall be faithful to your person,
And all my studies for my country's safety.
 Clown. Hum, hum, hum.
 Merl. Come, you are releas'd, sir.
 Clown. Cousin, pray, help me to my tongue again; you
do not mean I shall be dumb still, I hope?
 Merl. Why, hast thou not thy tongue?
 Clown. Ha! yes, I feel it now, I was so long dumb, I
could not well tell whether I spake or no.
 Prince. Is 't thy advice, we presently pursue
The bloody Saxons that have slain my brother?
 Merl. With your best speed, my lord;
Prosperity will keep you company.
 Cador. Take then your title with you, royal prince,
'Twill add unto our strength: Long live king Uter!
 Edol. Put the addition to 't that heaven hath given you:
The dragon is your emblem, bear it bravely,
And so long live and ever happy, styl'd
Uter Pendragon, lawful king of Britain.
 Prince. Thanks, Edol, we embrace the name and title,
And in our shield and standard shall the figure
Of a red dragon still be borne before us,
To fright the bloody Saxons.—O, my Aurelius,
Sweet rest thy soul; let thy disturbèd spirit
Expect revenge, think what it would, it hath,
The dragon's coming in his fiery wrath. [*Exeunt.*

ACT V.

Scene I. *Thunder, then music.*

Enter Joan *fearfully, the* Devil *following her.*

 Joan. Hence, thou black horror! Is thy lustful fire
Kindled again? Not thy loud-throated thunder,

Nor thy adulterate infernal music,
Shall e'er bewitch me more; O, too, too much
Is past already!
Devil. Why dost thou fly me?
I come a lover to thee, to embrace,
And gently twine thy body in mine arms.
Joan. Out, thou hell-hound!
Devil. What hound so e'er I be,
Fawning and sporting as I would with thee,
Why should I not be strok'd and play'd withal?
Wilt thou not thank the lion, might devour thee,
If he shall let thee pass?
Joan. Yes, thou art he;
Free me, and I'll thank thee.
Devil. Why, whither wouldst?
I am at home with thee, thou art mine own,
Have we not charge of family together?
Where is your son?
Joan. O, darkness cover me!
Devil. There is a pride which thou hast won by me,
The mother of a fame, shall never die:
Kings shall have need of written chronicles,
To keep their names alive, but Merlin none,
Ages to ages shall, like satellites,
Report the wonders of his name and glory,
While there are tongues and times to tell his story.
Joan. O, rot my memory before my flesh,
Let him be call'd some hell or earth-bred monster,
That ne'er had hapless woman for a mother!
Sweet death, deliver me!—Hence from my sight!
Why shouldst thou now appear? I had no pride
Nor lustful thought about me, to conjure
And call thee to my ruin, whenas at first
Thy cursèd person became visible.
Devil. I am the same I was.
Joan. But I am chang'd.
Devil. Again I'll change thee to the same thou wert,

To quench my lust.—Come forth, by thunder led,
My coadjutors in the spoils of mortals.   [*Thunder.*

             Enter Spirits.
Clasp in your ebon arms that prize of mine,
Mount her as high as pallid Hecate,
And on this rock I'll stand to cast up fumes
And darkness o'er the blue-fac'd firmament:
From Britain and from Merlin, I'll remove her,
They ne'er shall meet again.
    Joan. Help me some saving hand,
If not too late, I cry: Let mercy come!
              Enter MERLIN.
    Merl. Stay, you black slaves of night, let loose your hold,
Set her down safe, or by th' infernal Styx,
I'll bind you up with exorcisms so strong,
That all the black Pentagoron of hell,
Shall ne'er release you; save yourselves and vanish!
                        [*Exeunt Spirits.*
    Devil. Ha, what is he?
    Merl.   The child hath found his father.
Do you not know me?
    Devil. Merlin!
    Joan. O, help me, gentle son!
    Merl. Fear not, they shall not hurt you.
    Devil. Reliev'st thou her, to disobey thy father?
    Merl. Obedience is no lesson in your school,
Nature and kind to her commands my duty;
The part that you begot was against kind.
So all I owe to you is to be unkind.
    Devil. I'll blast thee, slave, to death, and on this rock
Stick thee as an eternal monument.
    Merl. Ha, ha, thy power's too weak; what art thou,
                      devil,
But an inferior lustful Incubus,
Taking advantage of the wanton flesh,
Wherewith thou dost beguile the ignorant?

Put off the form of thy humanity,
And crawl upon thy speckled belly, serpent,
Or I'll unclasp the jaws of Acheron,
And fix thee ever in the local fire.
  Devil. 'Traitor to hell! Curse that I e'er begot thee!
  Merl. 'Thou didst beget thy scourge; storm not, nor stir;
The power of Merlin's art is all confirm'd
In the fates' decretals:—I will ransack hell,
And make thy masters bow unto my spell.
Thou first shalt taste it.
              [*Thunder and lightning in the rock.*]
Tenebrarum precis, divitiarum et inferorum deus, hunc Incubum in ignis eterni abyssum accipite, aut in hoc carcere tenebroso in sempiternum astringere mando.
              [*The rock incloses the Devil.*]
So! there beget earthquakes or noisome damps,
For never shalt thou touch a woman more.—
How cheer you, mother?
  Joan. O, now my son is my deliverer,
Yet I must name him with my deepest sorrow.
                         [*Alarum afar off.*
  Merl. Take comfort now, past times are ne'er recall'd,
I did foresee your mischief and prevent it.
Hark, how the sounds of war now call me hence
To aid Pendragon, that in battle stands
Against the Saxons, from whose aid
Merlin must not be absent. Leave this soil,
And I'll conduct you to a place retir'd,
Which I by art have rais'd, call'd Merlin's bower.
There shall you dwell with solitary sighs,
With groans and passions, your companions,
To weep away this flesh you have offended with,
And leave all bare unto your aerial soul.
And when you die, I will erect a monument
Upon the verdant plains of Salisbury,
No king shall have so high a sepulchre,

With pendulous stones that I will hang by art,
Where neither lime nor mortar shall be us'd,
A dark enigma to the memory,
For none shall have the power to number them,
A place that I will hallow for your rest;
Where no night-hag shall walk, no ware-wolf tread,
There Merlin's mother shall be sepulchrèd.   [*Exeunt.*

SCENE II. *Enter* DONOBERT, GLOSTER, *and* Hermit.

Dono. Sincerely, Gloster, I have told you all:
My daughters are both vow'd to single life,
And this day gone unto the nunnery,
Though I begot them to another end,
And fairly promis'd them in marriage,
One to earl Cador, th' other to your son,
My worthy friend, the earl of Gloster.
Those lost, I am lost: they are lost, all's lost.
Answer me this then: Is 't a sin to marry?
  Herm. O no, my lord.
  Dono. Go to then, I will go no further with you,
I persuade you to no ill, persuade you then
That I persuade you well.
  Glost. 'Twill be a good office in you, sir.

Enter CADOR *and* EDWIN.

Dono. Which since they thus neglect,
My memory shall lose them now for ever.—
See, see the noble lords, their promis'd husbands!
Had fate so pleas'd, you might have call'd me father.
  Edw. Those hopes are past, my lord, for even this minute
We saw them both enter the monastery,
Secluded from the world and men for ever.
  Cador. 'Tis both our griefs we cannot, sir:
But from the king take you the time's joy from us;
The Saxon king Ostorius slain and Octa fled,

That woman-fury, queen Artesia,
Is fast in hold, and forc'd to re-deliver
London and Winchester (which she had fortified)
To princely Uter, lately styl'd Pendragon,
Who now triumphantly is marching hither
To be invested with the Briton crown.
   Dono. The joy of this shall banish from my breast
All thought that I was father to two children,
Two stubborn daughters, that have left me thus.
Let my old arms embrace, and call you sons;
For, by the honour of my father's house,
I'll part my estate most equally betwixt you.
   Edw., Cador. Sir, you are most noble.

Flourish. Enter EDOL *with drum and colours,* OSWALD *bearing the standard,* TOCLIO *the shield, with the red dragon pictured in them, two Bishops with the crown,* Prince UTER, MERLIN, ARTESIA *bound,* GUARD *and* Clown.

   Prince. Set up our shield and standard, noble soldiers.
We have firm hope that, tho' our dragon sleep,
Merlin will us and our fair kingdom keep.
   Clown. As his uncle lives, I warrant you.
   Glost. Happy restorer of the Britons' fame,
Uprising sun, let us salute thy glory:
Ride in a day perpetual about us,
And no night be in thy throne's zodiac.—
Why do we stay to bind those princely brows
With this imperial honour?
   Prince.   Stay, noble Gloster!
That monster first must be expell'd our eye,
Or we shall take no joy in it.
   Dono. If that be hinderance, give her quick judgment,
And send her hence to death; she has long deserv'd it.
   Edol. Let my sentence stand for all. Take her hence,
And stake her carcass in the burning sun,
'Till it be parch'd and dry, and then flay off
Her wicked skin, and stuff the pelt with straw

To be shown up and down at fairs and markets,
Two pence a piece. To see so foul a monster,
Will be a fair monopoly and worth the begging.
    Art. Ha, ha, ha.
    Edol. Dost laugh, Erictho?
    Art. Yes, at thy poor invention,
Is there no better torture-monger?
    Dono. Burn her to dust.
    Art. That is a Phoenix' death, and glorious.
    Edol. Ay, that's too good for her.
    Prince. Alive
She shall be buried, circled in a wall.—
Thou murderess of a king, there starve to death.
    Art. Then I'll starve death when he comes for his prey,
And i' the mean time I'll live upon your curses.
    Edol. Ay, it is good enough, away with her!
    Art. With joy, my best of wishes is before;
The brother's poison'd, but I wanted more.   [*Exit.*
    Prince. Why does our prophet Merlin stand apart,
Sadly observing these our ceremonies,
And not applaud our joys with thy hid knowledge?
Let thy divining art now satisfy
Some part of my desires; for well I know
'Tis in thy power to show the full event,
That shall both end our reign and chronicle.
Speak, learnèd Merlin, and resolve my fears,
Whether by war we shall expel the Saxons,
Or govern what we hold with beauteous peace
In Wales and Britain?
    Merl. Long happiness attend Pendragon's reign!
What heaven decrees, fate hath no power to alter:
The Saxons, sir, will keep the ground they have,
And by supplying numbers still increase,
Till Britain be no more. So please your grace,
I will, in visible apparitions,
Present you prophecies, which shall concern

Succeeding princes, which my art shall raise,
Till men shall call these times the latter days.
 Prince. Do it, my Merlin,
And crown me with much joy and wonder.
[*Merlin strikes.*

Hoboys. Enter a King in armour, his shield quartered with thirteen crowns. At the other door enter divers Princes who present their crowns to him at his feet, and do him homage; then enters Death and strikes him; he growing sick, crowns CONSTANTINE.   [*Exeunt.*

 Merl. This king, my lord, presents your royal son,
Who in his prime of years shall be so fortunate,
That thirteen several princes shall present
Their several crowns unto him, and all kings else
Shall so admire his fame and victories,
That they shall all be glad
Either through fear or love, to do him homage;
But death (who neither favours the weak nor valiant)
In the midst of all his glories, soon shall seize him,
Scarcely permitting him to appoint one
In all his purchas'd kingdoms to succeed him.
 Prince. Thanks to our prophet
For this so wish'd-for satisfaction,
And hereby now we learn that always fate
Must be observ'd, whatever that decree.
All future times shall still record this story
Of Merlin's learnèd worth, and Arthur's glory.
[*Exeunt.*

www.ingramcontent.com/pod-product-compliance
Lightning Source LLC
Chambersburg PA
CBHW020322240426
43673CB00039B/889